Industrial Policy for National Champions

CESifo Seminar Series
edited by Hans-Werner Sinn

See http://mitpress.mit.edu for a complete list of titles in this series.

Industrial Policy for National Champions

edited by Oliver Falck, Christian Gollier, and
Ludger Woessmann

CESifo Seminar Series

The MIT Press
Cambridge, Massachusetts
London, England

For information about special quantity discounts, please email special_sales@mitpress. mit.edu

This book was set in Palatino by Toppan Best-set Premedia Limited. Printed and bound in the United States of America.

Library of Congress Cataloging-in-Publication Data

Industrial policy for national champions / edited by Oliver Falck, Christian Gollier, and Ludger Woessmann.
    p.   cm. — (CESifo seminar series)
Includes bibliographical references and index.
ISBN 978-0-262-01601-8 (hardcover : alk. paper)
1. Industrial policy—European Union countries. 2. Europe—Economic integration.
3. Business and politics—European Union countries. 4. Competition, Unfair—
Europe. I. Falck, Oliver. II. Gollier, Christian. III. Woessmann, Ludger.
HD3616.E83I54   2011
338.94—dc22

                                                              2011001831

10 9 8 7 6 5 4 3 2 1

Contents

Series Foreword

This book is part of the CESifo Seminar Series. The series aims to cover topical policy issues in economics from a largely European perspective. The books in this series are the products of the papers and intensive debates that took place during the seminars hosted by CESifo, an international research network of renowned economists organized jointly by the Center for Economic Studies at Ludwig-Maximilians-Universität, Munich, and the Ifo Institute for Economic Research. All publications in this series have been carefully selected and refereed by members of the CESifo research network.

Acknowledgments

Initial versions of the contributions collected in this volume were first presented at the conference on "Do We Need National or European Champions?" at CESifo in Munich, Germany, in November 2007. The conference was part of the project "How to Construct Europe," funded by the German Leibniz Association, whose support we gratefully acknowledge. The included papers are a peer-reviewed selection from the set of papers presented at the conference. We hope that the volume documents a fruitful example of building bridges, bringing together leading scholarly perspectives from both sides of the Atlantic.

Our thanks go to all contributors for sharing their research results with an international audience. We would like to particularly thank the conference discussants, whose expertise helped substantially in improving the drafts: Cécile Aubert, Werner Boente, Adriaan Dierx, Tobias Kretschmer, Valerie Rabassa, Régis Renault, Michele Ruta, and Monika Schnitzer. The work by numerous anonymous referees who lent further support to the selection and improvement of the papers in this volume is also gratefully acknowledged. Our additional thanks for support during the finalization of the book project go to Pia Unte as well as John Covell, Dana Andrus, and Emily Taber from the MIT Press. Finally, we would like to thank the CESifo support staff, most notably Deirdre Weber, who ensured that the conference was a wonderful event.

Contributors

Philippe Aghion is the Robert C. Waggoner Professor of Economics in the Department of Economics at Harvard University.

Cécile Aubert is a Professor of Economics at the University of Bordeaux, France.

Sara Biancini is an Assistant Professor at the University of Cergy-Pontoise, France.

Oliver Falck is an Economist at the Ifo Institute for Economic Research at the University of Munich, Germany.

Kathy Fogel is an Assistant Professor of Finance at Sam M. Walton College of Business, University of Arkansas.

Christian Gollier is a Professor of Economics at the Toulouse School of Economics, France.

Stephan Heblich is a Lecturer in Economics at the University of Stirling, UK.

Bruno Jullien is Directeur de Recherche CNRS at the Toulouse School of Economics, France.

Randall Morck is Stephen A. Jarislowsky Distinguished Chair in Finance and Distinguished University Professor, University of Alberta; and Research Associate, National Bureau of Economic Research.

Massimo Motta is ICREA Research Professor at Universitat Pompeu Fabra and Dean of the Barcelona Graduate School of Economics, Spain.

Michele Ruta is an Economist at the World Trade Organization (WTO), Switzerland.

Paul Seabright is a Professor of Economics at the University of Toulouse, France.

Jens Suedekum is a Professor of Economics at the University of Duisburg-Essen, Germany.

Ludger Woessmann is a Professor of Economics at the University of Munich and Head of the Department of Human Capital and Innovation at the Ifo Institute for Economic Research, Germany.

Bernard Yeung is Dean and Stephen Riady Distinguished Professor in Finance and Strategy, National University of Singapore Business School.

I   Introduction

1 Arguments for and against Policies to Promote National Champions

Oliver Falck, Christian Gollier, and Ludger Woessmann

Governments around the world, and particularly within the European Union, are deeply divided about the proper role of industrial policy, with preferences ranging from neoliberal approaches to strong government support for national champions. Some politicians argue that hands-off governance facilitates the sellout of national economies, while others suggest that interventionist governments only hurt themselves when creating huge and inefficient corporations. Some arguments are based on national interest that comes at the detriment of foreign interest, which would call for a transnational coordination and supervision of industrial policies that foster national champions. Others argue that the world as a whole may be better off if national industrial policies succeed in spurring innovative firms that increase productivity and spark economic growth worldwide. The chapters collected in this volume provide new perspectives on these issues and discuss the pros and cons of government support for national champions.

The issue of government support for national champions derives added momentum from the recent financial and economic crisis. In the aftermath of the failure of the large US-based bank Lehman Brothers, which hit the gobal financial sector and threatened the existence of other banks, many politicians were happy to justify the subsidization of large banks with reference to their system-relevant role in a tightly interweaved financial sector. Following the same rationale, politicians feared that the bankruptcy of firms in other sectors that are characterized by a dense network of input–output relations, such as automotives, might hurt national interests and initiate a bandwagon effect and hence cause further bankruptcies that affect the labor market.

Beyond the innovative contributions of each chapter, with this combined volume we aim to add to the existing literature in three distinct areas. First, most contributions in this volume take a European perspective, which involves issues emerging from the European Union's substantial market integration. The volume thus extends on collections on industrial policy that focus on the United States (Krugman 1986) or Japan (Itoh et al. 1991). Second, this volume primarily studies industrial policy for national champions with the rigor of economic models and thus complements more qualitative overviews such as Bianchi and Labory (2008) or Sekkat and Buigues (2009). Third, given the recent topicality of government bailouts, this volume chooses to explore the specific theme of promotion of national champions rather than the broader topics of industrial policy. Most arguments in favor of or against policies to foster national champions can be grouped under three types of models (see Gollier and Woessmann 2009 for a policy-oriented review): "classical" models that discuss market imperfections in static equilibrium, models that stress the dynamic nature of an economy characterized by constant change through innovation, and models that depict the political economy of the decision-making process. The contributions in this volume cover all three types of arguments. Given the multiple dimensions of the arguments, there is no single definition of what constitutes a "national champion," and we allow each chapter to put forward the most suitable operationalization in its particular context.

In the view of many observers, arguments in favor of champions-promoting policies are most persuasively made in a dynamic context, so we start our collection with three chapters taking a dynamic economy view. In reality, though, most champions-promoting policies may be best understood from a political-economy perspective, so we next turn to two chapters that stress the political-economy view. The final three chapters are in the more classical tradition suggesting that national champions could conceivably have emanated from deviations of perfectly competitive markets.

1.1 Analyses in Dynamic Settings

In chapter 2, Philippe Aghion revisits the traditional case for protecting "infant industries." In such a setting the argument involves learning-by-doing effects that lead to downward-sloping cost curves, and government intervention at the industry's birth can be justified as a mean of speeding up production externalities. Government intervention could take the form of subsidizing or protecting national production. Aghion suggests an innovation-based model of economic growth to depict the effects of protection on domestic innovation and growth in such a setting. In his model, industrial policy is beneficial only in "extreme" situations, namely by offering temporary protection in small countries that are behind the global technology frontier and by targeted intervention in industrial niches.

In chapter 3, Kathy Fogel, Randall Morck, and Bernard Yeung analyze the dynamic effects of national champions and estimate the association between national champions and economic growth in standard cross-country growth regressions. They build on their previous research (Fogel, Morck, and Yeung 2008), which supports the Schumpeterian concept of creative destruction, in that higher turnover in a country's group of biggest businesses is associated with higher macroeconomic growth. In their analysis, they estimate the association between the turnover in corporate control of a country's big business and economic growth. They find no statistically significant association here and speculate that one possible explanation might be that control turnover is among the increasingly entrenched insiders who obtain corporate power.

In chapter 4, Cécile Aubert, Oliver Falck, and Stephan Heblich provide an evolutionary perspective on the effects of subsidizing national champions. Focusing on the role of locally bound spillovers, they consider national champions at different stages of the industry life cycle and show that it may be efficient for governments to subsidize innovative firms in their early stages and to protect mature firms from competition. In reality, however, they suggest that politicians may tend to concentrate on externalities at the mature stage of the lifecycle, which are either transitory or come at the expense of foreign-country consumers. This leads us to what, in a positive rather than normative sense, may be more powerful explanations of the emergence of policies that foster national champions: political-economy arguments.

1.2 Political-Economy Analyses

The next two chapters turn to examples of what Aghion in chapter 2 refers to as "the powerful political economy counterargument(s)" against policies to protect national champions.

In chapter 5, Massimo Motta and Michele Ruta approach the topic of national champions from the perspective of determinants of merger policy in globalized markets. They argue that arguments that assume benevolent national governments "are probably not the most useful in understanding governments' attitudes toward mergers." In their view, to be able to understand real-world merger policy, such economic arguments rather have to be accompanied by political-economy arguments. The authors point out that, first, depending on the location of the firms (home or abroad), mergers have different effects on consumers, merging firms, and nonmerging competitors; second, even though antitrust decisions can be delegated to independent authorities, governments still exert some influence on merger policy; and third, some groups in society are politically better organized than others to pursue their interest. As a consequence, as long as national governments are politically motivated, they will succumb to lobbying by domestic firms.

The general point that lobbying can lead to policies supporting "champions" with inefficient production is well established by now. But how exactly do such mechanisms work, and what kind of inefficiencies can emerge in practice? In chapter 6, Paul Seabright revisits the Airbus case—perhaps the most frequently mentioned European "champion" (see also Neven and Seabright 1995)—arguing that politically sponsored firms in safety-critical industries may be particularly prone to delivery delays. In a simple model of team production, he shows that the extent of this problem is greater, the more safety-critical the industry. This behavior is in direct contrast to that of profit-maximizing firms, which generally exert a great deal of effort to produce well in advance of deadlines in order to ensure that the occurrence of unexpected problems will not jeopardize the deadline. Politically sponsored firms will typically be less motivated to meet production deadlines because they generally receive a smaller proportion of the rents arising from meeting the deadlines. The ensuing delivery delays can be viewed as a "hidden cost" of the political sponsorship of industrial "champions."

1.3   Analyses in Static Settings

The "classical" argument in favor of policies to promote national champions comes from strategic trade theory. As Brander and Spencer (1985) have shown, policies to promote national champions are "efficient" from a national perspective if—because of increasing returns to scale—the domestic firm can extract monopoly rents on the foreign market, as long as national governments do not take into account the welfare of foreign residents. Thus, governments acting on behalf of their respective citizens should promote competition at home, but encourage monopolies of their national firms abroad. This type of beggar-thy-neighbor policies may be viewed as the basic argument in favor of promoting national champions.

In chapter 7, Christian Gollier and Bruno Jullien take up this strategic trade theory argument, placing it in a situation of inefficient financial markets. Under the assumption that inefficient financial markets create credit rationing, national firms are inhibited from exploiting their competitive advantage abroad. In this view, encouraging monopolies both abroad and in the home market may be "efficient" because it enables firms to self-finance their expansion abroad. In the tradition of static-economy arguments, policies to promote national champions based on such mechanisms are welfare maximizing from a national perspective but not from a global perspective. They create the usual prisoner's dilemma situation where in equilibrium, each national government will subsidize national firms, most of which are bound to fail to emerge as global champions.

In chapter 8, Sara Biancini models another type of noncompetitive market: national champions that arise from formerly public monopolies. With the liberalization of formerly monopolistic industries, sector-specific regulation is implemented to facilitate market entry and reduce the strategic advantage of the formerly public monopolies. This way regulation of the former monopolist turns into regulation of the "national champion" that deals in international markets. In a model with two firms and two regulators, Biancini shows that market integration can be welfare reducing because of its impact on the budget constraint of regulated firms. In her model, cooperation among regulators is a way to avoid globally suboptimal policies in which countries are willing to pay transfers to inefficient national producers.

In chapter 9, Jens Suedekum develops a model of Bertrand competition with economic patriotism. In his model there are two domestic firms and one foreign firm, and all compete in the domestic market. To model the implications of economic patriotism when it comes to a choice between creating a national champion and accepting a foreign takeover, Suedekum provides a scenario where there can either be a national merger that creates a national champion or a takeover of one of the national firms by the potentially more efficient foreign rival. A welfare-maximizing domestic competition agency is charged with approving any change in the ownership structure. In the model, decreasing transport costs make the foreign takeover more likely when the government is unbiased by economic patriotism. However, when the domestic government is biased by economic patriotism, promotion of the national champion is more likely.

1.4   Some Synoptic Observations

The chapters of this volume shed light on important new aspects of the question of whether governments should try to promote national champions. The richness of the different static, dynamic, and political-economy models provides a much more in-depth understanding of industrial policy than any individual model could. What becomes clear from the different perspectives, though, is that it is not easy to make a general case in favor of policies that promote national champions on purely economic grounds.

While several deviations from perfectly competitive markets can make champions-promoting policies "efficient" from a national point of view, such static-equilibrium considerations tend to be inefficient when taking the perspective of global welfare. In other words, international cooperation would make welfare-maximizing governments refrain from champions-promoting policies. There are more obvious arguments in favor of champions-promoting policies in dynamic models that advertise the infant industry argument, but it becomes clear that these are very special cases whose existence has to be doubted in the majority of real-world situations. The little empirical evidence that exists on the matter tends to suggest that, if anything, entry barriers and state control, including attempts to defend national champions, tend to reduce rather than spur technological catch-up and economic growth (Nicoletti and Scarpetta 2003), as does the stability that "champions"-promoting policies tend to provide to big business.

Real-world policies promoting national champions seem much more readily understandable in political-economy terms than in economic-efficiency terms. Governments may be inclined to succumb to the lobbying pressure of leveraged interests as long as the constituency of those who are paying for it is more dispersed. What is worse, political-economy arguments may suggest that what Aghion terms the "commonsense" approach to industrial policy, namely "experiment and then make sure you can stop the intervention if it turns out not to be efficient," may not be viable after all: if the main reason for champions-promoting policies to exist in the first place is that governments are subject to political pressure from vested interests, then stopping such policies may prove infeasible, be they efficient or not.

References

Bianchi, P., and S. Labory, eds. 2008. *International Handbook on Industrial Policy*. Cheltenham: Edward Elgar.

Brander, J., and B. Spencer. 1985. Export subsidies and international market share rivalry. *Journal of International Economics* 18 (1–2): 83–100.

Fogel, K., R. Morck, and B. Yeung. 2008. Big business stability and economic growth: Is what's good for General Motors good for America? *Journal of Financial Economics* 89 (1): 83–108.

Itoh, M., K. Kiyono, M. Okuno, and K. Suzumura, eds. 1991. *Economic Analysis of Industrial Policy*. New York: Academic Press.

Gollier, C., and L. Woessmann. 2009. Do we need national or European champions? In T. Büttner and W. Ochel, eds., *How to Construct Europe*, forthcoming.

Krugman, P., ed. 1986. *Strategic Trade Policy and the New International Economics*. Cambridge: MIT Press.

Neven, D., and P. Seabright. 1995. European industrial policy: The Airbus case. *Economic Policy* 10 (21): 313–58.

Nicoletti, G., and S. Scarpetta. 2003. Regulation, productivity and growth: OECD evidence. *Economic Policy* 18 (36): 9–72.

Sekkat, K., and P. Buigues. 2009. *Industrial Policy in Europe, Japan and the USA*. Basingstoke: Palgrave Macmillan.

II Analyses in Dynamic Settings

2 Some Thoughts on Industrial Policy and Growth

Philippe Aghion

2.1 Introduction

In the aftermath of WWII, many developing countries have opted for policies aimed at promoting new infant industries or at protecting local traditional activities from competition by products from more advanced countries. Thus several Latin American countries advocated import substitution policies, whereby local industries would more fully benefit from domestic demand. East Asian countries like Korea or Japan, rather than advocating import substitution policies, would favor export promotion, which in turn would be achieved partly through tariffs and nontariff barriers and partly through maintaining undervalued exchange rates. For at least two or three decades after WWII, these policies, which belong to what is commonly referred to as "industrial policy," remained fairly noncontroversial as both groups of countries were growing at fast rates.

However, the slowdown in Latin America as of the 1970s and in Japan as of the late 1990s contributed to the growing skepticism about the role of industrial policy in the process of development. Increasingly since the early 1980s industrial policy has been raising serious doubts among academics and policy advisers in international financial institutions. In particular, it was criticized for allowing governments to pick winners and losers in a discretionary fashion and consequently for increasing the scope for capture of governments by local vested interests. Instead, policy makers and growth/development economists would advocate general policies aimed at improving the "investment climate": the liberalization of product and labor markets, a legal and enforcement framework that protects (private) property rights, and

This chapter draws unrestrainedly from joint work with Peter Howitt.

macroeconomic stabilization. This new set of growth recommendations came to be known as the "Washington consensus," as it was primarily advocated by the IMF, the World Bank, and the US Treasury, all based in Washington, DC.

The Washington consensus advocates did have a case: for example, recent empirical work by Frankel and Romer (1999) and Wacziarg (2001) would point to a positive effect of trade liberalization on growth. Thus Wacziarg (2001) showed that increasing trade restrictions by one standard deviation would reduce productivity growth by 0.264 percent annually. Similarly Keller (2002, 2004) showed that 70 percent of international R&D spillovers are due to cross-country trade flows, and more recently, Aghion et al. (2008) pointed to large growth-enhancing effects of the trade liberalization and delicensing reforms introduced in India in the early 1990s, particularly in more advanced sectors or in Indian states with more flexible labor market regulations.

The main goal of this chapter is to see whether a case can still be made for policies aimed at supporting or protecting some local sectors, or whether the proponents of a full and unconditional liberalization have definitely won the debate.

2.2   The Traditional Infant Industry Argument

2.2.1   The Argument in a Nutshell

The infant industry argument, as formalized, for example, by Greenwald and Stiglitz (2006),[1] can be summarized as follows. Consider a local economy that comprises a traditional (agricultural) sector and a nascent (industrial) sector. The industrial sector's new activities involve high costs initially. However, production and the resulting learning-by-doing reduce these costs over time. Suppose that there are knowledge externalities between these new industrial activities and the traditional sector.

Two conclusions are immediately obtained in this setting. First, full trade liberalization will make it very costly for domestic industrial sectors to invest in learning-by-doing; so it involves producing but not selling in the short run, since domestic costs are initially higher than foreign costs. Second, the social benefits from learning-by-doing are not fully internalized by industrial sectors since they do not internalize the knowledge externalities they have on the agricultural sector.

It is the combination of these two considerations that justifies domestic policies aimed at (temporarily) protecting nascent industries.

Such policies may take the form of targeted subsidies or import restrictions, or they may involve nontargeted policies, for example, maintaining undervalued exchange rates, that will benefit the local industry as a whole as long as it does not import too many inputs from abroad itself.

2.2.2   Criticisms

The main objections to the infant industry argument have been empirical. Thus Krueger and Tuncer (1982) saw no systematic tendency for unprotected firms or industries in Turkey over the 1960s to display higher productivity growth than less protected industries. Moreover they saw no apparent tendency for a new industrial activity to display higher rates of growth than the overall industry to which it belongs.

However, the most compelling case against the traditional infant industry argument was recently made by Nunn and Trefler (2007), henceforth NT. NT's argument goes as follows: if we were to believe the infant industry argument above, we should see a positive correlation between growth and the extent to which the domestic tariff structure is skilled-biased, the idea being that learning-by-doing on new activities with knowledge spillovers on the rest of the economy should require more skills than other activities. Thus NT regress average per capita GDP growth, measured by the log of (y_{c1}/y_{c0}), where y_{c1} (resp. coefficient y_{c0}) denotes per capita GDP at the end (resp. the beginning) of the period, on the extent to which the tariff structure is skill-biased (which in turn is measured by the correlation coefficient between skill intensity and the level of tariffs across sectors). A straight cross-country regression with region and cohort fixed effects shows a positive and significant correlation between growth and the skill bias of the tariff structure.

Thus, at first sight, NT's regression results seem to confirm the infant industry argument. However, NT push the analysis further by regressing, for each sector in each country, per capita growth on both the country-level measure of skill bias of tariffs and a new (industry-level) tariff–skill interaction term: this latter term interacts the tariff for that particular industry with the ratio of skills over unskilled labor in that same industry. The intriguing result is that the coefficient for this industry-level tariff–skill interaction is negative and significant! In other words, the positive coefficient on the aggregate measure of skill-biased tariff found in the previous regression does not fully reflect the growth effect of protecting more skill-biased industries. Actually NT argue that the explanation for the positive coefficient also involves a third

variable, namely the quality of local institutions, that is positively correlated with growth and also with the government's propensity to
emphasize skill-intensive sectors.

Thus the Greenwald–Stiglitz story and/or, more generally, the case
for infant industry policies is only partly vindicated by the empirical
analysis.

2.3   The Discouragement Effect of Trade Liberalization

The analysis in this section covers the effects of trade liberalization on
innovation and growth in the domestic economy. In particular, I raise
the possibility that trade liberalization could inhibit growth in some
economies, and that this might in turn justify some form of temporary
protection.

2.3.1   Preliminary: The Closed-Economy Model

I first analyze innovation and growth in a closed economy, which I use
as benchmark case to analyze the effects of trade liberalization.

Production and National Income   There is a single country in which
a unique final good, which also serves as numéraire, is produced
competitively using a continuum of intermediate inputs according to

$$Y_t = L^{1-\alpha} \int_0^1 A_{it}^{1-\alpha} x_{it}^{\alpha} di, \qquad 0 < \alpha < 1, \tag{2.1}$$

where L is the domestic labor force, assumed to be constant, A_{it} is the
quality of intermediate good i at time t, and x_{it} is the flow quantity of
intermediate good i being produced and used at time t.

In each intermediate sector there is a monopolist producer who uses
the final good as the sole input, with one unit of final good needed to
produce each unit of intermediate good. The monopolist's cost of production is therefore equal to the quantity produced x_{it}. The price p_{it} at
which she can sell this quantity of intermediate good to the competitive
final sector is the marginal product of intermediate good i in the final
good production function (2.1).

The monopolist will choose the level of output that maximizes
profits, namely

$$x_{it} = A_{it} L \alpha^{2/(1-\alpha)}, \tag{2.2}$$

resulting in the profit level

$$\pi_{it} = \pi A_{it} L, \tag{2.3}$$

where $\pi \equiv (1-\alpha)\alpha^{(1+\alpha)/(1-\alpha)}$.

The equilibrium level of final output in the economy can be found by substituting the x_{it}'s into (2.1), which yields

$$Y_t = \varphi A_t L, \tag{2.4}$$

where A_t is the average productivity parameter across all sectors

$$A_t = \int_0^1 A_{it} di$$

and $\varphi = \alpha^{2\alpha/(1-\alpha)}.$ [2]

Innovation   Productivity growth comes from innovations. In each sector at each date there is a unique entrepreneur with the possibility of innovating in that sector. She is the incumbent monopolist and an innovation would enable her to produce with a productivity (quality) parameter $A_{it} = \gamma A_{i,t-1}$ that is superior to that of the previous monopolist by the factor $\gamma > 1$. Otherwise, her productivity parameter stays the same: $A_{it} = A_{i,t-1}$. In order to innovate with any given probability μ she must spend the amount

$$c_{it}(\mu) = (1-\tau) \cdot \phi(\mu) \cdot A_{i,t-1}$$

of final good in research, where $\tau > 0$ is a subsidy parameter that represents the extent to which national policies encourage innovation, and ϕ is a cost function satisfying

$$\phi(0) = 0 \quad \text{and}$$
$$\phi'(\mu) > 0, \quad \phi''(\mu) > 0, \qquad \text{for all } \mu > 0.$$

Thus the local entrepreneur's expected profit net of research cost is

$$V_{it} = E\pi_{it} - c_{it}(\mu)$$
$$= \mu \pi L \gamma A_{i,t-1} + (1-\mu)\pi L A_{i,t-1} - (1-\tau)\phi(\mu)A_{i,t-1}.$$

She will choose the value of μ that maximizes these expected profits.

Each local entrepreneur will choose a frequency of innovations μ^* that maximizes V_{it}. The first-order condition for an interior maximum is $\partial V_{it}/\partial \mu = 0$, which can be expressed as the research arbitrage equation:

$$\phi'(\mu) = \frac{\pi L(\gamma - 1)}{1 - \tau}. \tag{2.5}$$

If the research environment is favorable enough (i.e., if τ is large enough), or the population large enough, so that

$$\phi'(0) > \frac{\pi L(\gamma-1)}{1-\tau},$$

then the unique solution μ to the research arbitrage equation (2.5) is positive, so in each sector the probability of an innovation is that solution ($\hat{\mu} = \mu$), which is an increasing function of the size of population L and of the policies favoring innovation τ. Otherwise, there is no positive solution to the research arbitrage equation so the local entrepreneur chooses never to innovate ($\hat{\mu} = 0$).

Since each A_{it} grows at the rate $\gamma-1$ with probability $\hat{\mu}$ and at the rate 0 with probability $1-\hat{\mu}$, the expected growth rate of the economy is

$$g = \hat{\mu}(\gamma-1).$$

So we see that countries with a larger population and more favorable innovation conditions will be more likely to grow, and if they grow, will grow faster than countries with a smaller population and less favorable innovation conditions.

2.3.2 The Effects of Openness on Innovation and Long-Run Growth

Now let us open trade in goods (both intermediate and final) between the domestic country and the rest of the world, and we first take productivities in all domestic and foreign sectors to be given. Productivity-enhancing innovations are introduced in the next section.

To keep it simple, suppose that there are just two countries, called "home" and "foreign," that differ in terms of the size of population and the policies favoring innovation. Suppose that the range of intermediate products in each country is identical, that they produce exactly the same final product, and that there are no transportation costs. Within each intermediate sector, the world market can then be monopolized by the producer with the lowest cost. We use asterisks to denote foreign country variables.

To begin with, each country does no trade and hence behaves just like the closed economy described in the previous section. Then at time t we allow them to trade costlessly with each other. The immediate effect of this opening up is to allow each country to take advantage of more productive efficiency. In the home country, final good production will equal

$$Y_t = \int_0^1 Y_{it} di = L^{1-\alpha} \int_0^1 \hat{A}_{it}^{1-\alpha} x_{it}^{\alpha} di, \qquad 0 < \alpha < 1, \tag{2.6}$$

where $\hat{A}_{it}$ is the higher of the two initial productivity parameters:

$$\hat{A}_{it} = \max\{A_{it}, A_{it}^*\}.$$

Likewise in the foreign country final good production will equal

$$Y_t^* = \int_0^1 Y_{it}^* di = \left(L^*\right)^{1-\alpha} \int_0^1 \hat{A}_{it}^{1-\alpha} \left(x_{it}^*\right)^{\alpha} di, \qquad 0 < \alpha < 1. \tag{2.7}$$

The monopolist in sector i, whose intermediate good has productivity $\hat{A}_{it}$, can now sell to both countries and thereby achieve the profit level

$$\pi_{it} = \pi \hat{A}_{it}(L + L^*), \tag{2.8}$$

where once again $\pi \equiv (1-\alpha)\alpha^{(1+\alpha)/(1-\alpha)}$.

Innovation We now endogenize the growth of productivities A_{it} and A_{it}^*. Consider the innovation process in a given sector i. The country where the monopoly currently resides is on the global technology frontier for sector i, and the local entrepreneur will aim at making a frontier innovation that raises the productivity parameter from $\hat{A}_{it}$ to $\gamma \hat{A}_{it}$. If so, that country will retain a global monopoly in intermediate product i. In the other country the local entrepreneur will be trying to catch up with the frontier by implementing the current frontier technology. If she succeeds and the frontier entrepreneur fails to advance the frontier during that period, then the lagging country will have caught up, both countries will be on the frontier, and we can suppose that each entrepreneur will monopolize the market for product i in her own country. But if the frontier entrepreneur does advance the frontier, the entrepreneur in the lagging country will still remain behind and will earn no profit income.

Over time the lead in each sector will tend to pass from country to country, as long as the lagging sector is innovating. (Otherwise, the lead will remain with the country that starts with the lead when trade is opened up.) However, there will be no immediate leapfrogging of one country by the other because in order to retake the lead a country must first catch up. So, in between lead changes, there will be a period when the sector is level or neck and neck. The growth rate of productivity will be determined by the incentives to perform R&D in the different cases (when the country is the sole leader, when it is the laggard, and when the sector is level.) So we need to study each case in turn.

Three Cases   Three possibilities must be considered. A domestic sector leads over the corresponding sector in the foreign country (case A), or the domestic sector is at level (neck and neck) with its counterpart in the foreign country (case B), or the domestic sector lags behind its foreign counterpart (case C). More precise descriptions of these cases follow.

CASE A

Case A is where the lead in sector i resides in the home country while the foreign country lags behind. In this case the expected profit of the entrepreneur in the home country, net of R&D costs, is

$$EU_A = \mu_A \gamma (L + L^*) \pi + (1 - \mu_A)(L + (1 - \mu_A^*)L^*)\pi - (1 - \tau)\phi(\mu_A)$$

while the expected profit of the foreign entrepreneur is

$$EU_A^* = \mu_A^* (1 - \mu_A)\pi L^* - (1 - \tau^*)\phi(\mu_A^*),$$

where everything is normalized by the preexisting productivity level. That is, with probability μ_A the home entrepreneur will innovate, thus earning all the global profits in the market at productivity level γ times the preexisting level. If she fails to innovate, she will still earn all domestic profits in the market at the preexisting profit level, and if the foreign entrepreneur fails to innovate (which occurs with probability $1 - \mu_A^*$), she will also earn all the foreign profits in the market. In any event she must incur the R&D costs $(1 - \tau)\phi(\mu_A)$. Likewise the foreign entrepreneur will earn all the profits in the foreign market if she innovates and her rival does not, which occurs with probability $\mu_A^*(1 - \mu_A)$.

CASE B

Case B is where the sector is level. In this case the expected profits of the respective entrepreneurs net of R&D costs are

$$EU_B = (\mu_B(L + (1 - \mu_B^*)L^*)\gamma + (1 - \mu_B)(1 - \mu_B^*)L)\pi - (1 - \tau)\phi(\mu_B) \quad \text{and}$$
$$EU_B^* = (\mu_B^*(L^* + (1 - \mu_B)L)\gamma + (1 - \mu_B^*)(1 - \mu_B)L^*)\pi - (1 - \tau^*)\phi(\mu_B^*).$$

For example, the home entrepreneur innovates with probability μ_B, which earns her all the home profits for sure and all the foreign profits if her rival fails to innovate, whereas if both fail to innovate, she retains all the domestic profits.

CASE C
Case C is where the foreign country starts with the lead. By analogy with case A the expected profits minus R&D costs are, respectively,

$$EU_C = \mu_C(1-\mu_C^*)\pi L - (1-\tau)\phi(\mu_C) \quad \text{and}$$
$$EU_C^* = \mu_C^*\gamma(L+L^*)\pi + (1-\mu_C^*)(L^* + (1-\mu_C)L)\pi - (1-\tau^*)\phi(\mu_C^*).$$

EQUILIBRIUM INNOVATION AND GROWTH
The research arbitrage equations that determine the innovation rates in equilibrium are simply obtained by taking the first-order conditions for each of the above given expected profits minus R&D cost expression. Innovation rates in the domestic country thus satisfy

$$\frac{(1-\tau)\phi'(\mu_A)}{\pi} = (\gamma-1)(L+L^*) + \mu_A^* L^*,$$

$$\frac{(1-\tau)\phi'(\mu_B)}{\pi} = (\gamma-1)L + \mu_B^* L + (1-\mu_B^*)\gamma L^*,$$

$$\frac{(1-\tau)\phi'(\mu_C)}{\pi} = (1-\mu_C^*)L,$$

and symmetrically for innovation in the foreign country.[3]

In steady state there will be a constant fraction of sectors in each state, q_A, q_B, and q_C, with $q_A + q_B + q_C = 1$, while aggregate productivity will be

$$\hat{A}_t = q_A \hat{A}_{At} + q_B \hat{A}_{Bt} + q_C \hat{A}_{Ct},$$

where, for example, $\hat{A}_{At}$ is the average productivity level in sectors where the lead resides in the home country. It follows that the growth rate of aggregate productivity (and hence of each country's national income) in steady state will be

$$g = \eta_A g_A + \eta_B g_B + \eta_C g_C, \tag{2.9}$$

where for each state $S = A, B, C$, $\eta_S = q_S \hat{A}_{St}/\hat{A}_t$ is the share of aggregate productivity accounted for by sectors in state S in the steady state, and g_S is the expected growth rate of the leading technology $\hat{A}_{it}$ in each sector currently in state S.

Since the η's add up to one, this implies that the steady-state growth rate of the open economy is a weighted average of the productivity growth rates g_s. These are respectively

$$g_A = (\gamma - 1)\mu_A,$$
$$g_B = (\gamma - 1)(\mu_B + \mu_B^* - \mu_B \mu_B^*),$$
$$g_C = (\gamma - 1)\mu_C^*.$$

Our conclusions in the remaining part of the section will be derived from comparing the home country research arbitrage equations under openness with the closed economy research arbitrage equation (2.5), which we reproduce here for convenience:

$$\frac{(1-\tau)\phi'(\mu)}{\pi} = (\gamma - 1)L. \tag{2.10}$$

Scale and Escape Entry Comparing this closed economy research arbitrage equation with the one governing μ_A obtains

$$\frac{(1-\tau)\phi'(\mu_A)}{\pi} = (\gamma - 1)(L + L^*) + \mu_A^* L^*. \tag{2.11}$$

We see that when the home country has the technology lead (case A), it will innovate at a faster rate than when it was a closed economy because the right-hand side of the leader's research arbitrage equation (2.11) is larger than the right-hand side of the closed economy counterpart (2.10). This is because of two effects, scale and escape entry.

The scale effect arises because the successful innovator gets enhanced profits from both markets, not just the domestic market, thus giving her a stronger incentive to innovate. This is why (2.11) has the sum of size variables $L + L^*$ where (2.10) has just the domestic size variable L.

The escape entry effect arises because the unsuccessful innovator in the open economy is at risk of losing the foreign market to her foreign rival, a risk that she can avoid by innovating. By contrast, the unsuccessful innovator in the closed economy loses nothing to a foreign rival and thus does not have this extra incentive to innovate. Formally, this effect accounts for the extra term $\mu_A^* L^*$ that appears on the right-hand side of (2.11) but not in (2.10).

Comparing the closed-economy research arbitrage equation (2.10) to the one governing the home country's innovation rate in a level sector obtains

$$\frac{(1-\tau)\phi'(\mu_B)}{\pi} = (\gamma-1)L + \mu_B^*L + (1-\mu_B^*)\gamma L^*.$$

We see the same two effects at work. The term μ_B^*L is the escape entry effect. By innovating, the home entrepreneur can avoid the risk of losing the local market. The term $(1-\mu_B^*)\gamma L^*$ is the scale effect. By innovating, the home entrepreneur can capture (with some probability) the foreign market as well as the domestic market.

It follows that both μ_A and μ_B will be larger than the closed economy innovation rate μ. The same will be true for the foreign innovation rates μ_B^* and μ_C^*, which will both be larger than the foreign countries innovation rate when it was closed, μ^*.

The Discouragement Effect of Foreign Entry We saw above that a country behind the world technology frontier may be discouraged from innovating by the threat of entry because even if it innovates, it might lose out to a superior entrant. This is reflected in the research arbitrage equation governing the home country's innovation rate in case C, the case where it is the technological laggard:

$$\frac{(1-\tau)\phi'(\mu_C)}{\pi} = (1-\mu_C^*)L.$$

If the foreign country's innovation rate is large enough when it has the lead, then the right-hand side of this research arbitrage equation will be strictly less than that of the closed economy equation (2.10), so we will have $\mu_C < \mu$. This does not have a direct effect on the growth rate (2.9) because g_C depends only on the leader's innovation rate μ_C^*. That is, in this state the home country is just catching up, not advancing the global technology frontier. However, as we will see, a fall in μ_C will nevertheless have an indirect effect on growth by affecting the steady-state weights η_S in (2.9), which are the fractions of productivity accounted for by the sectors in each state.

How Trade Can Reduce Growth in One Country The fact that trade raises growth in both countries when either the countries are symmetrical or one country fails to innovate when behind suggests that trade will usually raise growth in both countries. But there can be exceptions. These exceptions must, of course, involve countries that are asymmetrical. For example, consider the case of a small country (home) whose policies used to be very unfavorable to innovation but have recently undertaken a reform to make the country more innovative. Suppose that these policies have been so successful that just before opening up to trade, the home country has a faster growth rate than the foreign country:

$$\mu > \mu^*,$$

but the reforms have been so recent that the home country is still behind the foreign country in all sectors. Then, after the opening up to trade, initially, all monopolies will reside in the foreign country; that is, all sectors will be in case C above. Now suppose furthermore that the discouragement effect is large enough that the home country does not innovate when behind ($\mu_C = 0$). Then, as we have seen, all monopolies will remain forever in the foreign country.

This is the case where, as we saw above, the home country's level of national income might actually fall when trade is opened up because the increased efficiency of the selection effect might be outweighed by the loss of profits from the home country monopolists that are forced out of business by foreign competition. What we can now see is that whether or not national income falls at first, the home country's growth rate from then on may be lower than if it had never opened up to trade.

More specifically, if it had not opened up for trade, then its growth rate would have remained equal to

$$g = (\gamma - 1)\mu,$$

whereas under open trade, its growth rate will be that of each sector in case C, namely

$$g' = (\gamma - 1)\mu_C^*.$$

So the home country growth rate will be reduced by trade if and only if $\mu_C^* < \mu$. Now we know from our analysis above that μ_C^* must exceed the innovation rate that the foreign country would have experienced under autarky,

$$\mu_C^* > \mu^*,$$

but this does not guarantee that it exceeds the innovation rate that the home country would have experienced under autarky. Indeed, if μ_C^* is close enough to μ^*, it will be strictly less than μ and the home country's growth rate will be reduced by trade.

This is where our assumption that the home country is small comes into play. If it is very small relative to the foreign country, then the scale effect of trade on the foreign innovation rate μ_C^* will be small. Since we are assuming that the home country never innovates when behind, there is no escape entry effect on μ_C^*. So, if the home country is small enough, then μ_C^* will indeed be close enough to μ^* that it falls below μ and the home country's growth rate is diminished by trade.

So we have a presumption that if there are instances where trade is bad for growth, they are probably in small countries that start off far behind the global technology frontier. We also have an example of how economic reform needs to be sequenced properly in order to have its desired effect. That is, generally speaking, a country's growth prospects are enhanced by liberalizing trade and by removing barriers to innovation. But, if these reforms are undertaken simultaneously, their full benefits might not be realized. Instead, it might be better to remove the barriers to innovation first and then to wait until several domestic industries have become world leaders before removing the barriers to international trade.

2.4 A Case for Targeted Intervention: Industrial Niches

The notion that the existing pattern of specialization may limit the evolution of comparative advantage over time has not received much attention in the growth literature so far. For example, in Romer (1990)'s product variety model the current set of inputs display the same degree of imperfect substitutability with respect to any new input that might be introduced, and therefore does not make one new input more likely than any other: this property stems directly from the fully symmetric nature of the Dixit–Stiglitz model of product differentiation upon which the Romer model is built. However, an important insight that emerges from the work of Young (1991), Lucas (1993), and more recently Haumann and Klinger (2007) is that successful growth stories are involving gradual processes whereby neighboring sectors experiment with new technologies one after the other because experimentation involves learning-by-doing externalities across sectors.

To illustrate the case for targeted intervention based on the existence of cross-sectoral externalities in the simplest possible way, consider the following toy model. Individuals each live for one period. There are four *potential* sectors in the economy, which we number from 1 to 4, but only one sector, namely sector 1, is active at date zero. Thus the economy at date 0 can be represented by the 4-tuple:

$$\Omega_0 = (1, 0, 0, 0),$$

where the number 1 (resp. 0) in column i refers to the corresponding sector i being currently active (resp. inactive). At date t, a sector that is active produces at the frontier productivity level $\bar{A}_t = (1+g)^t$. Once activated, a sector automatically remains active forever. Aggregate output at date t is

$$Y_t = A_t = N_t \bar{A}_t,$$

where N_t is the number of active sectors at date t.

R&D investments activate new sectors, but there is a cost of learning about faraway sectors. Specifically there is a fixed R&D cost $\gamma(1+g)^t$ of activating a sector in period t, but this is only possible if (1) the sector is adjacent to an already active sector or (2) the R&D cost $\gamma(1+g)^{t-1}$ was also incurred in that sector last period.

Consider first the economy under laissez faire. Being populated by one-period-lived individuals, the economy will never invest in a sector that is not adjacent to a sector already active. At best, a local entrepreneur will find it optimal to activate a sector adjacent to an already active sector. This will be the case whenever

$$\gamma < \theta,$$

where θ is the fraction of output that can be appropriated by a private innovator. Note, however, that if

$$\theta < \gamma,$$

then private firms will not explore new sectors, not even neighboring ones, even though it might be socially optimal to do so.

Coming back to the case where $\gamma < \theta$, in this case, the laissez-faire sequence of active sectors will be

$$\Omega_1 = (1, 1, 0, 0),$$
$$\Omega_2 = (1, 1, 1, 0),$$
$$\Omega_t = (1, 1, 1, 1), \qquad t \geq 3.$$

Now consider a social planner. The social planner will invest in sector 2 in period 1, whenever the cost $\gamma(1+g)$ of doing so is less than the net present revenue of activating sector 2, namely

$$\sum_{t=1}^{\infty} \frac{\bar{A}_t}{(1+r)^t} = \frac{1+g}{r-g},$$

that is, whenever

$$\gamma < \frac{1}{r-g}.$$

For g sufficiently close to r or for γ sufficiently small, this inequality is automatically satisfied, in which case it will also be optimal to invest in sector 3 in period 2 because at that date sector 3 will be adjacent to an already active sector (i.e., sector 2).

But, in addition, whenever γ is sufficiently small, it will be optimal to invest in sector 4 in period 1 because that will allow sector 4 to be activated in period 2, whereas otherwise it can only be activated in period 3. Investing in period 1 instead of period 2 in sector 4 will yield an additional

$$\frac{\bar{A}_2}{1+r}$$

and will cost an additional $\gamma(1+g)$. So, if γ is small enough, namely if

$$\gamma < \frac{1+g}{1+r},$$

the optimal sequence of active sectors will be

$$\Omega_1 = (1, 1, 0, 0),$$
$$\Omega_2 = (1, 1, 1, 0),$$
$$\Omega_t = (1, 1, 1, 1), \qquad t \geq 3.$$

The laissez-faire equilibrium is suboptimal because people do not invest far enough away from already active sectors. In this example, output will be lower than optimal in period 2 $(3\bar{A}_2$ versus $4\bar{A}_2)$ because individuals were not far sighted enough to invest in sector 4, which was too far away from already active sectors, in period 1.

Thus this model suggests a role for targeted industrial policy: namely to overcome the potential underinvestment in new sectors. In particular, if targeted subsidies were to be implemented by a government, we conjecture that such subsidies should be more growth enhancing: (1) if they target sectors that are currently inactive but close "input-wise" to already active sectors, and (2) if the country experiences low levels of financial development or low labor mobility or low average levels of education. The first part implies that the targeted sectors are more likely to benefit from learning-by-doing externalities from already active sectors. The second part makes it less likely that market forces will spontaneously take advantage of these externalities.

The idea that the product space is heterogeneous with an uneven density of active product lines and that the current density distribution of active sectors impacts on the evolution of comparative advantage is taken to the data by Hausmann and Klinger (2006), henceforth HK. HK measure the relatedness between two product lines by the probability $\varphi_{i,j}$ that on average countries exports enough of the two goods simultaneously.[4] Then HK define the density around good i in country c as the average relatedness of that product with other products exported by the same country, namely

$$density_{i,c,t} = \frac{k\varphi_{i,k,t} \cdot x_{c,k,t}}{k\varphi_{i,k,t}},$$

where $x_{c,k,t}$ is the volume of export of product k by country c at time t.

A main finding in HK is that the probability of a country exporting product i in year $t+1$ is positively and significantly correlated with the country's density around product i in year t. This in turn provides empirical support to the idea that countries move toward new product lines that are adjacent to existing lines, even though this may be suboptimal as discussed above.

At least two arguments can be opposed to targeted interventions of the kind suggested in this section: (1) such policies may serve as a pretext for government favors, particularly if input–output information can be manipulated by politicians or bureaucrats; (2) what guarantees that temporary support to industries will be terminated, especially if the investment turns out to be inefficient? One possible answer to these two objections would be to involve third parties (e.g., private partners) that would access input–output information and would also act as cofinanciers.

2.5 Conclusion

In this chapter we have tried to push the discussion on industrial policy a little further. In particular, we have identified (extreme) situations where temporary protection might be called for, and we have also tried to resurrect the case for targeted interventions.

An additional case for intervention can be made in relation to the business cycle. More specifically, recent work by Aghion, Hemous, and Kharroubi (2009) uses a sample of 45 industries across 17 OECD countries over the period 1980 to 2005 to show that growth in industrial sectors that are more dependent on external finance (using Rajan and Zingales's 1998 methodology) benefits more from more countercyclical fiscal policies, namely from policies that involve larger deficits in recessions (compensated by bigger surpluses during booms). Moreover it is rather the expenditure side than the revenue side of governments' budgets whose countercyclicality matters for growth in such sectors.

Whether these arguments are in some cases stronger than the powerful political economy counterargument(s), needs to be assessed depending on characteristics of the country or the sector, and also with regard to the economy's location in the business cycle. In any case, the general recommendation made by the Spence report with regard to industrial policy strikes us as stemming from common sense: namely experiment, and then make sure you can stop the intervention if it turns out not to be efficient.

Notes

1. See also Young (1991).

2. To derive this expression for Y_t, substitute the x_{it}'s into (2.1) to get

$$Y_t = L^{1-\alpha} \int_0^1 A_{it}^{1-\alpha} (A_{it} L \alpha^{2/(1-\alpha)})^\alpha di$$

$$= (\alpha^{2/(1-\alpha)})^\alpha L \int_0^1 A_{it}^{1-\alpha} A_{it}^\alpha di$$

$$= \zeta A_t L.$$

3. That is,

$$\frac{(1-\tau^*)\phi'(\mu_A^*)}{\delta} = (1-\mu_A)L^*,$$

$$\frac{(1-\tau^*)\phi'(\mu_B^*)}{\delta} = (\gamma-1)L^* + \mu_B L^* + (1-\mu_B)\gamma L,$$

$$\frac{(1-\tau^*)\phi'(\mu_C^*)}{\delta} = (\gamma-1)(L+L^*) + \mu_C L.$$

4. More specifically, relatedness between products i and j is measured by

$$\varphi_{i,j} = \min\left\{ P\left(\frac{x_i}{x_j}\right), P\left(\frac{x_j}{x_i}\right) \right\},$$

where $P(x_i / x_j)$ is the probability that a country exports (enough of) good i conditional upon exporting (enough of) good j.

References

Aghion, P., R. Burgess, S. Redding, and F. Zilibotti. 2008. The unequal effects of liberalization: Evidence from dismantling the license Raj in India. *American Economic Review* 98 (4): 1397–1412.

Aghion, P., D. Hemous, and E. Kharroubi. 2009. Cyclical budgetary policy, credit constraints, and Industry growth. Mimeo. Harvard University.

Frankel, J., and D. Romer. 1999. Does trade cause growth? *American Economic Review* 89 (3): 379–99.

Greenwald, B., and J. Stiglitz .2006. Helping infant economies grow: Foundations of trade policies for developing countries. *American Economic Review, Papers and Proceedings,* 96 (2): 141–46.

Hausmann, R., and B. Klinger. 2006. Structural transformation and patterns of comparative advantage in the product space. Working paper 128. CID.

Hausmann, R., and B. Klinger. 2007. The structure of the product space and the evolution of comparative advantage. Working paper 146. CID.

Keller, W. 2002. Technology diffusion and the world distribution of income: The role of geography, language, and trade. Mimeo. University of Texas.

Keller, W. 2004. International technology diffusion. *Journal of Economic Literature* 42 (3): 752–82.

Krueger, A., and B. Tuncer. 1982. An empirical test of the infant industry argument. *American Economic Review* 72 (5): 1142–52.

Lucas, R. 1993. Making a miracle. *Econometrica* 61 (2): 251–72.

Nunn, N., and D. Trefler. 2007. The political economy of tariffs and long-term growth. Mimeo. University of Toronto.

Rajan, R., and L. Zingales. 1998. Financial dependence and growth. *American Economic Review* 88 (3): 559–86.

Romer, P. 1990. Endogenous technological change. *Journal of Political Economy* 98 (S5): 71–102.

Wacziarg, R. 2001. Measuring the dynamic gains from trade. *World Bank Economic Review* 15 (3): 393–429.

Young, A. 1991. Learning by doing and the dynamic effects of international trade. *Quarterly Journal of Economics* 106 (2): 369–405.

3 National Champions and Economic Growth

Kathy Fogel, Randall Morck, and Bernard Yeung

3.1 Introduction

Schumpeter's (1912, 1942) view that economic growth arises through an ongoing process of *creative destruction*, as developed in the *New Endogenous Growth Theory* of, for example, Aghion and Howitt (1998), is increasingly solidly validated by empirical work. Bower and Christensen (1995), Christensen (1997), and others painstakingly document numerous case studies of the disruptive effects on existing businesses of many new technologies that nonetheless ultimately advance overall productivity. Fogel et al. (2008), noting that creative destruction implies the more extensive destruction of staid established firms by creative upstarts, find faster long-term economic growth in countries where large firms' long-term survival odds are lower. Chun et al. (2008) note that intensified creative destruction implies a widening gap between winner and loser firms, and find faster productivity growth in US industries exhibiting larger firm-specific performance variance. An economically significant association between creative destruction and economic growth, at least in developed economies in the later twentieth and early twenty-first centuries, is now widely accepted.

Precisely how the process of creative destruction works is, however, less certain. Even Schumpeter permitted a degree of ambiguity: Schumpeter (1912) argues that key innovations are best created and developed by entrepreneurs capitalizing new firms in financial markets, but thirty years later Schumpeter (1942) posits that R&D departments in large quasi-monopolistic firms have better access to the risk-tolerant capital creative destruction requires.

The theoretical importance of new firms to an economy's overall growth rests critically on the microeconomics of property rights. An employee in a large corporation has difficulty ensuring that her innovations belong to her, rather than her employer. For example, Shuji Nakamura invented the blue LED, which made flat screen full color displays possible, while working for Nichia Chemical Industries. To reward him, Nichia raised Nakamura's salary to US$140,000. Had he founded a new firm to develop his insight, Nakamura would be a multibillionaire. In frustration, he quit and moved to the United States, a country with a long tradition of innovators founding new giants.

For example, Alexander Graham Bell offered his telephone patents to Western Union, the telegraphy giant, for $100,000. Telephone communication was then feasibly only for local communication, and short-distance telegraphy was an insignificant market. Western Union's confidently unimaginative management declined Bell's offer, forcing the discarded inventor to found the tiny upstart that became AT&T.

Why were Nichia Chemical Industries and Western Union so ill-disposed toward what turned out to be revolutionary innovations? Shleifer and Vishny (1989) develop a model in which incumbent corporate insiders maximize their job security by committing their firms to technologies reliant on the insiders' particular expertise. Consistent with this, Betz (1993) documents how IBM's top researchers and managers, with careers built around mainframe computing, delayed moving into PCs to safeguard the value of their human capital. The career concerns of its key decision makers ultimately cost IBM its near monopoly over business computers. Klepper (2007) discusses analogous events in the US auto industry.

The model of managerial entrenchment Shleifer and Vishny (1989) develop is microeconomic, but it has implications for economywide growth. A country that protects its large established firms from harsh gales of creative destruction may safeguard entrenched insiders, like those Betz (1993) describes. But if this protection undermines the prospects of potentially rapidly growing new upstart firms and deter innovators, like Nakamura and Bell, long-term economywide growth could be compromised.

Schumpeter (1942) suggests that such protection might not have negative economywide consequences, arguing that the creation and successful development of an innovation often requires vast amounts of risk-tolerant capital that large established firms are well positioned to provide. While alternative sources of entrepreneurial capital exist— venture capital funds and public equity markets—the former demand sweeping control rights (Gompers and Lerner 2001) and the latter are an expensive source of funds (Ritter 1987). Large established firms could easily provide the funding innovative entrepreneurs need—if only the problems enumerated above could be sidestepped.

This suggests the possibility of a "kinder gentler" form of creative destruction, in which large established firms sponsor innovative new ideas and continually renew themselves while augmenting the economy's growth. The problems highlighted above that might deter innovation in large firms are ultimately problems of corporate governance. Enforceable contracts protecting employees' intellectual property rights over innovations they develop while at work seem entirely feasible as a matter of law, but large corporations' top managers virtually never provide such protection (Orkin and Burger 2005).

Much evidence shows that the insiders of large established firms put their self-interest aside if their job security is demonstrably at the public shareholders' pleasure (Shleifer and Vishny 1997b). For example, Gompers, Ishii, and Metrick (2003) and Bebchuk and Cohen (2005) document clearly superior performance in US firms whose managers can be more readily ousted by public shareholders.

Bertrand and Schoar (2003) further show that firms' strategies can change markedly when new top managers take control. Fama (1980) argues that a market for managerial labor services can ensure that new top managers are hired whenever the old ones become too self-interested, and Demsetz (1983) argues that a broader array of contracting solutions work toward this end. Regardless of the underlying microeconomic forces, if the top managers of large established firms can be induced to sponsor innovators, or to step aside if they fail to do so, creative destruction might proceed through existing national champions.

But entrenched managers are not the only impediment. Morck, Wolfenzon, and Yeung (2005), Bertrand and Schoar (2006), and others show that inept or self-interested controlling shareholders can also compromise their firms' performance, and may well be the most important class of entrenched insiders in many countries. Morck, Shleifer, and Vishny (1989) argue that corporate takeovers let new controlling shareholders renew old corporations. Shleifer and Vishny (1997b) go further, concluding that new controlling shareholders are the primary mechanism for correcting serious misgovernance. Hermalin and Weisbach (2003) concur, arguing that the mechanisms Fama (1980) and Demsetz (1983) envision work poorly, and Bebchuk and Cohen (2005) conclude that little improvement is possible in firms shielded from meaningful control changes.

If control can pass readily to more able or better motivated people, old large firms might not have to be replaced for innovation to take place. Whether control changes might augment economic growth by instilling innovation in large established firms is therefore an empirical question.

To explore these issues, we follow Fogel et al. (2008) by defining the "national champions" of 43 countries in 1975 as their ten largest employers as of that year.[1] They measure the business turnover of each country's national champions by counting those that disappear from the top-ten list over the subsequent twenty years, from 1976 to 1996, and document a statistically significant link between a higher rate of business turnover and faster economic growth, which we reproduce. To see if control turnover in these same national champions' top management can substitute for business turnover in national champions themselves, we use the same definition of national champions, but test for an analogous link between higher rates of turnover in corporate control and economic growth. We detect no statistically significant relationship between higher rates of turnover in who controls a country's top corporation and faster economy growth, if measured by increase in per capita GDP or by TFP growth.

If we measure economic growth by capital accumulation, we find a paradoxically negative relationship between that measure and control turnover. This is most marked in low-income countries, where the effect is economically large.

We could advance some explanations of the aforementioned statistically insignificant and paradoxical results. One possibility is that business turnover is a better indicator of creative destruction than control turnover. Likely, even with a change of corporate management, a company does not fundamentally change; corporate practices and routines remain largely the same (Nelson and Winter 1982). Thus the critical disruptive innovations have to come from new corporations with new routines. Another possibility is that our control turnover measures are not capturing genuine governance-enhancing control turnover. Control turnover, particularly in countries with weak institutions, might merely reflect a passing of corporate power to successively more entrenched insiders who attach successively higher value to the private benefits of control.

Such a case would occur if the control turnover entrusts corporate governance to those who draw successively higher utility from non-pecuniary private benefits of control, for example, from the pleasure of exerting power. Or, as is usual, it might occur if control turnover passes corporate governance to people who can extract pecuniary and nonpecuniary benefits more efficiently, for example, by channeling more wealth or by effectively leveraging more control or influence.

These speculations cannot presently be confirmed by our data, which we concede are rife with problems. We enthusiastically invite more study of these issues, and confirmation, rebuttal, or alternative explanations of our findings.

3.2   Data and Variables

This section describes the data and the key variables we used for our measurements. For some of the key variables we reuse variables from Fogel et al. (2008), and we reproduce the descriptions of such variables where appropriate.

3.2.1   Measuring Business Turnover and Control Turnover

Fogel et al. (2008) construct corporate survival rates by comparing lists of leading firms in Dun & Bradstreet's *Principal International Business* directories in 1975 and 1996. These data are based on surveys, and include both listed and unlisted firms, obviating the criticism of studies using, for example, DataStream, which listed firms are less important in some countries than others. Fogel et al. drop companies with fewer than 500 employees and countries with fewer than 10 such companies; as well as countries experiencing prolonged wars or civil wars. Communist block countries are not covered.

They supplement these data by collecting information on who controls each firm in their list in 1975 and again in 1996. This effort combines data from WorldScope, SDC Platinum, and Hoover's online, and the data are supplemented by archived Internet news providers like Forbes and individual companies' websites, Google searches, and library books on national economic histories, corporate histories, and business family histories. This effort is unsuccessful for many large firms in Arabic, African, and all East European countries, precluding these countries from our sample as well.

Given these data, we follow La Porta et al. (1999) and consolidate firms into corporate groups based on a 20 percent control threshold. For example, if 20 percent or more of three publicly traded firms are controlled by the same wealthy individual or family, and this family is the largest shareholder of these firms, we consolidate them into a single family group. If no owner votes over 20 percent, we call the firm "free-standing and widely held." We calculate the total number of employees for each group by adding up the employees of the firms belonging to that group, as provided by Dunn and Bradstreet. Using employee headcount lets us sidestep problems involving intragroup sales and overhead assets ownership that complicate financial consolidation efforts. The consolidation process resolves a list of top businesses, by which we mean "businesses or groups," for each of 1975 and 1996 in each of 44 countries.

We further follow Fogel et al. (2008) in creating five different lists for each country in 1975 and 1996, depending on the types of businesses counted. List I is maximally inclusive, and includes state-controlled, foreign-controlled, and financial-sector firms as well as nonfinancial private-sector firms. List II drops financial-sector firms on the grounds that these are typically differently regulated and often promised implicit or explicit state guarantees. List III drops further foreign-controlled businesses on the ground that they are less affected by local business conditions and institutions. List IV drops both financial sector firms and businesses that are state controlled in 1975, 1996, or at any time in between, including state-controlled listed firms with the government as a direct or indirect controlling shareholder, on the ground that all the qualifications above may apply to them. Our final list V is a minimally inclusive list, and includes only domestically controlled, private-sector nonfinancial businesses.

We consider several such lists, rather than focusing on a single one, because while finances, economic openness, and government intervention may contribute to growth, including these growth sources into a single list could inadvertently merely reproduce established results. Further, in many economies, large fractions of economic activity are due to all sorts of firms, so we expect some objections to the classifications we noted above. Financial firms can and do fail; locally based multinationals could be as independent of local conditions as the local subsidiaries of foreign multinationals; and firms controlled by politically connected business families might have budget constraints little harder than those of state-controlled enterprises (SCEs).

Business Turnover Rates   The next step is matching 1975 and 1996 lists. We follow Fogel et al. (2008) in defining the *business turnover rate* in each list as the fraction of 1975 top-ten firms that have disappeared by 1996. The turnover rate in each list is laboriously constructed using all the information sources listed above, and is supplemented where necessary with telephone calls to finance professors, bankers, and corporate archives in various countries. This reveals instances of name changes, superficial reorganizations of business groups under different family investment vehicles, and the like. We are highly confident that our business turnover rates are accurate.

In constructing our business turnover rates, we must define what we mean when we say a 1975 top-ten business has disappeared by 1996. If we require that the business no longer exists in any form, our turnover rates are very low across the board. Even companies that undergo spectacular bankruptcies can reemerge as shadows of their former selves—as is defined as the top-ten businesses of 1975 remaining in the top-ten lists in 1996, grow as fast as total GDP, retaining at least 10 percent of their 1975 workforce, or a combination of the criteria above.

We denote our business turnover rates $\Phi(n, w)$, with $n \in \{I, II, III, IV, V\}$ indicating which top-ten list is used and $w \in \{E, L\}$ indicating whether equal or labor weighting is used in its construction.

Control Turnover Rates   Next we define a *control turnover rate* in each list of top firms as one less the fraction of 1975 top-ten controlling owners who still control a top business in 1996. As noted above, we define control as a voting stake of 20 percent or more, exercised directly or indirectly, in the absence of another larger voting stake.

We define a *change in control* as a change in the identity of the business' controlling shareholder. Unfortunately, calling a control change is not always a simple exercise, and judgment calls are inevitable.

Most cases are straightforward. If a business has no controlling shareholder in 1975, but has a 20 percent voting blockholder in 1996, we say control has changed. Likewise, if the identity of the controlling owner changes from 1975 to 1996, say because it is taken over, we say control has changed. Obviously we do not count equity blocks acquisitions by another group company controlled by the old ultimate controlling shareholder, as these or merely reorganizations of the internal structures of business groups.

In many cases the controlling owner is a family or family trust. If the same family remains in control, we say control has not changed. This is because we cannot always isolate a particular point in time when a son takes over from a father, and thus cannot be sure whether or not a genuine generational transfer has occurred in the window we study. Also succession within a family may not be the radical change in control such as Shleifer and Vishny (1997b) envision as correcting governance problems (Bertrand and Schoar 2006). Rather, successive generations may grow increasingly entrenched, conservative, and resistant to innovative ideas (Pérez-González 2006; Morck and Yeung 2003, 2004; Morck, Wolfenzon, and Yeung 2005).

If the business has no controlling shareholder in 1975 and again in 1996, we say control changes if the identity of the CEO (the top executive, regardless of actual title) changes. Again, this is a judgment call. If the board (Hermalin and Weisbach 1988), institutional investors (Black and Coffee, 1994), or creditors empowered in a distressed or bankrupt firm successfully lobby to oust professional managers who blocked innovation, this is a genuine change in control. But Vancil (1987) shows that this likely overstates genuine control changes by documenting successions from patrons to protégés that clearly preserve existing management strategies and governance problems. We are unable to distinguish these cases from each other at present, so we accept the noise created by aggregating them. We hope to revisit this distinction in a subsequent study that more precisely isolates genuine turnover of corporate decision makers.

In a similar vein, state-controlled businesses might be said to be "under new management" if the government passes to a different party or a new dictator. However, the governance problems of state-controlled firms are likely to persist across regimes (Shleifer 1996; Shleifer and Vishny 1994a, b, 1997a). Consequently we say there is no control change if a 1975 state-controlled business remains state controlled in 1997. We do, however, consider 1975 state-controlled enterprises that are privatized by 1996 to have undergone control turnovers. We recognize that this induces a second set of problems, for privatizations may well accompany broader liberalizations that affect economic growth more broadly than through specific firms.

Because a subset of these events, namely bankruptcies or business failures, are used to define business turnover, our control turnover index correlates with business turnover, shown to advance growth (Fogel et al. 2008).

We concede that these judgment calls render our control turnover rates noisy. However, this is a first-pass study, and we hope to revisit these issues in further work that handles these issues with more precision. In the present exercise we opt for bright-line rules that render our data construction as transparent as possible.

We denote our control turnover rates $\Theta(n, w)$ with $n \in \{I, II, III, IV, V\}$, indicating which top-ten list is used, and $w \in \{E, L\}$, indicating whether equal or labor weighting is used in its construction.

Data   Table 3.1 presents our maximally inclusive *business turnover* and *control turnover* rates—that is, those based on list I of all available firms. We construct two versions of each turnover rate. One is *labor weighted*, and weights each employer or controlling shareholder by total employees in 1975. The second is equal weighted, and is the simple fraction of businesses or controlling shareholders dropping out of the list by 1996. The labor-weighted turnover rate weights larger businesses within the top ten more heavily; the equal-weighted turnover rates weigh all the top-ten businesses the same.

3.2.2   Economy Growth Rates

We follow Fogel et al. (2008) in gauging economy performance by long-term growth rates in per capita GDP, total factor productivity, and capital accumulation. These variables are constructed from per capita GDP and capital stock figures from Penn World Tables 6.2. All figures are purchasing power parity adjusted and deflated to 2000 international dollars. The most recent data year for most countries is 2003.

Absent other considerations, we would relate control turnover measured between 1975 and 1996 to economy growth in a window beginning around 1996. However, major economic crises in East Asia and parts of Latin America render economy-level data around 1996 highly atypical. We therefore follow Fogel et al. (2008) and define our long term, real per capita GDP growth rate from 1990 to 2003 as

$$\Delta \ln(y) = \ln(\textit{per capita GDP}_{2003}) - \ln(\textit{per capita GDP}_{1990}). \tag{3.1}$$

To distinguish economic growth due to an increased physical capital stock from growth due to improved productivity, we follow King and Levine (1994) and decompose overall economic growth into capital accumulation growth and total factor productivity (TFP) growth components. To do this, we construct a time series of total real physical capital stock estimates for each country $\{K_t\}$, with t measuring time in

Table 3.1
Business turnover and control turnover

	Business turnover		Control turnover	
	$\Phi(I,L)$	$\Phi(I,E)$	$\Theta(I,L)$	$\Theta(I,E)$
Argentina	0.688	0.700	0.859	0.900
Australia	0.331	0.500	0.883	0.900
Austria	0.167	0.400	0.214	0.500
Belgium	0.592	0.700	0.680	0.800
Bolivia	0.251	0.700	0.281	0.800
Brazil	0.529	0.500	0.529	0.500
Canada	0.599	0.600	0.922	0.900
Chile	0.560	0.600	0.677	0.800
Colombia	0.712	0.800	0.712	0.800
Denmark	0.437	0.600	0.938	0.900
Finland	0.220	0.200	0.519	0.500
France	0.436	0.600	0.537	0.700
Germany	0.237	0.300	0.717	0.800
Greece	0.618	0.700	0.666	0.800
Hong Kong	0.394	0.700	0.846	0.800
India	0.879	0.900	0.879	0.900
Indonesia	0.722	0.800	0.765	0.900
Israel	0.405	0.400	0.450	0.500
Italy	0.239	0.600	0.239	0.600
Japan	0.275	0.300	0.595	0.700
Malaysia	0.927	0.900	0.927	0.900
Mexico	0.236	0.500	0.544	0.800
Netherlands	0.202	0.600	1.000	1.000
New Zealand	0.795	0.800	1.000	1.000
Norway	0.699	0.700	0.909	0.900
Pakistan	0.772	0.600	0.772	0.600
Peru	0.541	0.500	0.638	0.700
Philippines	0.740	0.800	0.816	0.900
Portugal	0.657	0.800	0.709	0.900
Singapore	0.440	0.600	0.623	0.800
South Africa	0.475	0.600	0.716	0.800
South Korea	0.549	0.500	0.619	0.600
Spain	0.537	0.700	0.704	0.800
Sri Lanka	0.929	0.909	1.000	1.000
Sweden	0.215	0.500	0.518	0.800
Switzerland	0.204	0.400	0.934	0.900
Taiwan	0.608	0.800	0.608	0.800
Thailand	0.314	0.500	0.314	0.500
Turkey	0.792	0.900	0.792	0.900
United Kingdom	0.769	0.800	1.000	1.000
United States	0.469	0.500	1.000	1.000
Uruguay	0.510	0.700	0.641	0.800
Venezuela	0.263	0.600	0.297	0.700

Note: Business turnover is the fraction of top-ten 1975 businesses no longer in the top ten by 1996. Control turnover is the fraction of controlling owners of top-ten 1975 businesses no longer controlling a top-ten business by 1996. Both are based on list I, based on all available top businesses—financial, foreign-controlled, state-controlled, and private sector.

years and starting in 1950. We assume each country starts with a zero capital stock in 1950 and that real investment in capital stock depreciates at $\delta = 7$ percent per year and is augmented each year by real aggregate investment, denoted I_t. Each country's series of capital stock estimates is then constructed from the finite-difference equation

$$K_t = (1 - \delta)K_{t-1} + I_{t-1}. \tag{3.2}$$

Since the Penn World Tables data end in 2003, this is the last year for which we can estimate K_t.

Real per capita physical capital stock is then total real physical capital stock divided by total population. Each country's growth rate in real per capita physical capital is then simply the log of its per capita physical capital in 2003 minus that in 1990, denoted $\Delta \ln(k)$. Last, we follow Beck, Levine, and Loayza (2000) in estimating total factor productivity (TFP) growth as real per capita GDP growth minus 0.3 times real per capita capital growth. We denote the TFP growth rate variable Δtfp.

3.2.3 Control Variables
To control for other plausible factors affecting economic growth rates, we include additional control variables measured at the starting point of our growth window. We denote the vector containing these control variables $\underline{X}$.

Convergence Economic growth is thought to be subject to a convergence effect: higher growth rates are possible for poorer countries catching up to the developed economies but are much harder to sustain once the catch-up process is largely complete (e.g., Mankiw 1995).[2] Our primary control variables thus include measures of the initial conditions of each economy at the beginning of the growth window: the logs of per capita GDP, per capita capital stock, and education attainment in 1990. Per capita GDP is obtained from Penn World Tables 6.2, adjusted to purchasing power parity and 2000 international dollars. Per capita capital stock is constructed as in the previous section. Education attainment is from Barro and Lee (2001) and counts the total number of years of schooling in population aged 25 or older.

Natural Endowment An economy's natural endowment is also thought to play a key role in economic development (e.g., Romer, 1993;

Rodriguez and Sachs, 1999; Sachs, 2001; Sachs and Warner, 2001). We therefore include measures of each economy's "economic endowment"— its size, store of natural resources, and geographical characteristics known to correlate with trade and capital openness. Total GDP and total population measure country size. Natural resource dependency is the net imports (imports minus exports) of fuel, ore, and metal as a percentage of total GDP. Following Romer (1993) and Sachs (2001), we use the logarithm of a country's land area and an indicator variable, coded one for landlocked countries and zero for those with access to the sea, as exogenous measures of openness. Landlocked countries in our sample include Austria, Bolivia, and Switzerland. These variables, except the landlocked dummy, are from the online edition of World Development Indicators. The list of landlocked countries is gathered from the online version of the CIA World Factbook.

Some countries and regions, notably Latin America and East Asia, experienced financial and monetary crises just before or just after 1996. To ensure that these crises do not drive our result in any way, we augment our list of controls with regional indicator variables. The first is a Latin America indicator variable, set to one for countries in Central and South America countries and zero otherwise. The next is an Asian crisis indicator variable, set to one for economies affected by the 1997 to 1998 East Asian financial crises.

Institutions   We also control for institutional variables known to affect economic growth. The first variable is the Common Law legal system dummy first proposed by La Porta et al. (1998), who associate the Common Law with better government institutions and more developed financial markets. The Common Law indicator is set to one for countries with legal systems derived from British Common Law and to zero for all others.

Our second institutional variable is an autocracy–democracy index. Although democracy per se might not strongly predict economic growth (Barro 1996), it supports institutions that maintain the rule of law, enforce property rights, constrain vested interests, and level the playing field for new firms—all of which plausibly affect innovation and growth. Our autocracy–democracy index is *polity2*, from the Polity IV dataset constructed by the University of Maryland's Center for International Development and Conflict Management. This ordinal index ranges from minus ten for highly authoritarian governments to plus ten for stable democracies.

Last, we control for the respect state accords the property rights of private businesses. Property rights protection is known to affect the cost of capital, businesses' propensity to invest, the functional efficiency of capital allocation, and economic growth (e.g., Keefer and Knack 1995; Wurgler 2000; Bekaert, Harvey, and Lundblad 2005). Our measure is an *expropriation risk index* from La Porta et al. (1998), the risk of "outright confiscation" or "forced nationalization" as assessed by the International Country Risk Guide (ICRG), averaged across all years from 1982 through 1995. This index ranges from zero to ten, with higher scores greater property rights protection.

In a range of ancillary tests, we augment these key variables with yet more institutional development controls: indices measuring *corruption, rule of law, shareholder rights,* and *creditor rights,* all from La Porta et al. (1998); a *bureaucracy* index from ICRG, a *tax compliance* index from Global Competitiveness Report, a *political rights* index from Freedom House, and a *government crisis* index from La Porta et al. (2002).

3.2.4 Summary Statistics

Table 3.2 presents univariate statistics of the key variables described above. Based on our maximally inclusive list I, which covers all available top businesses, including financial, foreign-controlled, state-controlled as well as private-sector businesses, the employment-weighted turnover rate averages about 50 percent from 1975 to 1996 across all 43 countries in the sample while control turnover averages 70 percent. Cumulative long-term real per capita GDP growth averages about 24 percent for the 1990 to 2003 window, reflecting a 15 percent average real growth in total factor productivity and a 31 percent average real accumulation of physical capital.

3.3 Main Results

We now run regressions to see if corporate control turnover rates correlate with economy growth in the same way as business turnover rates. We replicate the result of Fogel et al. (2008) linking the toppling of formerly dominant firms to accelerated growth, and then search for a similar link between the changes in corporate control and accelerated growth. The former captures the rawest form of Schumpeter's (1912, 1942) process of "creative destruction," which emphasizes the destruction of old, dominant firms by new corporate upstarts as the fundamental engine of economic growth. The latter is intended to capture a

Table 3.2
Summary statistics of growth and control variables

		Mean	Standard deviation	Minimum	Maximum
Turnover measures					
Business turnover, labor weighted	$\Phi(I,L)$	0.510	0.221	0.167	0.929
Business turnover, equally weighted	$\Phi(I,E)$	0.623	0.172	0.200	0.909
Control turnover, labor weighted	$\Theta(I,L)$	0.697	0.220	0.214	1.000
Control turnover, equally weighted	$\Theta(I,E)$	0.793	0.149	0.500	1.000
Economic growth measures					
Per capita GDP growth, 1990 to 2003	$\Delta \ln(y)$	0.244	0.152	−0.180	0.607
Total factor productivity growth, 1990 to 2003	$\Delta \ln tfp$	0.151	0.105	−0.127	0.343
Capital accumulation growth, 1990 to 2003	$\Delta \ln(k)$	0.310	0.223	−0.175	0.916
Control variables	$\underline{X}$				
Log of GDP per capita, 1990	x_1	9.26	0.794	7.55	10.2
Log of per capita capital stock, 1990	x_2	9.88	1.08	7.41	11.3
Log of adult education attainment, 1990	x_3	1.91	0.378	0.829	2.49
Total GDP, 1990 (in trillions)	x_4	0.575	1.11	0.0172	6.78
Total population, 1990 (in millions)	x_5	60.7	134	3.05	850
Total land area (in millions km²)	x_6	1.33	2.46	0.00067	9.16
Natural resource dependency, 1990	x_7	0.0109	0.0674	−0.0551	0.3130
Common law legal origin	x_8	0.326	0.474	0.000	1.000
Democracy-autocracy index	x_9	4.52	6.58	−9	10
Expropriation risk	x_{10}	8.31	1.47	5.22	9.98

Note: Business turnover is the fraction of top-ten 1975 businesses no longer in the top ten by 1996. Control turnover is the fraction of controlling owners of top ten 1975 businesses who relinquish control of a top-ten business by 1996. Turnover indexes are based on list I, which covers all available top businesses including financial, foreign-controlled, state-controlled, and private-sector top businesses. The sample is the 43 countries listed in table 3.1 less Taiwan for net export of fuel, ore, and metal, less Hong Kong for democracy-autocracy, and less Bolivia for expropriation risk.

"kinder and gentler" form of creative destruction, in which changes in corporate control might allow old firms to reinvent themselves as conduits for innovation—a form in which only to old top echelon of corporate decision makers need be dislodged.

3.3.1 Business Turnover and Control Turnover Compared

Fogel et al. (2008) link faster turnover of the largest businesses in a country with accelerated per capita GDP growth, TFP growth, and capital accumulation. Since business turnover necessarily implies control turnover in our top-ten lists, the two sets of turnover rates are necessarily correlated.

We examine this correlation by regressing control turnover on business turnover,

$$\Theta(n, w) = a_1(n, w) + a_2(n, w)\Phi(n, w) + \Theta^{\perp}(n, w), \tag{3.3}$$

across our sample of countries. As above, $n \in \{I, II, III, IV, V\}$ indicating the top-ten list used and $w \in \{E, L\}$ indicates whether equal or labor weighting is used in the construction of the turnover rate. The intercept $a_1(n, w)$ and regression coefficient $a_2(n, w)$ are estimated using ordinary least squares.

The regression residuals from (3.3), denoted $\Theta^{\perp}(n, w)$, provide measures of control turnover for each country uncorrelated with business turnover. We interpret them as gauging how much control turnover, weighted either equally or by labor, we find in list n.

Table 3.3 summarizes the regressions represented by (3.3). The table confirms that our control turnover rate and business turnover rate estimates are highly correlated—the coefficient estimates on business turnover for indexes based on lists I through III are all positive and highly significant. However, the R^2's of these regressions indicate only about 30 percent of their variation is shared. When we turn to the turnover rates based on lists IV and V, from which state-controlled enterprises are excluded, we find markedly lower coefficients and R^2's. Thus *business turnover* and *control turnover* rates are far less collinear—suggesting a greater likelihood of an independent effect associated with control turnover.

3.3.2 Simple Correlation Coefficients

Table 3.4 presents simple correlations of countries' business turnover and control turnover rates with their various economic growth rates and control variables. The table includes only turnover rates

Table 3.3
Regressions of control turnover on business turnover

Top-ten list used		Weights used	Regression coefficient	T statistic	P-level	R^2
I	Maximally inclusive	Labor	0.559	4.40	(0.00)	0.315
		Equal	0.504	4.67	(0.00)	0.342
II	Drops financial businesses	Labor	0.546	4.11	(0.00)	0.287
		Equal	0.402	3.70	(0.00)	0.245
III	Drops foreign-controlled businesses	Labor	0.565	4.25	(0.00)	0.301
		Equal	0.426	3.92	(0.00)	0.268
IV	Drops one-time state-controlled businesses	Labor	0.272	2.35	(0.02)	0.116
		Equal	0.164	1.60	(0.12)	0.058
V	Nonfinancial, domestically controlled, private sector only	Labor	0.351	2.96	(0.01)	0.172
		Equal	0.296	2.56	(0.01)	0.135

Note: Business turnover is the fraction of top-ten 1975 businesses no longer in the top ten by 1996. Control turnover is the fraction of controlling owners of top-ten 1975 businesses who relinquish control of a top-ten business by 1996. Numbers in parentheses are probability values for rejecting the null hypothesis of zero coefficients. Probability values are based on heteroskedasticity-consistent standard errors. The regression coefficient is the estimate of $a_2(n, w)$, as defined in regression (3.3) of the text. List I covers all available firms; list II covers all firms from list I except financial firms; list III is list I less financial and foreign-controlled firms; list IV is list I excluding financial and state-controlled firms; and list V is list I excluding financial, foreign-controlled, and state-controlled firms. Sample is countries listed in table 3.1. Sample is the 43 countries listed in table 3.1. Numbers in parentheses are probability values for rejecting the null hypothesis of zero correlation coefficients. Correlation coefficients significant at 10 percent or better are in boldface.

constructed with our maximally inclusive list, which includes financial companies, state-controlled or foreign-controlled businesses, as well as domestic private-sector top businesses, and with our minimally inclusive list, which includes only nonfinancial private-sector domestically controlled businesses.

Note that business turnover rates based on the maximally inclusive list of top businesses are positively and significantly correlated with all three measures of growth, and that control turnover rates are somewhat less impressively correlated with economic growth. At first, this might be taken as linking both business turnover and control turnover to accelerated economic growth. However, caution is warranted because the turnover rates are correlated. The final column correlates the component of control turnover orthogonal to business turnover with economic growth and reveals no significant linkage. This is

Table 3.4
Correlations of turnover rates with economy growth rates and controls

| List used in turnover rate construction | Labor weighted turnover rate based on | | | | | |
| | List I | | | List V | | |
Economy growth rate or control variable	Business turnover	Control turnover	Orthogonal control turnover	Business turnover	Control turnover	Orthogonal control turnover
Real per capita GDP growth, 1990 to 2003	0.428 (0.00)	0.259 (0.09)	0.023 (0.88)	0.130 (0.41)	-0.068 (0.66)	-0.134 (0.39)
TFP growth, 1990 to 2003	0.423 (0.00)	0.276 (0.07)	0.046 (0.77)	0.210 (0.18)	0.014 (0.93)	-0.080 (0.61)
Capital accumulation, 1990 to 2003	0.307 (0.05)	0.155 (0.32)	-0.021 (0.89)	-0.035 (0.82)	-0.177 (0.26)	-0.179 (0.25)
Log of per capita GDP in 1990	-0.481 (0.00)	0.074 (0.64)	0.416 (0.01)	-0.348 (0.02)	0.260 (0.09)	0.444 (0.00)
Log of per capita capital assets in 1990	-0.515 (0.00)	0.027 (0.86)	0.382 (0.01)	-0.280 (0.07)	0.289 (0.06)	0.445 (0.00)
Log of adult education attainment in 1990	-0.351 (0.02)	0.214 (0.17)	0.496 (0.00)	-0.260 (0.09)	0.337 (0.03)	0.489 (0.00)
Log of total GDP in 1990	-0.0791 (0.61)	0.115 (0.46)	0.192 (0.22)	-0.419 (0.01)	-0.158 (0.31)	0.0172 (0.91)

Table 3.4
(continued)

List used in turnover rate construction	Labor weighted turnover rate based on					
	List I			List V		
Economy growth rate or control variable	Business turnover	Control turnover	Orthogonal control turnover	Business turnover	Control turnover	Orthogonal control turnover
Net export of fuel, ore and metal over GDP in 1990	−0.0768 (0.63)	−0.170 (0.28)	−0.154 (0.33)	**0.282** **(0.07)**	0.165 (0.30)	0.051 (0.75)
Common law dummy	**0.308** **(0.04)**	**0.358** **(0.02)**	0.224 (0.15)	−0.0504 (0.75)	−0.0089 (0.96)	0.0133 (0.93)
Democracy–autocracy	−0.0913 (0.57)	**0.272** **(0.08)**	**0.395** **(0.01)**	**−0.261** **(0.10)**	**0.271** **(0.08)**	**0.418** **(0.01)**
Expropriation risk	**−0.431** **(0.00)**	0.0599 (0.71)	**0.367** **(0.02)**	**−0.366** **(0.02)**	0.214 (0.17)	**0.399** **(0.01)**

Note: Business turnover is the fraction of top-ten 1975 businesses no longer in the top ten by 1996 weighted by 1975 employees. Control turnover is also labor weighted, and measures the fraction of controlling owners of top-ten 1975 businesses no longer controlling of a top-ten business in 1996. Orthogonalized control turnover is the residual from regressing control turnover on business turnover. Turnover rates are all based on list I (all available top businesses) and list V (excludes financial, foreign-controlled, and state-controlled businesses). Sample is 43 countries listed in table 3.1 less Taiwan for net export of fuel, ore and metal, less Hong Kong for democracy–autocracy, and less Bolivia for expropriation risk.

roughly equivalent to regressing growth on both measures of turnover; which procedure (not shown) also confirms the statistical significance of business turnover rates and the insignificance of control turnover rates in explaining economy growth.

Our minimally inclusive turnover rates are less interesting in the table, for none is statistically significantly related to growth at conventional levels. However, neither these insignificant results, nor the insignificant results for the orthogonalized control turnover rates are the final word. We must control for the initial conditions, endowment effects, and institutional effects discussed above.

The table suggests that including these control variables might matter, for higher levels of per capita GDP, capital stock and education in 1990 and greater democracy all correlate with both depressed business turnover rates and elevated orthogonalized control turnover rates. That is, more developed economies—as indicated by higher per capita GDP, capital assets, education levels, or democracy scores—have lower business turnover rates but higher control turnover rates.

3.3.3 Multiple Regressions with Controls

We replicate the regressions in Fogel et al. (2008), which are similar to the now standard approach of Mankiw (1995), but include our *control turnover* rates as an extra explanatory variable. Our regressions are thus of the form

$$g = b_0 + b_1 + b_2\Theta(n,w) + \underline{c}\underline{X} + e \tag{3.4}$$

with g one of our growth rates, $\Delta\ln(y)$, $\Delta\ln(k)$, or Δtfp; Φ one of our business turnover rates, Θ one of our control turnover rates, and $\underline{X}$ a vector of the controls for initial conditions, economy initial endowments, and institutional factors described above. The regression coefficients estimated are the intercept, b_0; the explanatory power of business turnover, b_1; the added explanatory power of control turnover, b_2; and the coefficients of the various controls, the vector $\underline{c}$. The regression residuals are denoted e.

Table 3.5 reports the regression coefficients b_1 and b_2 from variants of (3.4) using turnover rates constructed from all five lists of top businesses. Only initial conditions, the logs of per capita GDP, capital stock, and education, are included as controls. Supplementing these with the natural endowment and the institutional development controls, discussed above, generates qualitatively similar results (not shown).

Table 3.5
Business turnover, control turnover and economic growth

Control turnover construction		Δln(y)		Δlntfp		Δln(k)	
List	Weights	Business turnover	Control turnover	Business turnover	Control turnover	Business turnover	Control turnover
I	Labor	**0.410** (0.00)	−0.101 (0.44)	**0.256** (0.01)	−0.031 (0.73)	**0.512** (0.02)	−0.233 (0.20)
	Equal	**0.514** (0.00)	−0.263 (0.19)	**0.311** (0.01)	−0.099 (0.40)	**0.676** (0.02)	−0.547 (0.11)
II	Labor	**0.396** (0.01)	−0.090 (0.48)	**0.235** (0.02)	−0.029 (0.75)	**0.538** (0.02)	−0.205 (0.22)
	Equal	**0.342** (0.08)	−0.210 (0.33)	0.181 (0.19)	−0.060 (0.65)	**0.536** (0.07)	−0.501 (0.14)
III	Labor	**0.379** (0.01)	−0.093 (0.45)	**0.223** (0.03)	−0.032 (0.71)	**0.520** (0.03)	−0.206 (0.20)
	Equal	**0.387** (0.02)	−0.234 (0.25)	**0.215** (0.07)	−0.083 (0.53)	**0.574** (0.04)	−0.504 (0.11)
IV	Labor	**0.183** (0.09)	−0.175 (0.19)	0.117 (0.14)	−0.067 (0.44)	0.221 (0.16)	**−0.362** (0.07)
	Equal	**0.250** (0.05)	−0.262 (0.27)	**0.152** (0.10)	−0.047 (0.74)	**0.327** (0.09)	**−0.719** (0.06)
V	Labor	0.166 (0.12)	−0.178 (0.14)	0.105 (0.17)	−0.083 (0.30)	0.202 (0.16)	**−0.317** (0.07)
	Equal	**0.266** (0.04)	−0.275 (0.17)	**0.166** (0.07)	−0.098 (0.42)	**0.335** (0.08)	**−0.589** (0.06)

Note: Business turnover is the fraction of top-ten 1975 businesses no longer in the top ten by 1996. Control turnover is the fraction of controlling owners of top-ten 1975 businesses no longer controlling a top-ten business by 1996. Growth is 1990 to 2003 per capita GDP growth, Δln(y), total factor productivity growth, Δlntfp, or per capita capital accumulation, Δln(k). Δlntfp is Δln(y) − 0.3Δln(k). Control variables are the log of per capita GDP, log of per capita capital assets, and log average years of education for adults aged 25 and over. All financial variables are measured in 1990 using US dollars at purchasing power parity deflated to year 2000 levels. Probability values are based on heteroskedasticity-consistent standard errors. Only coefficient estimates on business turnover indexes are shown. List I covers all available firms; list II covers all firms from list I except financial firms; list III is list I less financial and foreign-controlled firms; list IV is list I excluding financial and state-controlled firms; and list V is list I excluding financial, foreign-controlled, and state-controlled firms. Sample is the 43 countries listed in table 3.1. Numbers in parentheses are probability values for rejecting the null hypothesis of zero coefficients. Boldface indicates significance at 10 percent or better.

The table confirms Fogel et al. (2008), who link faster business turn-over to faster *per capita* GDP; TFP and capital growth rates are repli-cated, in that the estimates of b_1 are significant and positive. Including control turnover as an added variable in their regressions thus leaves the positive association they detect between business turnover and economic growth essentially unaffected. The overall pattern of results in table 3.5 suggests that creative destruction relies on business turnovers.

Our variables of primary interest in (3.4) are the control turnover rate measures themselves. Although these attract *negative* coefficients throughout, they are always insignificant in regressions explaining per capita GDP and TFP growth rates. Nonetheless, the uniformly positive coefficients lend little comfort to the hypothesis that readier control turnover augments economic growth. Control turnover and business turnover are, of course, positively correlated, so we might be detecting a mere multicollinearity effect reflected in negative insignificant coef-ficients on the less powerful control turnover measure.

However, closer inspection belies this for greater control turnover, if measured excluding state-controlled firms from the top-ten lists, is actually significantly associated with slower capital accumulation, though the significance levels never defeat a 5 percent threshold. Recall that these are the control turnover measures shown above to be least correlated with their corresponding business turnover measures.

These findings are highly robust. Residual analysis and scatter plots show that outliers are not to blame either for the general insignificance of control turnover in explaining per capita GDP growth and TFP growth or for the significance of control turnover in explaining capital accumulation. Using the alternative window of 1990 to 2000 to estimate economy growth rates generates qualitatively similar results, by which we mean that the pattern of signs and significance levels in the table remains unchanged.

Controlling for measures of country size, like the logarithm of total GDP in 1990 or that of total population in 1990, likewise generates qualitatively similar results. Adding various measures of openness, like the log of the country's land area or a "landlocked" dummy variable, and alternative measures of institutional development, like our corrup-tion, rule of law, bureaucracy, tax compliance, political rights, or gov-ernment crisis measures, also yield qualitatively similar results. We further control for macroeconomic volatility using, in turn, the variance of each country's per capita GDP growth, inflation rate, and the variance of monetary aggregate (M2) growth. Including these controls also generates qualitatively similar results to those in the tables. Finally, regressions with OLS standard errors, instead of heteroskedasticity-consistent standard errors, yield qualitatively similar results too.

In summary, we find no evidence that control turnover might augment GDP or TFP growth rates after accounting for business turnover. Business turnover rates are significantly and robustly correlated with elevated growth rates across the board, as in Fogel et al. (2008)—even in the presence of our control turnover rate estimates—consistent with growth through creative destruction entailing business turnover. In contrast, we find no evidence of a reinforcing effect from control turnover. If anything, our findings link readier control turnover to slower growth, at least if growth is measured by capital accumulation. The negative link is significant if we exclude state-controlled firms from the top-ten lists used to construct the turnover rates, but the difference in p-levels is small—around 11 percent versus around 7 percent.

3.3.4   High-Income versus Low-Income Countries
Aghion et al. (2005) show that the economics underlying rapid growth is likely to differ qualitatively between highly developed countries and developing countries. The former are already near the global technological frontier, and can best grow rapidly by developing innovations that raise their productivity levels. This requires innovation, and thus calls for creative destruction, to expand the production possibilities frontier outward. Developing countries, in contrast, can often grow rapidly by using off-the-shelf technology to "catch up" with the developed world. This demands vast capital investment to replicate existing technologies but does not necessarily call for innovation or creative destruction.

To explore this dichotomy, we partition our sample into high-income and low-income countries, defined as having 1990 per capita GDP levels above or below the sample median. Our high-income subsample primarily consists of OECD countries, and our low-income subsample mostly includes developing countries in Asia and South America.

Table 3.6 reproduces the regressions of table 3.4 using each subsample. These regressions have scarce degrees of freedom, so the p-levels must be interpreted with caution. The exercise is perhaps better considered "curve fitting" than classical statistics.

We again replicate the finding of Fogel et al. (2008) that elevated business turnover rates are most strongly associated with accelerated

Table 3.6
High-income versus low-income countries

Panel A: Regressions on subsample of 22 median or above median per capita GDP countries

Growth rate turnover rate list and weighting	$\Delta\ln(y)$		$\Delta\ln tfp$		$\Delta\ln(k)$	
	Business turnover	Control turnover	Business turnover	Control turnover	Business turnover	Control turnover
I Labor	**0.187** **(0.09)**	0.024 (0.77)	**0.180** **(0.10)**	0.006 (0.95)	0.022 (0.84)	0.063 (0.52)
Equal	**0.240** **(0.09)**	0.000 (1.00)	**0.268** **(0.06)**	-0.029 (0.78)	-0.093 (0.52)	0.098 (0.49)
II Labor	0.162 (0.13)	0.056 (0.51)	0.153 (0.14)	0.034 (0.67)	0.029 (0.75)	0.072 (0.47)
Equal	0.180 (0.14)	0.087 (0.48)	0.186 (0.13)	0.063 (0.58)	-0.020 (0.88)	0.081 (0.59)
III Labor	**0.176** **(0.10)**	0.038 (0.64)	**0.167** **(0.10)**	0.021 (0.79)	0.031 (0.75)	0.058 (0.52)
Equal	**0.236** **(0.05)**	0.039 (0.71)	**0.228** **(0.07)**	0.031 (0.77)	0.026 (0.84)	0.026 (0.84)
IV Labor	0.135 (0.12)	0.053 (0.40)	0.119 (0.16)	0.033 (0.63)	0.055 (0.37)	0.067 (0.54)
Equal	**0.190** **(0.04)**	0.234 (0.12)	**0.186** **(0.04)**	**0.283** **(0.05)**	0.013 (0.88)	-0.163 (0.25)
V Labor	**0.136** **(0.09)**	0.030 (0.57)	0.117 (0.12)	0.015 (0.81)	0.062 (0.26)	0.051 (0.61)
Equal	**0.213** **(0.02)**	0.088 (0.36)	**0.196** **(0.03)**	0.144 (0.18)	0.057 (0.46)	-0.187 (0.11)

Table 3.6
(continued)

Panel B: Regressions on subsample of 21 below median per capita GDP countries

Growth rate turnover rate list and weighting	Δln(y) Business turnover	Δln(y) Control turnover	Δlnffp Business turnover	Δlnffp Control turnover	Δln(k) Business turnover	Δln(k) Control turnover
I Labor	**0.888** **(0.05)**	−0.509 (0.32)	**0.416** **(0.09)**	−0.148 (0.60)	**1.572** **(0.09)**	−1.205 (0.21)
I Equal	**0.924** **(0.05)**	−0.820 (0.14)	0.421 (0.15)	−0.304 (0.31)	**1.678** **(0.04)**	**−1.721** **(0.08)**
II Labor	**1.023** **(0.03)**	−0.596 (0.24)	**0.454** **(0.10)**	−0.203 (0.51)	**1.898** **(0.03)**	−1.309 (0.14)
II Equal	0.689 (0.33)	−0.786 (0.24)	0.168 (0.71)	−0.231 (0.56)	**1.736** **(0.09)**	**−1.850** **(0.08)**
III Labor	**0.853** **(0.02)**	−0.448 (0.28)	0.359 (0.14)	−0.122 (0.65)	**1.647** **(0.01)**	−1.088 (0.11)
III Equal	0.764 (0.14)	−0.765 (0.24)	0.229 (0.52)	−0.224 (0.58)	**1.782** **(0.01)**	**−1.804** **(0.05)**
IV Labor	0.044 (0.94)	−0.431 (0.29)	0.041 (0.92)	−0.176 (0.55)	0.008 (0.99)	**−0.850** **(0.10)**
IV Equal	0.264 (0.68)	−0.671 (0.22)	0.071 (0.87)	−0.238 (0.49)	0.641 (0.51)	**−1.443** **(0.07)**
V Labor	−0.064 (0.92)	−0.219 (0.62)	−0.086 (0.85)	−0.052 (0.88)	0.072 (0.93)	−0.555 (0.30)
V Equal	0.180 (0.83)	−0.442 (0.51)	−0.052 (0.92)	−0.094 (0.83)	0.774 (0.55)	−1.158 (0.25)

Note: Business turnover is the fraction of top-ten 1975 businesses no longer in the top ten by 1996. Control turnover is the fraction of controlling owners of top-ten 1975 businesses who relinquish control of a top-ten business by 1996. Growth is 1990 to 2003 per capita GDP growth, Δln(y), total factor productivity growth, Δlnffp, or per capita capital accumulation, Δln(k). Δlnffp is Δln(y) − 0.3Δln(k). Control variables are the log of per capita GDP, log of per capita capital assets, and log average years of education for adults aged 25 and over. All financial variables are measured in 1990 using US dollars at purchasing power parity deflated to year 2000 levels. Probability values are based on heteroskedasticity-consistent standard errors. Only coefficient estimates on business turnover indexes are shown. List I covers all available firms; list II covers all firms from list I except financial firms; list III is list I less financial and foreign-controlled firms; list IV is list I excluding financial and state-controlled firms; and list V is list I excluding financial, foreign-controlled, and state-controlled firms. Numbers in parentheses are probability values for rejecting the null hypothesis of zero coefficients.

Panel A: Low-income countries include Argentina, Bolivia, Brazil, Chile, Colombia, Greece, India, Indonesia, South Korea, Malaysia, Mexico, Pakistan, Peru, Philippines, South Africa, Sri Lanka, Taiwan, Thailand, Turkey, Uruguay, and Venezuela. Numbers in parentheses are probability values for rejecting the null hypothesis of zero coefficients.

Panel B: High-income countries include Australia, Austria, Belgium, Canada, Denmark, Finland, France, Germany, Hong Kong, Israel, Italy, Japan, Netherlands, New Zealand, Norway, Portugal, Singapore, Spain, Sweden, Switzerland, United Kingdom, and United States.

growth in the private sectors of high-income countries but that business turnover in their state-controlled sectors seems to matter more for low-income countries.[3] Adding control turnover rates as an additional explanatory variable in their regressions does nothing to alter this finding.

The variables of interest in this exercise, our control turnover rates, attract positive insignificant coefficients across in all specifications run across the high-income country sample. However, their coefficients become negative across their low-income sample, and even attain significance in explaining capital growth rates. Remarkably, the negative point estimates of control turnover in the capital growth regressions across low-income countries average about −1.3—three times larger than the −0.4 average in the full sample regressions. These magnitudes imply unambiguously economically significant effects. For example, using the equally weighted list I index and holding all other variables at their mean, reducing control turnover by one standard deviation (0.12) adds 20.7 percent to the capital accumulation rate—a 60 percent increase above its mean.

The negative relation between control turnover and capital accumulation rates does not change qualitatively if we include country characteristic variables: country size, region dummies, natural resource dependency, a landlocked dummy, log of land area, or our growth rate variance measures. In all cases but one, including other institutional development control variables, such as rule of law, corruption, political rights, shareholder rights, creditor rights, leaves the coefficient magnitudes roughly unchanged, but increases the p-levels—though not to the point of insignificance for control turnover rates based on some at least some variants of the top-ten lists. The unique exception is our expropriation risk control, whose inclusion renders all versions of the control turnover rate entirely insignificant and reduces their coefficients strikingly. Thus the negative relationship between control turnover and capital accumulation may well operate through some mechanism that relates to government expropriation risk.

3.4   Conclusions

In summary, after controlling for a country's business turnover rate as well as key measures of its current level of development, natural resource endowment, and institutional development, management control turnover has no discernable relationship to per capita GDP growth or TFP growth and a possible negative relationship with capital accumulation. The latter is especially important in low-income countries. In high-income countries no relationship between control turnover and any of the three economy growth measures is apparent once the controls are included.

Our results suggest that across a broad cross section of countries, "robust" creative destruction, in which competition from rising innovative firms actually destroys old national champions, is required for rapid growth. Merely replacing the top managers or controlling shareholder of an aging champion has no discernable link to accelerated overall growth.

The results improve our understanding of creative destruction. First, the creation and implementation of innovation may depend not only on who control the corporation but also on corporate routines, even if the new controlling party genuinely intends to innovate. Nelson and Winter (1982) show that a company handles its business by a multitude of established hierarchical and operation procedures, which they term "routines." Routines are difficult to change, even by new corporate controlling party. They empower established interest in maintaining a hierarchy that may not be conducive to innovation. It follows that commercializing disruptive innovations, the foundation of creative destruction, involves the establishment of new corporations with new routines. Yet new corporate routines could alone be important innovations that lead to creative destruction, though our results show that turnovers in corporate control do not readily lead to change in routines.

Second, while the displacement of an established large firm by a new commercially successful firm typically represents creative destruction, change in management control does not necessarily lead to the same outcome. This observation is supported by Vancil (1987), Hermalin and Weisbach (1988, 2003) and others who argue that change of top management does not constitute real change. Indeed even privatized firms may turn out to be ineffectual if the new managers are politically connected cronies of top politicians, and genuine changes are difficult to distinguish from broader effects of general liberalizations.

Private benefits the insiders controlling great corporations derive from their positions are known to be huge (e.g., Dyck and Zingales 2004; Nenova 2003; Rajan and Zingales 2003a, b). These benefits, pecuniary and especially nonpecuniary, may be sufficient to preclude innovative strategies emerging out of voluntary contracting between current controlling insiders and, say, innovators lower in the ranks, innovative outsiders, or outside investors seeking more innovative strategies. Napoleon Bonaparte wrote, "Power is my mistress. I have worked too hard at her conquest to allow anyone to take her away from me." Buying out many CEOs and powerful business families might be little easier than bribing the Corsican to renounce his empire.

Our findings might be interpreted boldly as a general rejection of managerial labor markets (Fama 1980), other contracting solutions to governance problems (Demsetz 1983), or the market for corporate control (Shleifer and Vishny 1997b) as effective mechanisms for augmenting economic growth in the aggregate. This would argue against corporate governance reform that facilitates control turnover, for example, being an effective measure for accelerating economy-level growth rates.

However, we are reluctant to press our results this far. First, our findings pertain only to the very largest firms in national economies; any or all of these mechanisms might be far more effective in smaller firms and this might suffice to impact aggregate growth rates. Second, our results are cross-country regressions. Changes in corporate control might only be economically effective in countries with institutions that can magnify their effects. Finally, some control changes could matter more than others, and our data treat all equally.

The genuine mystery in our results is that economies in which corporate insiders are more readily displaced actually accumulate capital assets more slowly. One optimistic possibility is that superior corporate governance in these economies depresses corporate savings, which would otherwise be inefficiently large and wasted on uneconomical corporate expansion, as in Jensen (1986). However, that would mean we should expect higher economy growth rates to accompany suppressed savings rates. This was not observed.

A disturbing possibility is that the market for corporate control could seriously malfunction in economies where private benefits of control are extremely high. As noted above, in such an economy the increased pecuniary wealth derivable from innovation and faster growth might well be insufficient to compensate entrenched insiders for their nonpecuniary private benefits of control. Where the oligarchs dominating such an economy prefer bribing illiterate peasants with monetary inducements, they remain in power and the economy remains impoverished because this is Pareto optimal. Indeed, where oligarchs can expand their empires to enhance their private benefits, the less likely they will surrender their control. This circumstance calls for an egalitarian analysis of the issues involved as it is hardly comforting to honest citizens of such unfortunate countries or to economists.

A "race to the bottom" in corporate governance is postulated by Bebchuk and Ferrell (2001) to explain the competition between US states to erect ever more powerful barriers against hostile corporate takeovers. Bebchuk et al. (2000), Rajan and Zingales (2003ab), Morck et al. (2005), and others postulate that such a race to the bottom in general institutional development might occur in institutionally weak countries; and much anecdotal evidence supports this.

Our finding that controlling for expropriation risk nullifies the statistical and economic importance of the control turnover measure suggests that a rapacious government is somehow involved where control turnover is rendered an impediment to growth. Remember, the likelihood of risk of "outright confiscation" or "forced nationalization" is a variable that reflects extreme leftist or populist tendencies in politics. Why might a "race to the bottom" in corporate governance be more likely in leftist or populist developing countries? We can surmise that in such highly politicized economies the expertise is in rent-seeking as the best way to leverage corporate control into personal power, wealth, and influence. So in such countries the market for corporate control is likely to concentrate governance power in the hands of the most able political rent seekers—an outcome that understandably dampens investors' enthusiasm to save and foreigners' propensity to invest. Fortunately, in such cases we should expect slower economy growth rates to accompany the inefficiently suppressed savings rates. This also is not observed. Moreover this explanation suggests other measures of rent-seeking potential would agree with our expropriation risk measure. We must conclude by acknowledging only that we have detected a mysterious negative correlation between control turnover and capital accumulation. The possible explanation is an incomplete list of speculative hypotheses. Further work is obviously needed to confirm or refute our finding, and to consider other possible explanations more thoroughly.

Acknowledgments

We are grateful for insightful comments and suggestions by Philippe Aghion, Oliver Falck, Paul Seabright, and seminar participants at the CESifo conference "Do We Need National or European Champions." Remaining errors are due to the authors.

Notes

1. What constitutes a "national champion" is legitimately debatable. We take "national" to mean headquartered in the country and "champion" to mean a top-ten provider of jobs in the country. We fully accept alternative definitions of "national champion" as potentially more meaningful in various contexts.

2. For more details on growth convergence, see Barro and Sala-i-Martin (1995).

3. Note that "business turnover" in state-controlled enterprises does not include nationalizations or privatizations but only the disappearance of the businesses. In contrast, "control turnover" does count such changes in the control of these businesses.

References

Aghion, P., G.-M. Angeletos, A. Banerjee, and K. Manova. 2005. Volatility and growth: Financial development and the cyclical composition of investment. Working paper. Harvard University.

Aghion, P., and P. W. Howitt. 1998. *Endogenous Growth Theory*. Cambridge: MIT Press.

Barro, R. 1996. Democracy and growth. *Journal of Economic Growth* 1 (1):1–27.

Barro, R., and J. W. Lee. 2001. International data on educational attainment: Updates and implications. *Oxford Economic Papers* 53 (3):541–563.

Barro, R., and X. Sala-i-Martin. 1995. *Economic Growth*. New York: McGraw-Hill.

Bebchuk, L., and A. Ferrell. 2001. Federalism and takeover law: The race to protect managers from takeovers. In *Regulatory Competition and Economic Integration*, ed. D. Esty and D. Geradin, 68–94. Oxford: Oxford University Press.

Bebchuk, L., and A. Cohen. 2005. The costs of entrenched boards. *Journal of Financial Economics* 78 (2):409–433.

Bebchuk, L., R. Kraakman, and G. Triantis. 2000. Stock pyramids, cross ownership and dual class equity: The mechanisms and agency costs of separating control from cash flow rights. In *Concentrated Corporate Ownership*, ed. R. Morck, 295–318. Chicago: University of Chicago Press.

Beck, T., R. Levine, and N. Loayza. 2000. Finance and the sources of growth. *Journal of Financial Economics* 58 (1–2):261–300.

Bekaert, G., C. Harvey, and C. Lundblad. 2005. Does financial liberalization spur growth? *Journal of Financial Economics* 77 (1):3–55.

Bertrand, M., and A. Schoar. 2003. Managing with style: The effect of managers on firm policies. *Quarterly Journal of Economics* 118 (4):1169–1208.

Bertrand, M., and A. Schoar. 2006. The role of family in family firms. *Journal of Economic Perspectives* 20 (2):73–96.

Betz, F. 1993. *Strategic Technology Management*. New York: McGraw-Hill.

Black, B., and J. Coffee, Jr. 1994. Hail Britannia? Institutional investor behavior under limited regulation. *Michigan Law Review* 92 (7):1997–2087.

Bower, J., and C. Christensen. (January–February 1995). Disruptive technologies: Catching the wave. *Harvard Business Review*, 43–53.

Chun, H., J.-W. Kim, R. Morck, and B. Yeung. 2008. Creative destruction and firm-specific performance heterogeneity. *Journal of Financial Economics* 89 (1):109–135.

Christensen, C. 1997. *The Innovator's Dilemma*. Boston: Harvard Business School Press.

Demsetz, H. 1983. The structure of ownership and the theory of the firm. *Journal of Law & Economics* 26 (2):375–393.

Dyck, A., and L. Zingales. 2004. Private Benefits of Control: An International Comparison, Journal of Finance. *American Finance Association* 59 (2):537–600.

Fama, E. 1980. Agency problems and the theory of the firm. *Journal of Political Economy* 88 (2):288–307.

Fogel, K., R. Morck, and B. Yeung. 2008. Big business stability and economic growth: Is what's good for General Motors good for America? *Journal of Financial Economics* 89 (1):83–108.

Gompers, P. A., and J. Lerner. 2001. The venture capital revolution. *Journal of Economic Perspectives* 15 (2):145–168.

Gompers, P. A., J. L. Ishii, and A. Metrick. 2003. Corporate governance and equity prices. *Quarterly Journal of Economics* 118 (1):107–115.

Hermalin, B., and M. Weisbach. 1988. The determinants of board composition. *Rand Journal of Economics* 19 (4):589–606.

Hermalin, B., and M. Weisbach. 2003. Boards of directors as an endogenously determined institution: a survey of the economic literature. *Economic Policy Review* 9 (1):7–26.

Jensen, Michael C. 1986. "Agency Costs of Free Cash Flow, Corporate Finance, and Takeovers," *American Economic Review*. [May.] *American Economic Association* 76 (2):323–329.

Keefer, P., and S. Knack. 1995. Institutions and economic performance: Cross-country tests using alternative institutional measures. *Economics and Politics* 7 (3):207–227.

King, R., and R. Levine. 1994. Capital fundamentalism, economic development, and economic growth. *Carnegie-Rochester Conference Series on Public Policy* 40: 259–92.

Klepper, S. 2007. Disagreements, spinoffs, and the evolution of Detroit as the capital of the U.S. automobile industry. *Management Science* 53 (4):616–631.

La Porta, R., F. Lopez-de-Silanes, and A. Shleifer. 1999. Corporate ownership around the world. *Journal of Finance* 54 (2):471–517.

La Porta, R., F. Lopez-de-Silanes, and A. Shleifer. 2002. Government ownership of banks. *Journal of Finance* 51 (1):265–301.

La Porta, R., F. Lopez-de-Silanes, A. Shleifer, and R. Vishny. 1998. Law and finance. *Journal of Political Economy* 106 (6):1113–1156.

Mankiw, N. G. 1995. The growth of nations. *Brookings Papers on Economic Activity* (1):275–310.

Morck, R., A. Shleifer, and R. W. Vishny. 1989. Alternative mechanism of corporate control. *American Economic Review* 79 (4):842–852.

Morck, R., D. Wolfenzon, and B. Yeung. 2005. Corporate governance, economic entrenchment and growth. *Journal of Economic Literature* 43 (3):655–720.

Morck, R., and B. Yeung. 2003. Agency problems in large family business groups. *Entrepreneurship: Theory and Practice* 27 (4):367–382.

Morck, R., and B. Yeung. 2004. Family control and the rent-seeking society. *Entrepreneurship: Theory and Practice* 28 (4):391–409.

Nelson, R. P., and S. Winter. 1982. *An Evolutionary Theory of Economic Change.* Cambridge, MA: Belknap Press.

Nenova, T. 2003. The value of corporate voting rights and control: A cross-country analysis. [June.] *Journal of Financial Economics, Elsevier* 68 (3):325–351.

Orkin, N., and S. Burger. 2005. Employee invention rights in the twenty-first century. *Labor Law Journal* 56 (1):82–89.

Pérez-González, F. 2006. Inherited control and firm performance. *American Economic Review* 96 (5):1559–1588.

Rajan, R., and L. Zingales. 2003a. The great reversals: The politics of financial development in the twentieth century. *Journal of Financial Economics* 69 (1):5–50.

Rajan, R., and L. Zingales. 2003b. *Saving Capitalism from the Capitalists: Unleashing the Power of Financial Markets to Create Wealth and Spread Opportunity.* New York: Crown Business.

Ritter, J. 1987. The costs of going public. *Journal of Financial Economics* 19 (2):269–281.

Rodriguez, F., and J. Sachs. 1999. Why do resource-abundant economies grow more slowly. *Journal of Economic Growth* 4 (3):277–303.

Romer, D. 1993. Openness and inflation: Theory and evidence. *Quarterly Journal of Economics* 108 (4):870–903.

Sachs, J. 2001. Tropical underdevelopment. Working paper 8119. NBER, Cambridge, MA.

Sachs, J., and A. Warner. 2001. The curse of natural resources. *European Economic Review* 45 (4–6):827–838.

Schumpeter, J. 1912. *Theorie der Wirtschaftlichen Entwicklung.* Leipzig: Duncker and Humblot.

Schumpeter, J. 1942. *Capitalism, Socialism and Democracy.* 3rd ed. New York: Harper.

Shleifer, A. 1996. Origins of bad policies: control, corruption and confusion. *Rivista di Politica Economica* 108 (3):599–617.

Shleifer, A., and R. Vishny. 1989. Management entrenchment: The case of manager specific investments. *Journal of Financial Economics* 25 (1):123–139.

Shleifer, A., and R. Vishny. 1994a. Politicians and firms. *Quarterly Journal of Economics* 109 (4):995–1025.

Shleifer, A., and R. Vishny. 1994b. Politics of market socialism. *Journal of Economic Perspectives* 8 (2):165–176.

Shleifer, A., and R. Vishny. 1997a. *The Grabbing Hand*. Cambridge: Harvard University Press.

Shleifer, A., and R. Vishny. 1997b. A survey of corporate governance. *Journal of Finance* 52 (2):737–784.

Vancil, R. 1987. *Passing the Baton: Managing the Process of CEO Succession*. Boston: Harvard Business School Press.

Wurgler, J. 2000. Financial markets and the allocation of capital. *Journal of Financial Economics* 58 (1):187–214.

4 Subsidizing National Champions: An Evolutionary Perspective

Cécile Aubert, Oliver Falck, and Stephan Heblich

4.1 Introduction

One mission of the EU Lisbon Strategy is to make Europe "the most competitive and dynamic knowledge-based economic region in the world." Although there are many different ways to reach this goal, the idea of an industrial policy that promotes European or national champions as the best way to compete in a globalized world has become (again) en vogue among European politicians.

While the desirability of promoting champions is the object of much discussion, it is not always clear what a champion is, nor what type of champion will receive the most attention from politicians (Maincent and Navarro 2006). In a rapidly changing business environment, national champions can be up-and-coming firms engaged in creative destruction, innovative firms operating at or close to the technology frontier, or large firms that maintain employment in a region or confer prestige on the politicians who support and protect them. In this chapter we argue that these different types of champions occur at different phases of a product life cycle. According to Gort and Klepper's (1982) knowledge-based view, the phases along a product life cycle are defined as follows. The very "early" phase is best characterized by experimentation undertaken in the quest for a dominant product variant—leading to high firm turnover. In the "intermediate" phase, some product variants dominate the growing market—leading to firm growth and firm entry but very little exit. In the "mature" phase, firms concentrate on process innovations to reduce production costs and there will be a certain amount of market entry by new firms that copy the established product and benefit from low production costs (e.g., a low-paid workforce). National firms must keep pace with the speed of process innovation, develop new products along another life cycle, or exit the market (see also Klepper 1996, 1997).

According to Aghion et al. (2009), for firms at the technology frontier, constant innovation is the only way to escape competition. However, firm failure only occurs in competitive markets. If a firm feels fairly confident that the government will protect and support it, no matter what its position in the market, the firm may not spend much time, money, or effort on innovation. As voters are uncomfortable with an economy founded on unpredictable firm selection (leading to fast but erratic growth) and prefer slow but smooth growth (Roe 2003), politicians up for reelection will prefer to subsidize firms or industries that are in danger of becoming losers in a process of creative destruction (Dewatripont and Seabright 2006). Because firms are well aware of this, their incentive to invest in research, to innovate, and to relocate their assets in more profitable activities is reduced. This well-known insight explains the diffidence of many economists toward national champion policies.

We, however, argue that different knowledge externalities are generated at each stage of a product's life cycle, and that these externalities may warrant government intervention, even in the absence of lobbying and capture, to foster investment and efficient redeployment of assets. Investment subsidies or protection from competition may be socially beneficial. Examples of costly policies by politicians concerned with reelection are also discussed.

In this chapter we focus on industries where firms need to innovate and develop new products to survive. Several market imperfections may justify intervention. First, competition is unlikely to lead to efficient levels of innovation and of redeployment of assets in the presence of externalities and information leakages. We argue that such externalities are important in the industries we consider. Second, competition may not lead to efficiency in the presence of imperfect credit markets. Therefore we consider two types of interventions that may improve overall efficiency, namely subsidizing innovative firms at early stages, and protecting firms with mature products from competition. We use the assumption of a benevolent politician to compare how these two ways would impact the promotion of national champions. We consider the case where both forms of intervention raise the incentive of local firms to invest in R&D activity. This will be particularly beneficial when such investments generate positive local externalities, including, for example, tacit knowledge acquired by firms and employees and/or processes adopted from other industries (such spillovers are commonly assumed in the endogenous growth literature). Some form of intervention is also beneficial when competitors may copy a new good or technology without bearing R&D costs—thus expropriating, to some extent, the research efforts of innovators. However, as we will argue, the investments undertaken due to government intervention may not be adequate.

The existing champions-related literature concentrates on the distribution of rents. Not surprisingly, a large part of this literature finds its foundation in the strategic trade policy literature. In this latter strand of research, markets are characterized by worldwide imperfect competition and suppliers from around the world compete to capture excess rents. To retain the largest possible share of these excess rents within national borders, governments may artificially bolster the position of domestic firms, for instance, through state aid. Spencer and Brander (1983) offer a theory of government intervention that provides an explanation for industrial strategy: domestic net welfare is improved by capturing a greater share of the output of rent-earning industries. However, this can result in a collectively wasteful subsidy war.

In our contribution, we adopt a different approach and focus on how governmental intervention alters incentives to (1) invest in R&D in the early phase of the life cycle and (2) relocate resources in later phases of the life cycle when the product becomes mature. In our very simple model, firms initially decide whether or not to invest in research, and later on whether to change activities, given that there are informational spillovers. On the one hand, these spillovers may allow imitation, thus discouraging investment in research. On the other hand, knowledge spillovers are known to be an important location factor in support of regional agglomeration, leading to positive external economies. Hence there is a dual nature to information spillovers. Accordingly we assess the impact of subsidizing research during the early stage and protecting firms in mature industries. Subsidies and aid to domestic firms are widespread and may benefit from an exemption from European Commission (EC) rules if they "facilitate the development of certain economic activities . . . or economic areas" (art. 87, EC Treaty). Protection is also far from being unusual and the merger between the two French firms GDF and Suez in 2008, protecting the latter from hostile takeover by non-French companies, may provide an example of it. We suggest a very simple model that mostly aims at highlighting the different types of externalities associated with innovation and production, and the main policy choices a government can make. Policy makers could use this framework for calibration and assessment of the expected benefits and externalities associated to a given project.

While we obtain theoretical justifications for intervention by assuming benevolent politicians, real-world politicians are likely to be motivated by reelection concerns. We provide illustrations drawn from actual experience of inefficient promotion of national champions.

4.2   Promoting Champions along a Life Cycle

4.2.1   Experimentation in the Early Phase of the Life Cycle

In the early phase of the life cycle, customer preferences are diverse and entrepreneurial virtues, such as flexibility and openness to the unexpected, are needed to address these preferences. High responsiveness to consumer preferences and willingness to experiment with processes borrowed from other industries are essential to success. This experimentation phase is characterized by high firm turnover, which, on the one hand, leads to fruitful innovation but, on the other hand, makes scale economies in production unlikely, a topic well discussed in the "infant industry" literature. The infant industry arguments were initially formulated by Alexander Hamilton at the end of the 18th century, and then expanded by Friedrich List, most particularly in his 1841 book, *The National System of Political Economy*. John Stuart Mill believed that industries should be protected only temporarily, that is, while they are learning new technologies. More recent studies have defined and restricted the applicability of the theory (see, e.g., Bardhan, 1971). Champions in this early phase of the life cycle can be described as *entrepreneurial firms.*

As argued above, politicians seeking reelection wish to smooth the evolution of the early phase of the life cycle—a process best described as creative destruction. Schumpeter (1942: 85) describes it as follows: "But . . . it is not the kind of [price] competition which counts but the competition for the new commodity, the new technology, the new source of supply, the new type of organization (the largest-scale unit of control for instance)—competition which commands a decisive cost or quality advantage and which strikes not at the margins of the profits and the outputs of the existing firms, but at their foundations and at their very lives." However, this attempt to smooth the evolution of the early stage of the life cycle may have severe consequences, and can, ironically enough, even result in destroying the process of creative destruction itself. Seabright (2005) argues that incumbent firms expanding into the infant industry sector are the greatest beneficiaries of public subsidizing as they are already politically well connected; that is, they are successful lobbyists. Such a policy harms the process of creative destruction in two ways. First, concentrating on incumbent firms prevents the positive effects of what Aghion et al. (2009) term "entry-competition," namely competition resulting from the threat of new entry. Furthermore politicians are reluctant to admit that one of their projects has failed unless they are absolutely forced to do so by some spectacular or public event. However, allowing projects to fail and disappear is an important part of the process of creative destruction.

4.2.2 Economies of Scale in the Intermediate Phase of the Life Cycle

Once the industry matures, firms having successfully emerged from the early phase of the life cycle begin to realize economies of scale in production as the number of product variants narrows. At this stage firms improve and extend the selected variants in an increasingly routinized and predictable process. At the beginning of this phase, the opportunity for dramatic product improvements (not innovations) along with excess profits attracts new entrants. With time the resulting competition creates a need for constant innovation as the only way to survive. Given the importance of successful innovation, R&D activities and knowledge production become an internal, bureaucratically controlled process in large firms and their key suppliers. The routinization of the innovation process increases the predictability of its outcome and thus contributes to firm competitiveness (Baumol 2002a). Toward the end of this phase, products become increasingly routinized and subsequent (incremental) innovations depend largely on previous experience. When combined with decreasing excess profits due to the larger number of market participants, this eventually creates a barrier for new entry. However, internal innovation and scale economies together result in rapidly growing firms. We call these firms *routinized firms*.

In this phase of the life cycle, politicians, regardless of their reelection goals, have no incentive to intervene as growth is smooth and stable. Routinized firm innovation "tends to be conservative, seeking products whose applicability is clear and whose markets are relatively not speculative. The bureaucratic control typical of innovative activity in the large firm serves to ensure that the resulting changes will be modest, predictable and incremental." (Baumol 2002b) Accordingly, as firm exit is rare during this intermediate phase of the life cycle and the number of firms generally increases, there is no need for politicians to interfere or intervene.

4.2.3   Public Recognition in the Mature Phase of the Life Cycle

In the mature phase of the life cycle, a small number of product variants dominate the market. Firms now concentrate on process innovation in order to make the production process more effective. These process innovations originate from the firms' internal learning-by-doing. Competitors that cannot keep pace with the speed of process innovation are forced to exit the market.

Some firms in the mature phase of the life cycle can best be described as *big projects*, because of their size or because of the media coverage their projects attract. Politician seeking reelection may be inclined to subsidize these big projects in order to prevent their market exit, even though exit and, again, creative destruction is the driving force behind process innovation at this phase of the life cycle. Seabright (2005) asks: "What do we know about the biases of politicians in selecting investment projects for public support? They tend to be large, they tend to produce products that are highly visible in the press and media (affording many photo-opportunities for the politicians concerned), and they tend to be comparatively insulated from competition—both because this makes them less risky to finance and because it avoids awkward questions about their comparative performance with similar projects that do not receive public support."

Based on empirical findings by Gort and Klepper (1982), Figure 4.1 illustrates net firm entry, namely changes in the number of firms over time. Assuming that, in the absence of intervention, the number of local firms follows this curve of industry evolution, we obtain the following implications. In the early phase, trial and error stimulate the process of creative destruction, where exit often quickly follows entry. Many firms, in a life or death struggle, are competing to create the dominant product variant, which results in a relatively high firm turnover rate during this phase of the life cycle and a relatively low number of firms in the market. As this search process brings about winners and losers, we are, again, dealing with a turbulent emerging market likely to attract political attention. In contrast, the second phase of the life cycle is already experiencing growth and thus is less likely to be the focus of political attention. Finally, the mature phase, where efficiency increases

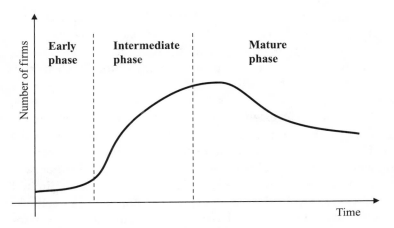

Figure 4.1
Stages along the product life cycle (source: Klepper 1996)

cause firm exit, is, again, a stage at which politicians are likely to feel tempted to intervene.

A major objection against such a national-champions policy is that in a period of global competition, protectionist policies pursued by one country may give rise to the risk of that country falling behind the technology frontier if other countries are relying on competition to spur innovation. Such a noncompetitive environment will not strengthen, but instead actually weaken the domestic firms. It deters investment and relocation of activities in new products or markets.

To examine these welfare effects more precisely, the following section isolates and formalizes several reasons for subsidizing innovative activities or promoting national champions along the three phases of the life cycle described above. Under the conditions spelled out below, the promotion of national champions may be welfare-improving from the point of view of the country or region where the national champion is located. We simply aim at providing an initial framework for classifying benevolent reasons to intervene and promote champions at a theoretical level.

4.3 A Simple Model of Intervention in Changing Industries

4.3.1 The Model

We consider a sector in which R&D is necessary to develop new products. Research has uncertain results and its outcome is initially confidential, providing the innovator with near-monopoly profits. But knowledge eventually leaks out (as for noncodifiable knowledge that cannot be described in a patent). This happens, for instance, when employees "job hop" from the innovator to competitors (Fallick et al. 2006) or simply when competitors reverse engineer the innovator's product or service. An innovator is thus initially protected by secrecy, but may later be to some extent expropriated from the research investment as knowledge spills over and competitors copy the technology or product. For simplicity, we will assume that there is only one local firm, the "innovator," but the analysis would be similar if the invention was copied in the short run by some local firms only, providing limited downward pressure on prices, and later on by nonlocal competitors. Once knowledge leaks out to foreign or nonlocal competitors, the innovator may continue producing the same product or can relocate their assets—by inventing and producing other products in the same sector, or producing and selling in different geographical areas. At each stage externalities are generated.

Innovation   A potential innovator has initial assets A and must borrow to invest a fixed amount I, $I > A$, in order to develop a new product. After I is invested, the innovator privately "invents" a new product with probability p, $0 < p < 1$, in which case she obtains observable profits at date 1. The invention then becomes public, and the innovator faces foreign competition at date 2 if she remains in the same sector. She can obtain reservation profits by relocating her physical assets and skills to another activity (possibly inventing a new product in the same domain, or geographically moving).

The exact timing is as follows:

Date 0: The innovator borrows and invents a new product with probability p. Knowledge externalities are generated, of value L_0.

Date 1: If the investment is successful, the innovator obtains (near-monopoly) profits, π_1, and consumers benefit from the new good and get surplus CS_1. Process externalities are generated, of value L_1.

Date 2: Foreign firms can now produce the good. The innovator can choose between remaining on this market and relocating.

If the innovator stays in the market, competition drives its profits to π_2 and consumer surplus to CS_2. Externalities of value L_2 are generated by local production.

If the innovator relocates her assets, she gets $\underline{\pi}$ and consumer surplus is now $\underline{CS}$ (as there is one less firm on the market). These levels depend on the degree of asset specificity.

Expectations are denoted with operator E (with $E(\pi_2|\pi_1)$ being the expected value of date 2 profits given date 1 profits, for instance.

Externalities   Local production of the new good may create positive externalities in the area: employees and researchers may benefit from learning-by-doing; the innovation may speed up other local research projects, possibly due to knowledge spillovers (Feldman 1994; Feldman and Audretsch 1999); local employment may generate complementarities favoring a "big push" (Rosenstein-Rodan 1943; Murphy et al. 1989). We denote by L_i, $L_i \geq 0$, the gains associated with these potential externalities at stage i, $i = 0, 1, 2$, and $L = L_0 + pL_1 + pL_2$.

Domestic social welfare (from the point of view of a benevolent government) is the sum of the innovator's profits, consumer surplus and externalities (foreign imitators' profits are not taken into account).

Investing in innovation (stage 0) may create a stock of "competencies" and knowledge of value for future projects independently of the success or failure of the initial research; this may be particularly likely in the pharmaceutical industry and other industries at the frontier of scientific knowledge.

In other sectors (e.g., new information technologies), most of the value will arise from developing a particular product: the benefit accrues at stage 1, as workers have to create new processes and learn by doing.

Externalities obtained from mature production at stage 2 are most likely to be employment related: the specific employment generated in the field may be of additional value, compared to local employment in other sectors, for instance, because employment in this field is a better match with local employee skills, or because production helps to develop new skills in the area. Such additional benefits are also likely to arise when the region faces high redundancy rates where laid-off employees have difficulty finding new jobs (mining regions are typical examples). Note that this last type of externality is the most visible one, especially to voters, and may receive excess media attention compared to the two other types.

We assume that the government is unable to assess the quality of an innovator's "idea"—that is, the profits she will make in case of success, π_1 and π_2, contrary to specialized bankers and venture capitalists, who may obtain expert information. It can be argued that "innovators" and experts, including specialized venture capitalists, have a better understanding of the true potential of a new product, software, technology, and so forth, than do politicians. We rule out the possibility of using a revelation mechanism to obtain this information. In our context, this would require regulation of prices or quantities, which would be quite unusual in the industries we are looking at and particularly complex due to the number of competitors; in addition, a government may be unable to regulate firms that are selling, but not producing, domestically (regulating only a fraction of active firms further adds to the complexity of incentive issues, e.g., see Aubert and Pouyet 2006).

In a world with credit constraints, borrowing entails costs. The innovator is protected by limited liability and the opportunity costs of raising funds are normalized to zero. Borrowing on an imperfect credit market costs $r(I - A)$ per unit borrowed, where $r(\ldots)$ is an increasing function of the amount borrowed, $I - A$. Borrowing $I - A$ thus imposes a total expected reimbursement of $(I - A)(1 + r(I - A))$. Let us denote by $\Pi(I - A)$ the minimum level of profit necessary to pay back borrowings: $\Pi(I - A) = (I - A)(1 + r(I - A))/p$. Given that lenders have complete information over expected profits, an innovator with an idea yielding profits of $\pi_1 + \pi_2$, with $\pi_1 + \pi_2 < \Pi(I - A)$ will not receive financing.

Governmental Intervention The "government" is assumed to be benevolent, unless otherwise stated, and cares only for local welfare, not including foreign firm profits (which might be zero anyway, if second-period competition is strong). There are two ways for the government to intervene:

- it can grant a subsidy s, s > 0, to the innovator,
- or it can protect her from foreign competition.

For clarity, we consider them separately to compare their relative benefits.

Protecting the local firm from competition increases her profits from π_2 to π_2^p, where $\pi_2 < \pi_2^p$. Protection reduces consumers surplus, as the market becomes less competitive, from CS_2 to CS_2^p, $CS_2 > CS_2^p$.

When the government grants a subsidy s to innovative activities, we assume for consistency that the outside option of relocating allows the firm to obtain a (possibly null) subsidy $\underline{s}$, in $[0, s]$. (if the outside option consists in launching a new project in a related sector, the innovator will indeed benefit from the subsidization policy). Rather than a subsidy, the government may prefer to grant a subsidized loan. Yet as the innovator is protected by limited liability, a loan does not solve potential moral hazard issues, and would not differ much from a subsidy in our subsequent analysis.

The government will choose a level of intervention based on the expected average values of π_1, π_2, π_2^P, $\underline{\pi}$, CS_1, CS_2, and $\underline{CS}$ for the industry considered (as we do not specify functional forms, this computation offers little insight and is not done here). The next subsections investigate how the two policies considered affect the decision to relocate assets in other activities, and the decision to undertake R&D.

4.3.2 The Decision to Redeploy Assets

Let us consider the decision to relocate assets at the end of the first period: that is, to use them in an alternative use instead of continuing to produce the now mature product. It would be socially optimal to relocate whenever $\pi_2 + CS_2 + L_2 < \underline{\pi} + \underline{CS}$.

The innovator will decide to relocate when $\pi_2 < \underline{\pi}$ in the absence of protection and subsidization of research, when $\pi_2 < \underline{\pi} + s$ if new research activities are subsidized, and when $\pi_2^P < \underline{\pi}$ if there is protection. The last inequality is more demanding than the first, while the second one is less so: wide subsidization fosters relocation; protection has the opposite effect.

Protection has the drawback of delaying the relocation of productive assets and human skills (as exemplified in mining industries in France and the United Kingdom). It may, however, be socially optimal if L_2 is very large—meaning local employment is highly valued and cannot be fully relocated.

Subsidization of research activities may be an efficient strategy if the innovator underinvests in the absence of intervention, which, as we argue below, is particularly likely to be the case if new activities improve the local stock of knowledge (high externalities, $L_0 + L_1$). Yet, in some settings, subsidization may have the adverse effect of inducing inefficient relocation. However, this impact may be of limited consequence when one considers consumer welfare alone (when L_2 is close to zero), as consumers will be served by foreign firms. Subsidization thus seems to fare better than protection with respect to asset relocation decisions unless it involves lasting local unemployment or disqualification (L_2 is high).

4.3.3   The Decision to Undertake Research

It would be optimal to invest in research whenever

$$p[\pi_1 + CS_1 + \max\{\pi_2 + CS_2 - (\underline{\pi} + \underline{CS}), 0\} + L_1 + L_2] + L_0 \geq I . \tag{4.1}$$

The innovator decides, in the absence of government intervention, to conduct research if and only if

$$p[\pi_1 + \max\{\pi_2 - \underline{\pi}, 0\}] \geq I + (I - A)r(I - A). \tag{4.2}$$

Several reasons may justify government intervention:

Imperfect market competition: Unless the innovator is able to perfectly price discriminate at date 1 (when she benefits from a knowledge advantage), her profits are lower than social welfare (i.e., $CS_1 > 0$) and innovation may not occur frequently enough. This also holds in the second period if competition remains imperfect after the entry of foreign competitors.

Imperfect credit markets: Financing costs above the opportunity cost of funds may dissuade investment in a socially optimal activity. This happens if condition (4.1) is satisfied in the absence of financing costs, but is no longer so when a financing cost $(I - A)r(I - A)$ adds to the investment cost I.

Local spillovers: Obviously, if there are strictly positive externalities at any stage $(L > 0)$, the innovator does not internalize the benefits of information leakage and of local employment, and does not innovate enough (she may also relocate too often as we have seen).

These scenarios imply that from the local welfare perspective, the level of R&D is too low.

Innovation under Subsidization of Research Activities   The potential innovator will invest I in R&D, under a subsidy, if and only if

$$p[\pi_1 + \max\{\pi_2 - (\underline{s} + \underline{\pi}), 0\}] \geq I - s + (I - s - A)r(I - s - A) .$$

Subsidization offers an immediate net gain to the investor as it reduces the interest rate, making more projects viable. It is particularly beneficial for small firms that have low levels of initial assets to be invested and also suffer from credit constraints. It has, however, the drawback of potentially inducing overinvestment, particularly by large firms that already have low interest rates thanks to self-financing.

As with any type of grant, a subsidy may give rise to moral hazard with beneficiaries diverting monetary resources to activities other than the one intended to be subsidized. Protection may appear more attractive as diversion is not an issue.

Innovation under Protection of Mature Firms   The potential innovator will invest if and only if

$$p[\pi_1 + \max\{\pi_2^P - \underline{\pi}+, 0\}] \geq I + (I - A)r(I - A).$$

Protection from foreign competition is of more or less value depending on the firm's expectations about its product's value in the second period or, more precisely, of π_2^P, which increases with this value. Protection has no impact on investment decisions if the firm expects to relocate in the second period anyway (however, the decision to relocate is chosen less often under protection). Protection may foster investment in projects that have a high second-period value. It may thus allow for a better screening of projects in terms of their expected value.

In addition, protection will allow a firm to obtain financing when its profits in the absence of protection were too low to ensure loan repayment: $\pi_1 + \max\{\pi_2, \underline{\pi}\} < \Pi(I - A) \leq \pi_1 + \pi_2^P$,

where $\Pi(I - A) = [I + (I - A)r(I - A)]/p$.

This aspect of protection has more impact for innovators with small initial resources A, and less for sectors in which innovations are undertaken by large firms that do not need much external financing. Protection may thus be particularly beneficial for smaller firms, contrary to the general practice of protecting firms that are "too big to fail."

4.3.4   A Discussion of Some Issues

Protection and the Cost of Public Funds   We have seen that protection tends to inefficiently delay relocation of assets, particularly if there are few externalities in mature industries. However, there is one argument in favor of using the protection strategy, an argument that is particularly relevant in the case of less developed countries. If using public funds to subsidize is costly, then protection of mature industries may be preferred. This effect should not be ignored. Spending one dollar on subsidies actually costs one dollar *plus* an amount called "the cost of public funds" which represents, among other things, administrative costs, the distorting impact of taxation, tax evasion, and corruption, and the shadow cost of the state's budget constraint. It is generally believed that this cost of public funds is around 0.3 for the United States, between 0.3 and 0.5 for European countries and Japan, and above 0.7 for less developed countries (Laffont and Tirole 1993). In less developed countries, administrative costs tend to be high, corruption is more widespread, and the opportunity value of funds is also quite high. Indeed Auriol and Warlters (2005) estimate that the cost of public funds amounts to 1.17 for 38 African countries. This high cost may explain why many less developed countries are particularly interested in protecting their domestic markets.

Note in this context that moral hazard is more likely to raise issues in developing countries than in more developed countries (though this is not always true). If information asymmetries are more severe in LDCs, subsidies are at a higher risk of being misused—contrary to protection for which money diversion is not an issue.

Nonbenevolent Governements   When governments cannot commit, extortion or holdup of firms' profits is an issue, as in Ades and Di Tella (1997). In our context, fear of extortion would deter investment in innovation. It may also delay redeployment of assets if the new activity is more prone to extortion. Firm owners and managers may be expected to value nonmonetary benefits (that cannot be seized by the government) relatively more than profits; this might favor resources diversion at the innovation stage, and no redeployment during the mature phase. The value of subsidization is reduced from the point of view of the government as a nonnegligible part of the subsidy is likely to be diverted. This issue is likely to be more relevant for some developing countries that have weak institutions.

In democratic regimes, reelection concerns may also distort policies. Redundancy and bankruptcy attract media attention and may have an adverse and immediate impact on a politician's chance of reelection. Anticipating this, the head of the government may prefer to support less risky projects or protect employment and ownership in mature industries. Spending time or money on firms in the early phases of the life cycle, which is more useful for small firms than large ones, is less likely to attract attention and has medium- or long-run effects only. Protecting mature industries may thus appear a more attractive option.

A concern for reelection, as it would lead to protecting mature firms, could be formally similar to the government associating an excessively high value to L_2. If this value is higher than its true level, there would be an overemphasis on policies that delay asset relocation leading to inefficient, excess stability in the local industry. In the long run this would deter innovation and impede growth in the region, as the products of mature firms eventually become obsolete while only few local firms innovate.

When foreign firm competition intensifies, though, as happens under increased globalization, protecting mature industries becomes particularly costly in terms of welfare. In this context Aghion et al. (2009) introduce the notion of an escape-competition effect where constant innovation is the only way to escape competition, secure a stable market position, and guarantee at least a certain level of employment. We briefly return to this issue in section 4.5, with real-life examples.

A Summary   To summarize, protection from competition reduces consumer surplus and is likely to cause inefficiencies in the relocation of resources. It may, however, be socially optimal when externalities generated by mature firms (L_2 high) would be lost when relocating the workforce. For instance, this may occur in downsizing sectors already marked by high unemployment and where workers are highly specialized. Here protection could be used to protect employees from unemployment and all the related social costs unemployment brings. Protection from competition may also be optimal for developing countries that lack financial resources to use other promotion tools. Last, protection may also be useful when subsidies are likely to be diverted from innovation activities because of moral hazard: in order to later benefit from protection, the firm must innovate now to obtain an incumbency in the future. Protection thus reinforces incentives to invest, contrary to subsidies, which have value both as means of investment, and as resources to be diverted from innovation activities.

Subsidies may be optimal for industries undertaking high-tech and long-term or fundamental research, namely those industries in which much value is created by simply searching for an invention. However, subsidization is not necessary when innovation is undertaken by large firms, or by subsidiaries of such firms, that do not face credit constraints.

In practice, the most visible government intervention tends to involve the protection of mature industries, as we discuss in section

4.5. These firms are unlikely to face much credit constraint and may not generate as many externalities as less visible firms; their protection is thus likely to be excessive. It is likely that voters are more aware of the short-term social adjustment costs incurred by allowing a mature firm to go bankrupt or undergo important restructuring, than they are of the long-term competitive benefits achieved through improving local knowledge stocks and hence being innovative at the technology frontier. As a consequence, protection becomes a more attractive policy for rational politicians seeking reelection.

4.4 The Importance of Local Knowledge and Research

Developing production processes and human capital involves important externalities as has been shown by the success of high-tech "belts." A closer examination of these examples highlights how internal organization and institutions have played a role in this success, which are exactly the type of externalities we have in mind when we refer to "externalities at the development stage," denoted L_1. For instance, Rosenberg (1990) attributes the success of the best private research laboratories (Bell Labs., IBM, Dupont, Dow Chemical, Eastman Kodak, etc.), and the appropriability of the fruits of their research, to the close intellectual proximity maintained between the basic research laboratories and the development and production wings of these firms (Dasgupta 1988).

A comparison of the famous Silicon Valley in California with Route 128 in the Boston, Massachusetts, area is particularly interesting. Both are high-tech districts, but they evolved in widely divergent ways. In 1965 Route 128 had approximately three times more high-technology employment than did Silicon Valley. Today, however, Silicon Valley is way, way ahead in the high-tech game. Saxenian (1994) attributes Silicon Valley's success to two major differences between it and Route 128. First, companies in Silicon Valley relied on vertical disaggregation, from which emerged competing modular suppliers (Baldwin and Clark 1997:85), whereas companies along Route 128 focused on vertical integration. Second, technological knowledge diffused much more rapidly in Silicon Valley than along Route 128.

Knowledge diffusion is a double-edged sword. Rapid knowledge diffusion undermines the appropriability of "exclusive" rents arising from the lock in of knowledge. However, knowledge diffusion across a network of firms can act as a multiplier, resulting in the creation of new knowledge and, therefore, additional but "collective" rents open to all network participants. Of course, whether this multiplier is a benefit is critically dependent on the extent to which the individual (or firm) will have access to the collective rents, namely the intensity of knowledge diffusion. Implicit and explicit institutions play an important role in this context as they can provide a foundation for trust in reciprocity, which will help assure that each network member is willing to feed the network with new knowledge (Powell 1990).

Job hopping is one of the simplest methods of knowledge diffusion. Gilson (1999) and Hyde (2003) argue that the only way this type of knowledge diffusion can be stopped is by means of a postemployment covenant not to compete. Employees who enter into such covenants are not permitted to work for competitors for a fixed length of time (usually two years) after termination of employment for any reason. Returning to the Silicon Valley versus Route 128 example, it is interesting that Massachusetts allows noncompete covenants but California does not. Accordingly "any firm connected to the personal networks through which information and employees flowed in Silicon Valley could benefit from the best innovation produced in the entire cluster rather than the best innovation produced by their own, proprietary research and development efforts" (Fallick et al. 2006).

The Silicon Valley example highlights the advantage of unhampered knowledge flows over restricted knowledge flows within a regional network. In Silicon Valley the absence of legal restrictions on job mobility led to a vertical disintegrated business culture of *coopetition*. Firms *cooperate* in creating a regional knowledge stock that, in turn, becomes the foundation of their *competitiveness* in global markets. Knowledge came to be seen as a regional club good and each company connected to the network could benefit from it. This resulted in a regional "standing-on-shoulders" effect that gained companies a competitive advantage over regions where companies could build only on their own internal knowledge. However, such an environment can only exist when there is trust in reciprocity (Powell 1990), namely in the absence of free-riding. Every rational company would desire to benefit from other firms' ideas and knowledge circulation within the network while, at the same time, locking in its own knowledge. If this was a dominant strategy, the regional standing-on-shoulders effect would not occur. However, if the law eliminates the possibility of locking in knowledge—as in California—cooperation becomes the dominant strategy and thus helps overcome problems of collective action that would eventually produce a regional disadvantage. In the absence of external institutions, social sanctions, acting as a kind of informal institution, can produce the same result (Ellickson 1991).

Given the comparative advantage of regional cooperation over isolation, it becomes desirable to engage in a network strategy such that it is in each company's own interest to cooperate, leading to an intense flow of knowledge. However, in the absence of explicit institutions, there is a risk of free-riding that can be avoided only by adequate implicit trust-supporting institutions. Depending on the regional network's structure, there are two ways of generating trust, both relying on a firm's regional embeddedness.

In networks of equals (i.e., small- and medium-sized firms) where firms are usually owner led, trust results from the owner's regional embeddedness and his or her social ties. The literature on industrial districts (Piore and Sabel 1984; Becattini 1990) highlights the advantages of coopetition resulting from trust in reciprocity due to strong social ties. The stronger the social ties within a network, the higher the probability of being caught out as a free-rider. If free-riding leads to an exclusion from the network, its costs usually exceed its benefits. Well-known examples of districts using social ties as a regulation are the textile and leather industry in northern Italy and manufacturing industry in southern Germany. These strongly export-oriented manufacturing sectors with many small- and medium-sized companies, often family owned, are highly specialized and yet competitive in the global market. However, as they usually serve niche markets, they are not highly visible and are rather "hidden champions" (cf. Audretsch et al. 2009).

In the case of hierarchical networks dominated by a large firm, trust does not prevail per se. Large companies' organizational structures are usually not compatible with relationships based on social ties. In this environment the big player's potential to become a real champion is determined by its ability to act as a network pilot. As a network pilot, the real champion needs to convince other firms in the region of the network's profitability. To do so, game theory would suggest the importance of a positive signal, usually some kind of self-commitment, from the network pilot. In giving this signal, the network pilot demonstrates its commitment to the network and thus contributes to strengthening and expanding the network. This idea is complementary to the French view of a national champion, which stresses such an entity's social responsibility. Social responsibility should be understood as all efforts contributing to build up, foster, and intensify the network.

Thus once a network pilot has managed to build up a regional network, (i.e., the network pilot has gained other companies' trust), additional social responsibilities come into play. At this point the entire network of firms needs to engage in various regional activities to stimulate regional dynamics and thus generate positive externalities for its members. With regard to network care and development, the network pilot may still bear most of the responsibility, but maintaining the network is in the pilot's own self-interest and thus the costs of the obligation (time and expense) can be justified. However, to create and maintain an all-embracing regional network, the large company members must not be too dominant, and positive externalities from participating must be perceptible to all members, independent of size. This is especially important as small companies are believed to be a driving force of innovation (Audretsch 1995). Supporting small companies and startups thus means that fresh knowledge will be produced, eventually increasing the network's pool of knowledge. One way to contribute to knowledge production is to provide corporate venture capital to startups (Gompers 2002); another way is to join forces with universities.

Other social responsibilities profitably engaged in by a regional network of firms might include sponsoring and donating to cultural institutions, such as festivals, concerts, exhibitions, and other bohemian projects in the region. This activity will enhance a region's amenities and make it more attractive to creative persons or those with high potential, thus not only keeping the current labor pool in place but expanding it with highly skilled workers (Glaeser et al. 2001; Florida 2002; Falck et al. 2009).

4.5 Strategic and Political Reasons to Promote Champions

4.5.1 Supporting the Lame Ducks

As discussed in section 4.3, it may be welfare-increasing to protect mature firms in the presence of specialized employment, tacit knowledge, and local networks. However, there may be other, nonbenevolent reasons why a public authority may want to intervene and favor insufficiently competitive firms (lame ducks).

Strategic Trade Policy or How to Beggar My Neighbor   One argument for supporting "lame ducks" is found in the strategic trade policy literature. Let us assume that there is a market for some arbitrary good. The market is characterized by worldwide imperfect competition and suppliers from around the world compete to capture excess rents. To retain the largest possible share of the excess rents within national borders, governments may be inclined to artificially bolster the position of domestic firms in this market, perhaps through state aid. As mentioned in the introduction, Spencer and Brander (1983) presented a theory of government intervention explaining industrial strategy. Positive welfare effects from subsidization of local firms are not guaranteed, for at least two reasons. First, local firms operating in imperfect markets do not earn excess rents only from foreign markets but also from home markets, leading to a loss of consumer surplus in the home country. This is reflected by $CS_2^P < CS$ in our model. Second, the subsidy-ridden noncooperative international equilibrium is suboptimal, leading to subsidy wars. The multilateral prohibition of subsidies, should such an agreement prove possible, would increase the welfare of all countries.

National Champions Are Mortal   Another argument in favor of protecting established firms in the temporary presence of sizable externalities (i.e., L_2 becomes negligible with time) involves structural change and unemployment. Cohen (1995: 30) states that "there is little need to dwell upon the *lame ducks* other than to remind the reader that a national champion is mortal." A dynamic economy, by definition, undergoes constant structural change, due, among other things, to different industry growth rates of production and demand (for an overview, see Pianta and Vivarelli 2007). Structural change has geographical implications too, as industries are not evenly distributed geographically (for a European discussion, see Midelfart-Knarvik and Overman 2002). Industries that do not change and grow will eventually die. This will obviously have serious negative effects on employment in the short run, but industry death can have long-term effects on employment too, particularly when the labor market is inflexible and immobile (externality L_2 in our model). In this situation state intervention can merely delay the inevitable, but politicians, with short-term horizons, especially when up for reelection, may wish to smooth out the process of decline and thus ease social tension. A famous example is former German Chancellor Gerhard Schröder's 1999 attempt to rescue one of

the biggest construction companies in Germany—Philipp Holzmann AG. Due to mismanagement and a far-too-optimistic view concerning a possible construction boom in eastern Germany, Philipp Holzmann AG accumulated more than 2.4 billion German marks of debt, which put the firm's survival in great danger. In a highly visible and celebrated move, Chancellor Schröder offered debt guarantees from the state. However, the firm's death was only delayed, not averted, and in early 2002, Philipp Holzmann AG went bankrupt.

This "save the lame duck at all costs" or "too big to fail" (Vives 2001) phenomenon has gained a new dimension in the financial crises in the years 2008 and 2009. In the aftermath of the case of Lehman Brothers, single banks are regarded to be system-relevant, meaning their failures are expected to affect all agents in the financial sector. Subsequently the same argument has been brought forward for firms in other key industries, such as automotives. So eventually the crisis shows that this sort of big champion is theoretically mortal but in reality "too big to fail" and thus becomes a *big-project firm*, as discussed next.

4.5.2 The Temptation to Support "Big-Project" Firms

High Visibility The French Concorde project is an excellent example of Seabright's (2005) point that politicians are tempted to select for public investment support those projects that are both highly visible in the media and comparatively insulated from competition. Being more or less isolated from competition, the project failed because it was more engineer- than customer-driven. Another example is the European Airbus project. The Airbus project has been celebrated in the media as a shining example of successful European champion-oriented industrial policy. Indeed there is a simulation study by Neven and Seabright (1995) concluding that Airbus was likely to earn a comfortable rate of return on the public investment made. Thus it was a good investment from a pure rate-of-return perspective. However, the effect of Airbus' entry on consumer surplus is not clear: the gains from competition may be offset by lost economies of scale and the Airbus-induced exit of McDonnell-Douglas. In our model we assume that competition benefits consumer welfare, $CS_2^p < CS_2$, as this is the most common case (all potential beneficial effects from protection are embedded in profits π_2^p and externalities L_2). In the absence of competition, however, there is no guarantee that the benefits from economies of scale will be passed on to consumers.

Strategic Industries and Security of Supply Yet another reason advanced for government intervention has to do with security of supply. Strategic industries that secure national supply with essential resources produce an externality L_2 different from employment that might also justify state intervention. Take the European gas market as an example. Only a small fraction of total European gas consumption is actually produced in Europe. Much of the gas is imported from politically unstable countries, making disruption of supply quite possible. Gas is mainly transported via inter-urban pipelines, another source of risk, both political and physical. Moreover construction of pipelines results in high sunk costs. As national production is limited, the only way to reduce these risks is to diversify gas imports, that is, build more pipelines, leading, of course, to even higher sunk costs. Therefore it is often argued that a national or European firm (a heavyweight champion) is needed to guarantee the security of gas supply. And it then seems acceptable that a vertically integrated gas supplier will earn excess profits from consumers on its home market to compensate for investing in the very expensive, but necessary for diversity and safety, pipelines and other infrastructure. Indeed this argument was viewed favorably and perhaps had a hand in the eventual approval of the merger of E.ON and Ruhrgas. E.ON, already one of Germany's largest energy companies, intended to acquire a 60 percent majority in the gas company Ruhrgas, resulting in E.ON/Ruhrgas becoming Europe's biggest energy company. Preliminarily permission for the merger was denied by the Federal Cartel Office on the ground that the merger would have detrimentally strengthened E.ON's already dominant position. However, the merger gained ministerial approval for reasons of security of supply (for details, see Sinn 2002).

Nevertheless, natural monopolies (characterized by high sunk costs) can erode over time—especially through technical progress. The supply of liquefied natural gas (LNG), which is transported by specially designed sea vessels and road tankers, may, in the future, increase, thus diversifying gas supply and reducing reliance on pipelines, making state protection of the pipeline owners (the heavyweight champions) less desirable, a turn of events predicted by our model: protection delays relocation decisions.

4.6   Conclusion

The aim of this contribution was to provide a different approach from that usually found in the literature on national-champion-oriented policies. While the existing literature mainly concentrates on the distribution of rents, we look at their creation. In doing so, we adopted an evolutionary perspective and considered how government intervention along the product life cycle can alter a firm's incentives to (1) invest in R&D in the early phase of the life cycle and (2) relocate resources during later phases of the life cycle when the product is mature. In a simple model we analyzed a firm's decision on whether or not to invest in research, given that there are knowledge spillovers. Such spillovers carry the risk of imitation by foreign firms, and that discourages research investment. Yet knowledge spillovers also play an important role in geographical location decisions to the extent that they generate positive regional externalities.

We assessed the impact of subsidizing research during early stages of the life cycle and the impact of protecting firms in mature industries. We found certain situations where subsidization of SMEs is an efficient strategy, including those cases (1) where credit constraints prevent small- and medium-sized firms from entering the market, thus hindering the positive entry competition effect, and (2) where subsidies have a multiplicative effect by creating spillovers in the early phase of the life cycle. Protection from competition may also be efficient when public funds are costly or when monetary resources may be diverted rather than invested. However, these findings proved only applicable to competitive economies at the technology frontier and under the assumption of a benevolent government. Our real-world examples show that subsidizing historically produced undesired results as do politicians seeking reelection who concentrate on protecting firms in the mature phase of the life cycle. This evidence suggests a skeptical view of the value of protection and that such a policy should be approached with great caution, especially during an election cycle when the assumption of a "benevolent" politician might be particularly inadequate.

Supra-national bodies such as the European Union may limit the discretion of politicians, and mutual scrutiny from its members may be useful in this context. However, *indirect* promotion, by means of providing an innovation-supportive environment, may hold greater promise as shown in Falck et al. (2010). A proper environment may include local transportation infrastructure along with supporting institutions such as business incubators, universities, and research institutes, that is, institutions that support local knowledge flows but whose products benefit the entire region, not just one company. This kind of policy, which is aimed at local championship instead of national or

European champions, is becoming increasingly popular and is known as cluster-oriented policy (Porter 1998).

References

Ades, A., and R. Di Tella. 1997. National champions and corruption: Some unpleasant interventionist arithmetic. *Economic Journal* 107 (443): 1023–42.

Aghion, P., R. Blundell, R. Griffith, P. Howitt, and S. Prantl. 2009. The effects of entry on incumbent innovation and productivity. *Review of Economics and Statistics* 93 (1): 20–32.

Aubert, C., and J. Pouyet. 2006. Incomplete regulation, market competition and collusion. *Review of Economic Design* 10 (2): 113–42.

Audretsch, D. B. 1995. *Innovation and Industry Evolution.* Cambridge: MIT Press.

Audretsch, D. B., O. Falck, and S. Heblich. 2009. Who's got the aces up his sleeve? Functional specialization of cities and entrepreneurship. *Annals of Regional Science.* doi:10.1007/s00168-009-0353-0.

Auriol, E., and M. Warlters. 2005. The marginal cost of public fund in Africa. Policy research working paper 3679. World Bank.

Baldwin, C. Y., and D. B. Clark. 1997. Managing in an age of modularity. *Harvard Business Review* 75 (5): 84–93.

Bardhan, P. K. 1971. An optimum subsidy to a learning industry: An aspect of the theory of infant industry protection. *International Economic Review* 12 (1): 54–70.

Baumol, W. J. 2002a. *The Free-Market Innovation Machine: Analyzing the Growth Miracle of Capitalism.* Princeton: Princeton University Press.

Baumol, W. J. 2002b. Entrepreneurship, innovation and growth: The David–Goliath symbiosis. *Journal of Entrepreneurial Finance and Business Ventures* 7: 1–10.

Becattini, G. 1990. The Marshallian industrial district as a socio-economic notion. In F. Pyke, G. Becattini, and W. Sengenberger, eds., *Industrial Districts and Inter-firm Co-operation in Italy.* Geneva: International Institute for Labour Studies, 37–51.

Cohen, E. 1995. France: National champions in search of a mission. In J. Hayward, ed., *Industrial Enterprise and European Champions.* Oxford: Oxford University Press, 23–47.

Dasgupta, P. 1988. The welfare economics of knowledge production. *Oxford Review of Economic Policy* 4 (4): 1–12.

Dewatripont, M., and P. Seabright. 2006. Wasteful public spending and state aid control. *Journal of the European Economic Association* 4 (2–3): 513–22.

Ellickson, R. 1991. *Order without Law.* Cambridge: Harvard University Press.

Falck, O., S. Heblich, and S. Kipar. 2009. Incumbent innovation and domestic entry. *Small Business Economics.* doi:10.1007/s11187-009-9219-1.

Falck, O., S. Heblich, and S. Kipar. 2010. Industrial innovation: Direct evidence from a cluster-oriented policy. *Regional Science and Urban Economics.* doi:10.1016/j.regsciurbeco.2010.03.007.

Fallick, B., C. A. Fleischman, and J. B. Rebitzer. 2006. Job-hopping in Silicon Valley: Some evidence concerning the microfoundations of a high-technology cluster. *Review of Economics and Statistics* 88 (3): 472–81.

Feldman, M. 1994. *The Geography of Innovation*. Boston: Kluwer Academic.

Feldman, M., and D. B. Audretsch. 1999. Innovation in cities: Science-based diversity, specialization and localized competition. *European Economic Review* 43 (2): 409–29.

Florida, R. 2002. *The Rise of the Creative Class*. New York: Basic Books.

Gilson, R. J. 1999. The legal infrastructure of high technology industrial districts: Silicon Valley, Route 128, and covenants not to compete. *New York University Law Review* 74 (3): 575–629.

Glaeser, E., J. Kolko, and A. Saiz. 2001. Consumer city. *Journal of Economic Geography* 1 (1): 27–50.

Gompers, P. A. 2002. Corporations and the financing of innovation: The corporate venturing experience. *Federal Reserve Bank of Atlanta Economic Review* 87: 1–17.

Gort, M., and S. Klepper. 1982. Time paths in the diffusion of product innovations. *Economic Journal* 92 (367): 630–53.

Hyde, A. 2003. *Working in Silicon Valley: Economic and Legal Analysis of a High-Velocity Labor Market*. New York: Sharpe.

Klepper, S. 1996. Entry, exit, growth, and innovation over the product life cycle. *American Economic Review* 86 (3): 562–83.

Klepper, S. 1997. Industry life cycles. *Industrial and Corporate Change* 6 (1): 145–81.

Laffont, J.-J., and J. Tirole. 1993. Cartelization by regulation. *Journal of Regulatory Economics* 5 (2): 111–30.

Maincent, E., and L. Navarro. 2006. A policy for industrial champions: From picking winners to fostering excellence and the growth of firms. Industrial and Economic Reforms paper 2. Enterprise and Industry Directorate-General.

Midelfart-Knarvik, K., and H. Overman. 2002. Delocation and European integration: Is structural spending justified? *Economic Policy* 17 (35): 321–59.

Murphy, K. M., A. Shleifer, and R. W. Vishny. 1989. Industrialization and the big push. *Journal of Political Economy* 97 (5): 1003–26.

Neven, D., and P. Seabright. 1995. European industrial policy: The Airbus case. *Economic Policy* 10 (21): 313–58.

Pianta, M., and M. Vivarelli. 2007. *Unemployment, Structural Change, and Globalization*. International Labour Organization.

Piore, M., and C. Sabel. 1984. *The Second Industrial Divide. Possibilities for Prosperity*. New York: Basic Books.

Porter, M. E. 1998. *On Competition*. Boston: Harvard Business School Press.

Powell, W. 1990. Neither market nor hierarchy: Network forms of organization. *Research in Organizational Behavior* 12: 295–336.

Roe, M. 2003. *Political Determinants of Corporate Governance*. Oxford: Oxford University Press.

Rosenberg, N. 1990. Why do companies do basic research (with their own money)? *Research Policy* 19 (2): 165–74.

Rosenstein-Rodan, P. N. 1943. Problems of industrialisation of eastern and south-eastern Europe. *Economic Journal* 53:202–11.

Saxenian, A. 1994. *Regional Advantage: Culture and Competition in Silicon Valley and Rte. 128*. Cambridge: Harvard University Press.

Schumpeter, J. A. 1942. *Capitalism Socialism and Democracy*. New York: Harper.

Seabright, P. 2005. National and European champions—Burden or blessing? *CESifo Forum* 2/2005: 52–55.

Sinn, H. W. 2002. *Fusion E.ON-Ruhrgas—Die volkswirtschaftlichen Aspekte*. Munich: Ifo Institute for Economic Research.

Spencer, B., and J. Brander. 1983. International R&D rivalry and industrial strategy. *Review of Economic Studies* 50 (4): 707–22.

Vives, X. 2001. Restructuring financial regulation in the European Monetary Union. *Journal of Financial Services Research* 19 (1): 57–82.

III Political-Economy Analyses

5   Mergers and National Champions

Massimo Motta and Michele Ruta

5.1   Introduction

In recent years a number of mergers (sometimes between firms located in the same country, sometimes between firms located in different countries) have attracted a lot of media attention because of alleged protectionist positions taken by politicians and authorities of the countries that in one way or another have been involved in such mergers. The European Commission's Directorate General for Competition has often had to intervene, either with declarations or by taking formal actions, asking member states not to hinder mergers involving foreign firms and perceived as undesirable from the point of view of national interests.

During the first two years (November 22, 2004 to November 21, 2006) of Mrs. Neelie Kroes's mandate as Commissioner for Competition, she was mentioned on the first page of *The Financial Times* 18 times, and 6 of which referred to mergers that raised political tensions across countries. Among such mergers, let us recall *ABN-Amro/Antonveneta* (a Dutch bank's bid to take over an Italian bank was opposed in various ways by the then governor of Banca d'Italia, the relevant authority at the time for bank mergers), *HypoVereinsbank/Unicredit* (the Polish government tried to block the creation of the large Polish subsidiary of the new Italian-German bank), *E-On/Endesa* (the takeover bid made by the German energy group was hindered by the Spanish government, which instead sponsored a domestic merger between Endesa and Gas Natural), and *Gas de France/Suez* (again sponsored by the French government in reaction to a possible bid by rival Italian energy firm ENEL). This list could, of course, be complemented by a number of other merger cases where in various forms the suspicion that national governments were promoting or defending *national champions* arose.

In this chapter we investigate why different countries have opposing interests and try to favor or oppose particular combinations of international firms' assets, and study under which circumstances there might be a conflict between such behavior and economic efficiency.

Of course, there may be very different arguments behind governments' attitudes toward mergers in an international economy, and some of these arguments may be purely political (perhaps reflecting a purely nationalistic citizens' dislike of foreigners). Here we focus on economic and political economy arguments, and we will see that these already offer some possible explanations of the opposing interests on mergers.

One could think that the protectionist attitudes of some governments toward mergers in international markets are just another application of the policy of building "national champions" that has been familiarized by the well-known literature on "strategic trade policies." However, we argue that standard "strategic trade policy" arguments are probably not very helpful in understanding governments' attitudes toward mergers. To go beyond these arguments, we informally present a political economy model of merger decisions, and argue that it can shed light on the conflicting positions often taken by different countries with respect to mergers.

5.2 Mergers and Strategic Trade Policies

5.2.1 Standard Strategic Trade Policy Arguments

One of the most appealing explanations for the creation of national champions is given by the strategic trade policy literature (Brander and Spencer 1983, 1985; Eaton and Grossman 1986).[1] The main insight of this literature is that when markets are oligopolistic, government intervention can shift profits from foreign to domestic firms.

For instance, a national government may subsidize domestic firms' output or exports, by reducing their costs and therefore making them more aggressive in international markets where they would increase their market share to the detriment of foreign rivals. The increase in domestic firms' profits will in turn raise national welfare.[2]

Figure 5.1 illustrates this argument. Suppose there is a firm h based in country H, and a firm f based in country F. Assume that they sell a homogeneous good (in a third country only for simplicity), they have identical marginal cost c, and that they are competing in quantities (or, more generally, actions are strategic substitutes), so that their best-reply

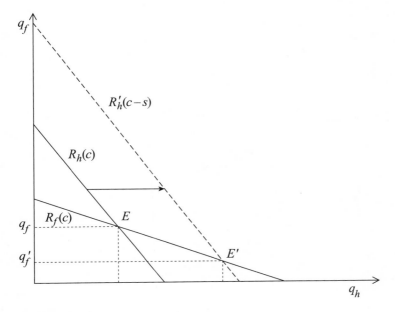

Figure 5.1
Subsidy s to firm h (strategic substitute)

functions, R_h and R_f are negatively sloped. Absent any subsidy, the quantities sold by each firm are those corresponding to the equilibrium point E. Suppose now that country H's government subsidizes its domestic firm h. This will have the effect of decreasing the marginal costs faced by firm h from c to $c-s$ and making it behave more aggressively in the market. This effect is illustrated by a shift in the best-reply function of firm h, from $R_h(c)$ to $R_h(c-s)$, and will in turn move the equilibrium from point E to point E'. At the new equilibrium, firm h has a larger share of the market and higher profits than at point E. In turn country H's welfare will also increase, since its welfare is given by the sum of consumer surplus (here zero, as the market is located in a third country)[3] and of producer surplus (the subsidies are just a transfer between domestic groups).

Of course, despite the initial enthusiasm toward such arguments, especially among policy makers (finally, economic theory could provide reasons to justify economic interventions!), it soon appeared clear that strategic trade policy theories were not that convincing.

First of all, if several governments used subsidies, all firms in international markets would increase outputs, and all profits would

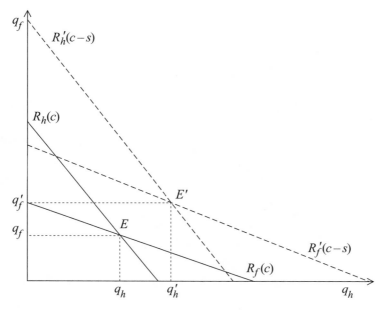

Figure 5.2
Both governments intervene

decrease: it would be better for governments to commit to free trade. This is illustrated by figure 5.2, which depicts the case where both governments subsidize their domestic firm. At the new equilibrium E' market shares are like in the absence of the intervention, but now both firms have increased their outputs, so equilibrium prices and profits will be lower: government intervention entails a welfare loss in both countries.

Second, if raising public money entailed inefficiencies, one would not easily recommend the use of subsidies.

Third, and probably most important, if it is known that a government is willing to subsidize firms in certain sectors, this would trigger inefficient rent-seeking behavior and it is far from being clear that the government would end up helping the right firms, rather than distributing aid to unprofitable and inefficient firms which turn out to have more political clout.

Fourth, the nature of these arguments is highly sensitive to the nature of product market competition. Consider again the case where there is only one government which intervenes, but assume that foreign

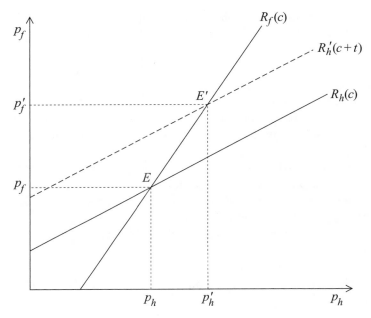

Figure 5.3
Strategic complements: Tax, not subsidy

firms react to the domestic firms' *more* aggressive behavior by being more aggressive as well (i.e., assume strategic complementarity). In that case, a subsidy would decrease welfare.

This is illustrated by figure 5.3, where it is assumed that firms compete in prices (or more generally firms' actions are strategic complements). The figure shows that if country H's government taxes the domestic firm, it will make it less aggressive (for any given price set by firm f, firm h finds it optimal to set a higher price), causing an upward shift of its best-reply function from $R_h(c)$ to $R_h(c+t)$. Since by strategic complementarity the rival will react by behaving less aggressively as well, at the new equilibrium both firms will have similar market shares but both set higher prices and enjoy higher profits. In turn this improves welfare of country H.

In other words, a subsidy would be optimal when market actions are strategic substitutes, but a tax would be optimal when actions are strategic complements. Since it is impossible to design economic policy on the basis of the mode of competition (which is to a large extent

unobservable, and would in any case change from sector to sector), it
follows that strategic trade policy provides a weak argument to justify
economic interventions.

5.2.2 Strategic Merger Policy

All these qualifications made, it should be said that strategic trade and
industrial policy arguments remain very popular and are often invoked
to justify government intervention in the economy and in particular
protectionist policies.

Therefore it is interesting to ask whether strategic policy arguments
may lie behind "national champions" positions on mergers in an international economy: for instance, would such arguments explain why a
government may want to promote a merger between domestic firms?
As a first step to answer this question, consider the effects of a merger
in a domestic economy. We will build on this benchmark analysis to
see what the effects of mergers in an international economy are, and
investigate whether "strategic trade policy" arguments make sense in
the context of mergers.[4]

Mergers in a Domestic Economy To understand the impact of a
merger between two firms operating in an oligopolistic industry, it is
convenient to first consider the case where the merger does not entail
efficiency gains (in other words, the merger does not modify the costs
of the firms which take part in it).

NO EFFICIENCY GAINS

When two competing firms merge, their market power will increase.
Before the merger, at the time of deciding which price to set (or which
quantity to sell), each firm would face a number of competitive constraints: a given price increase might lead consumers to switch to any
of the rivals, determining a certain reduction in profits. After the
merger, the merging firms coordinate their decisions and understand
that they face weaker competitive constraints, as there is one less independent rival to which consumers could switch if they decided to
increase prices. (Think of a merger to monopoly as the extreme case:
before the merger each of the duopolists knows that if it would solely
increase prices it would lose customers to the rival; after the merger, it
can increase prices without fear that customers would switch to any
rival.) As a result the merger will lead to a less aggressive action (a
price increase, or a fall in output, depending on which one is the

strategic variable) of the merging firms. Depending on the nature of competition in the industry, rivals may react by being also less aggressive (if actions are strategic complements) or by being more aggressive (if actions are strategic substitutes). However, it can be proved that the net effect of the merger is a price increase or a reduction in total output.[5] This means that the merger, absent efficiency gains, will decrease both consumer surplus and total welfare. Interestingly, and important for our analysis later on, if the merger does not entail efficiency gains, the profits of the outsiders will increase: this is because the price increase (or output reduction) of the merging firms will benefit the industry as a whole, and above all, the outsiders which can free-ride on the less aggressive action of the insiders. (As a matter of fact, it is even possible that a merger would not be profitable when there are strategic substitutes, as the more aggressive reaction by the outsiders would outweigh the benefit of a less aggressive action by the insiders.)[6]

Figure 5.4 illustrates the effect of the merger for the case where actions are strategic complements (but, as said above, qualitative results

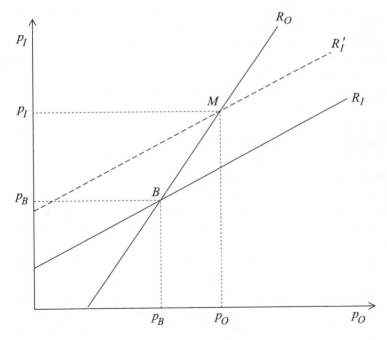

Figure 5.4
Merger, no efficiencies

would not change under strategic substitutes). The outsiders' best-reply function is given, whereas the effect of the merger is to make the insiders less aggressive, shifting their best-reply function from R_I to R_I'. As a result the equilibrium moves from point B (before the merger) to point M (with the merger), leading to higher industry prices and profits, and lower consumer and total welfare.

MERGERS WITH EFFICIENCY GAINS

When the merger entails sufficiently large cost savings (the insiders' costs decrease from c to ec, where $e < 1$ measures the reduction in costs: the lower e, the stronger the efficiency gain), the impact of the merger is considerably different. The merger makes the merging firms more efficient: rather than increasing their prices, lower costs will lead the insiders to be more aggressive in the marketplace (they will decrease their prices, or increase their output, depending on their strategic variable). The reaction of the outsider will depend on whether actions are strategic substitutes (in that case they will be less aggressive) or strategic complements (they will become more aggressive as well), but it can be shown that if efficiency gains are important enough, the final effect of the merger will be to lower industry prices and to increase output. Therefore, with sufficiently important efficiency gains, the merger will increase consumer and total welfare. Note also that in this case the outsiders will *lose* from the merger, since the more competitive insiders will be able to grab a bigger share of the market at the new equilibrium.

Figure 5.5 illustrates this case. Absent efficiency gains, the merger would lead the insiders to have the best-reply function $R_I'(e = 1)$, but the stronger the cost savings, the more their best-reply function will shift downward. The figure depicts a best-reply function R_I^e associated to a merger with efficiency gains which are important enough for the new equilibrium point after the merger to be at M^e where prices are lower than at the equilibrium point B that would prevail absent the merger.

More generally, the level of the efficiency gains is crucial to understand the impact of a merger. Figure 5.6 illustrates the effects of a merger in a closed economy as a function of the reduction in costs (from c to $ec \le c$) created by the efficiency gains. To understand the figure, recall that a lower value of e is associated to a higher level of efficiency gains. In the interval $[e_{\pi I}, 1]$; that is, if there are small or no efficiency gains, the merger may not take place under strategic substitutes. If

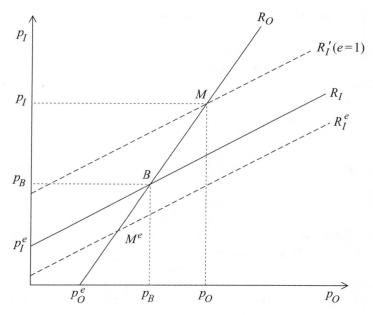

Figure 5.5
Merger, with efficiency gains

	$e_{CS} = e_{\pi O}$	e_W	$e_{\pi I}$	$0 \quad e$
$\pi_I \uparrow$	$\pi_I \uparrow$	$\pi_I \uparrow$	No merger takes place	
$\pi_O \downarrow$	$\pi_O \uparrow$	$\pi_O \uparrow$		
$CS \uparrow$	$CS \downarrow$	$CS \downarrow$		
$W \uparrow$	$W \uparrow$	$W \downarrow$		

Figure 5.6
Effects of a merger on profits of insiders, outsiders, consumer surplus, and aggregate welfare

firms choose outputs, the insiders would decrease their output, but the outsiders would increase it; hence prices would not increase enough to compensate the insiders for the fall in market share. (However, this region disappears if the actions are strategic complements: the merger would always be profitable for insiders then.)

When e falls in the interval $[e_W, e_{\pi_I}]$, both insiders and outsiders gain from the merger, but both consumer welfare and total welfare decrease (this is the case where efficiency gains are small).

When e belongs to the interval $[e_{CS}, e_W]$, efficiency gains are larger, so the increase in profits of all firms outweighs the (small) reduction in consumer surplus, resulting in higher welfare.

Finally, in the area where efficiency gains are very important, that is, $e < e_{CS}$, insiders' profits, consumer surplus and total welfare all increase, whereas outsiders are the only ones who lose from the merger (as the more competitive insiders subtract market shares from them).

A First Look at Mergers in an International Economy   We can now build on our knowledge of the effects of a merger in a domestic economy to explore whether "strategic trade policy" arguments may explain protectionist attitudes toward mergers, and in particular the favorable treatment of mergers between domestic firms: are such domestic mergers a way to build national champions?

Given the role played by efficiency gains, it is convenient to separately consider the cases where efficiency gains are absent and where they are sufficiently important.

MERGER WITHOUT EFFICIENCY GAINS

If the merger does not entail efficiency gains, that is, if it does not decrease insiders' unit costs, then after the merger the insiders will be *less* aggressive in the marketplace (i.e., the merger will be like a tax on output, rather than a subsidy to it).

If actions are strategic substitutes, that is, if foreign rivals will react by being more aggressive, then domestic firms' profits would decrease. If actions are strategic complements, that is, if foreign rivals will react by being less aggressive, domestic firms'—as well as outsiders'—profits would indeed increase (not by shifting oligopoly rents but rather by weakening competition in the market place).

However, note that if the product is also sold in the domestic country, then—independently of whether actions are strategic substitutes or complements—domestic consumers would lose from the merger.

Unless the domestic market is very small, the fall in domestic consumer surplus would tend to outweigh the gain (if any) in domestic firms' profits. In this case therefore there would be no reason for the domestic government to sponsor such a merger.[7]

MERGER WITH EFFICIENCY GAINS

If instead the merger did lead to conspicuous efficiency gains, then insiders would indeed become more competitive in international markets and would increase their overall market share and profits (independently of whether actions are strategic substitutes or complements). In this case there would indeed be a reason for the domestic government to promote the domestic merger, but note that there would be no harm to welfare: more inefficient foreign firms might want to complain, but consumers (wherever they are located) would be better off, and the merger should be approved. Opposing views among different countries might, of course, arise in this case, but we could not really talk about "protectionist behavior" that should be stigmatized.

Further we feel that it is not (or not only) a drive toward efficiency-enhancing concentrations which inspired governments' actions in most of the mergers mentioned above, and suspect that to understand such actions we would have to move beyond the assumption that governments are welfare-maximizers. To this purpose we propose to study this issue within a political economy approach that we discuss in what follows.

5.3   A Political Economy Approach

Merger policy, not differently from any other economic policy, is decided in a political economy environment. This simple observation has several important implications. First, as mergers have different effects on consumers, merging firms and nonmerging competitors, the location of the relevant market and firms (at home or abroad) matters. Second, antitrust decisions can be fully or partly delegated to independent authorities, but generally governments attempt to exert some influence on merger policy (which, depending on the country, may go from generic pressures to veto power on the final decision). Third, some groups in society are politically better organized than others to pursue their interests because of collective action problems.

We start by providing an informal description of a model that allows us to capture these features of merger policy.[8] We define merger policy

$x \in \{0, 1\}$ as a simple binary choice, where x can take the value of 0—*allow the merger*—or 1—*reject the merger*.[9] We assume that a merger to be effective needs to be approved by an authority in charge of merger policy. The decision of the authority, however, can in practice be influenced (or reversed) by the government with some exogenous probability, capturing informal political influence or a formal reversal clause that the government might appeal to. This opens the question of how the government formulates its position on the merger. As in the classic works of Bernheim and Whinston (1986) and Grossman and Helpman (1994), we assume that politicians' preferences are shaped by a combination of social welfare considerations and political influence by lobby groups representing the interests of firms.

More precisely, the political economy environment in which merger policy takes place is described by a three stage process (refer to figure 5.7). At the first stage, the merger is proposed and lobbies representing the interests of firms (insiders and the outsider) offer political contributions to the government contingent on its position on the merger.[10] At the second stage, the antitrust decision is taken. We assume that at this stage the characteristics of the merger are common knowledge. With some exogenous probability $\xi \in [0, 1]$, to be further specified later, merger policy is determined by the government. We assume that the objective function of the government is a weighted average of aggregate welfare and political contributions. The weight on this second term is often referred to as the *political bias*. With probability $(1 - \xi)$, the antitrust authority decides whether or not to allow the merger, based on social welfare considerations only.[11] The probability ξ is meant to capture in a general way the influence of the government on the

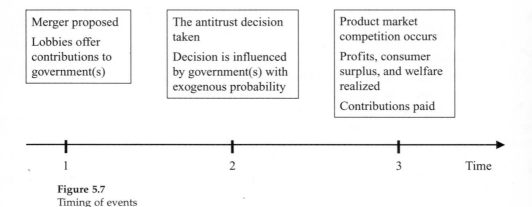

Figure 5.7
Timing of events

authority, with low values of ξ being associated to weak political influence on antitrust decisions. At the last stage, product market competition takes place, political contributions to the government are paid, and profits, consumer surplus, and welfare are realized. The political game is solved by backward induction and we limit attention to the equilibrium with truthful contributions (i.e., where payments from firms reflect the effect of merger decisions on their payoffs).

As discussed in the previous section, mergers can have substantially different effects in a closed or in an open economy environment. Moreover in an open economy environment itself there might be important differences as countries can be part of an international union with a common antitrust authority (as in the EU) or have separate authorities. We therefore assume that there are two regions (or countries), A and B, and consider three different scenarios to take into account these possibilities.

DOMESTIC MERGERS
The market and the firms are all located within national borders. Here A and B are regions of the same country. The merger decision is taken by the authority and can be influenced by a "politically motivated" national government with some exogenous probability $\xi_U \in [0, 1]$. This is our benchmark case.

NON-EU MERGERS
A and B are fully independent political units, with two separate authorities and national governments. The merger decision is taken by the authority where the market is located—either A or B—and can be influenced by the local government with some exogenous probability $\xi_j \in [0, 1]$, where j is either A or B. The authority maximizes national social welfare, while the objective function of the national government is a linear combination of national welfare and political contributions from domestic firms.

EU MERGERS
A and B delegate sovereignty on merger policy to an authority that allows or blocks the merger based on union social welfare considerations. However, the antitrust decision can still be influenced by "politically motivated" national governments with probability $\xi_A \in [0, 1]$ and $\xi_B \in [0, 1]$ respectively (where $\xi_A + \xi_B \leq 1$).

We now take a closer look at these three cases.

5.3.1 Domestic Mergers

This section deals with a situation where all firms are located in the same country, but two different agents—say, the antitrust authority and the economics minister—are involved in the merger decision process. This situation may well describe several cases where there has been a conflict between domestic decision makers. For instance, in the *E-On/ Ruhrgas* German energy merger, the Bundeskartellamt, which is the relevant competition authority in Germany (and the Monopolkommission, which has an advisory role) did not want to approve the merger, but the German government decided to authorize the merger (under German law, the BKA can be overruled by the economics minister). In the case of the (failed) merger project between *Gas Natural/Endesa*, both Spanish firms, the Tribunal de Defensa de la Competencia (the relevant Spanish competition authority), did not express a favorable opinion of the concentration, whereas the Spanish government openly approved of it.

In this case A and B are two regions of the same country and merger policy is

$$x = \begin{cases} x_U^G & \text{with probability } \xi_U, \\ x_U^A & \text{with probability } (1-\xi_U), \end{cases}$$

where superscripts G and A stand for government and authority respectively (and the subscript U is for the union of the two regions, i.e., the country in this case). We first look at the decision of the authority and then study the choice of the government.

As the objective function of the authority corresponds to total welfare, the authority approves a merger if and only if the merger is efficient ($e \leq e_U = e_W$). Aggregate welfare maximization implies that only those mergers that involve sufficiently large efficiency gains are approved by the authority; all other mergers (for which $e > e_U$) are rejected.

We next study how special interests influence merger policy preferences of the government. Politicians can be influenced by lobbies representing the interests of merging firms and outsiders.

Recall from the previous section that for any $e \in [e_{\pi o}, e_{\pi I}]$ (i.e., for low efficiency gains), both merging firms and outsiders will benefit from the merger. In this case lobbies representing the interests of insiders and competitors might both choose to exert pressures on politicians to have the merger approved. Notice, however, that for $e \leq e_U$ the merger is efficient and a politician would endorse it even in the absence of political pressures. In this case lobbies optimally set political contributions equal to zero at the first stage; the merger is approved by the authority and the government has no reason to oppose the decision. For $e > e_U$ (i.e., inefficient merger), the authority rejects the merger and lobbies set contributions so as to induce the government to oppose the authority's decision. Because of these political pressures the government endorses at least some mergers that would be rejected by the authority on the basis of efficiency (those for which the realization of the efficiency level falls in the area $e_U < e < e_U^G$, where e_U^G is the threshold efficiency value for the politically motivated government).

However, for $e < e_{\pi o}$, merging firms and outsiders have opposing interests and will lobby in opposite directions. The government nevertheless always supports the merger. The reason is twofold. First, consumer surplus is always larger if the merger is approved when $e < e_{\pi o} = e_{CS}$. Second, the lobby of insiders can always offer higher political contributions than the lobby representing the outsider. Figure 5.8 summarizes the political economy of domestic mergers.

The main result here is that even when both the government and the authority belong to the same country, they may have opposing views about a particular (domestic) merger. This is because the government's position is affected by political contributions, which distort its objective function away from total welfare considerations. As a result politicians may be ready to accept mergers that are not very efficient but that are profitable enough for firms to lobby the government. This is summarized by different "intervention" thresholds between the authority and the government.

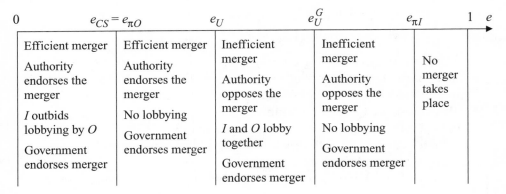

Figure 5.8
Political economy of *domestic mergers*

5.3.2 Non-EU Mergers

We now start addressing the political economy of mergers in international markets. The first case is the one where countries A and B are open to trade, but fully politically independent. Each country has an antitrust authority that maximizes national welfare and a politically motivated government that can influence (reverse) the decision of its national authority with probability ξ_j, with $j = A, B$. This case may be useful to understand mergers between non-EU firms, for instance, *Gencor/Lohnro*, *Boeing/McDonnell Douglas*, or *General Electric/Honeywell*, but which had important effects in the EU markets and were subject to the European Commission's jurisdiction. In this case the two decision makers of our model might be seen as the Directorate General for Competition (as antitrust authority) and the member states' governments as "political" agent (they can affect the final decision of the European Commission, which is a collegial body where Commissioners belonging to all the member states are present, and whose final decision does not necessarily coincide with the one recommended by the Competition Commissioner), whereas the non-EU governments do not have any saying in the decision.

The location of firms and consumers now matters and, depending on this, the merger has different effects on the welfare of country A and B. To focus ideas, we assume that the insiders are located in country A (representing the non-EU economy), while the outsider and the market are in B (the EU).

The authority in B decides whether to approve or block the merger. This decision can be influenced (or reversed) by the government in B with probability ξ_B. In this case, merger policy is

$$
x = \begin{cases} x_B^G & \text{with probability } \xi_B, \\ x_B^A & \text{with probability } (1 - \xi_B). \end{cases}
$$

There are two contrasting effects on social welfare in country B. For high-efficiency levels implied by the merger in country A ($e \leq e_{\pi o} = e_{CS}$), the outsider loses, but consumers gain. This second (positive) effect always dominates and the authority in B approves the merger. The opposite holds true for mergers in the area ($e > e_{\pi o} = e_{CS}$). Therefore a welfare-maximizing authority in B will approve a merger if and only if $e \leq e_B^A = e_{\pi o} = e_{CS}$. Notice, however, that the authority in B approves less mergers than what would be optimal from a (total) social welfare point of view (i.e., $e_B^A < e_W$) as it does not internalize the effect on the profits of the insiders.

The government in B is subject to lobbying by the outsider as non-merging competitors are always hurt by the decision of the authority. Whether lobbying is successful or not in this case is ambiguous and depends on the political bias of the government (i.e., the weight on political contributions in its objective function). More precisely the government in B can always be induced by the outsider to endorse the merger if the political bias is sufficiently high (i.e., if the weight on contributions is large).

In this case there is potentially a stark conflict between the different decision makers because the situations where the merger harms welfare coincides with the situations where national profits would increase, and vice versa. Some commentators have suggested that the *Boeing/Mc Donnell Douglas* case reflected a tension between efficiency arguments on one side and protectionist arguments on the other side. Arguably, the merger between the two American firms (located in country A in our example) might have been procompetitive (according to many, McDonnell-Douglas was bound to exit the industry anyhow), and therefore EU consumers would have been better off, but rival EU firm Airbus might have been hurt by the merger, which explains why many voices rose against the merger (in our example, the EU corresponds to country B). The final decision (after long discussions within the European Commission) to approve the merger subject to some remedy may be compatible with the hypothesis that the Competition Directorate—caring for consumer welfare only—favored the merger despite of the opposing views expressed by some member states and possibly represented within the Commission as a collegial body. Refer to figure 5.9 for a summary of this case.

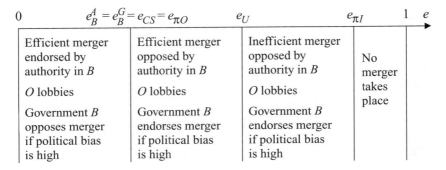

| 0 | $e_B^A = e_B^G = e_{CS} = e_{\pi O}$ | e_U | $e_{\pi I}$ | $1 \quad e$ |

Efficient merger endorsed by authority in B	Efficient merger opposed by authority in B	Inefficient merger opposed by authority in B	No merger takes place
O lobbies	O lobbies	O lobbies	
Government B opposes merger if political bias is high	Government B endorses merger if political bias is high	Government B endorses merger if political bias is high	

Figure 5.9
Political economy of *Non-EU mergers:* Insiders in A, market and outsider in B

5.3.3 EU Mergers

This section deals with EU mergers. This includes cases where a
domestic merger between two firms located in the same EU country
had effects on other EU countries (e.g., *Volvo/Scania* in Sweden) and the
many cases where firms of different EU nationalities were involved,
such as *E-On/Endesa*, *Edison/EdF*, and *HVB/Unicredit*. In these cases the
relevant competition authority (the European Commission) and the EU
governments involved took different positions. Note that even though
there may be only one decision maker (the European Commission) that
is formally invested with the power of allowing or prohibiting the
merger, member countries' governments might have several ways to
affect the final outcome of the merger. For instance, they could try to
increase the costs of the merger by changing the market rules, as when
the Spanish authorities imposed a number of restrictive conditions
(contested by the European Commission) for E-On's (failed) takeover
of Endesa, or when the Italian government changed the corporate governance rules of Edison, or when it announced that it would consider
unbundling of Telecom Italia's fixed network, following AT&T's interests in taking over TI. Or they could affect the Commission's decision
by voicing opposition within the Commission as a whole through their
Commissioner. This motivates our interest in understanding the political economy determinants of the position of member governments'
relative to the merger.

Consider a scenario where countries A and B are part of an international union, with a single antitrust authority, and each national government affects the antitrust decision with probability ξ_j. Merger policy
in the international union is as follows:

$$x = \begin{cases} x_A^G & \text{with probability } \xi_A, \\ x_B^G & \text{with probability } \xi_B, \\ x_U^A & \text{with probability } (1 - \xi_A - \xi_B). \end{cases}$$

We will consider two types of mergers that have distinctive features:
within-country and cross-border EU mergers. As the union authority
maximizes total welfare, it will approve a merger if and only if $e \leq e_U^A = e_W$
(i.e., wherever efficient) and reject it otherwise, independently of the
type of merger. Governments of A and B possibly have a different view
and we therefore need to address these two cases separately.

Within-Country Mergers   The position of national governments on
the merger is influenced by the location of the market and firms and

their political bias. We assume that the market is in country B as this corresponds to the more interesting practical cases. To simplify the discussion, we consider the two limit cases: fully benevolent governments which only act to maximize national welfare (i.e., with no political bias) and selfish governments which exclusively care about lobbying contributions (i.e., with maximal political bias).

BENEVOLENT NATIONAL GOVERNMENTS

If national governments have no political bias and maximize national welfare, no lobbying takes place. In this case the location of the market matters.

In country A there are no consumers and the government only takes into account the effect of the merger on the profits of the insiders (which are both located in A). Therefore the government in A endorses the merger if and only if $e \le e_A^G = e_{\pi I}$ (i.e., whenever the merger is proposed because profitable to the insiders). As for the benevolent government in B, it endorses the merger if and only if $e \le e_B^G = e_{CS} = e_{\pi O}$, as the effect of the merger on consumer welfare always dominates the effect on the outsider. This implies that for $e \le e_{\pi O}$, the union authority approves the merger and no national government opposes this decision. For $e_{\pi O} < e \le e_W$, the authority approves the merger and the decision is opposed by government B. For $e_W < e \le e_{\pi I}$, the authority would block the merger. In this case the government of A opposes the authority's decision.

The position on the merger of the union authority and the (benevolent) national governments are summarized in figure 5.10. Notice that no lobbying ever takes place in this case since we are analyzing the

0	$e_B^G = e_{CS} = e_{\pi O}$	$e_U^A = e_W$	$e_A^G = e_{\pi I}$	1	e
Efficient merger endorsed by union authority	Efficient merger endorsed by union authority	Inefficient merger opposed by union authority	No merger takes place		
Governments A and B endorse merger	No lobbying	No lobbying			
	Government A (B) endorses (opposes) merger	Government A (B) endorses (opposes) merger			

Figure 5.10
Political economy of *within-country EU mergers*: Benevolent governments, insiders in A, market and outsider in B

extreme situation where both governments are benevolent; that is, they
care only about their country's welfare. No firm would find it convenient to pay contributions as it could not affect the position of the
government by means of this action.

POLITICALLY MOTIVATED NATIONAL GOVERNMENTS
The opposite case is the one where national governments only care
about political contributions. In this case the location of the market
does not matter as governments pose no weight on the effect of the
merger on the general electorate and, hence, on consumer surplus.
Moreover lobbying is always successful: firms can set their contributions slightly positive on the policy option they prefer (e.g., reject the
merger) and zero on the alternative (e.g., approve the merger). This will
always induce selfish governments to follow the wishes of special
interests.

For $e \leq e_{\pi o}$, the authority approves the merger. The insiders in A
benefit from the merger and (successfully) lobby government A for
endorsement. The outsider in B, however, loses from the merger for a
low realization of e and lobbies its government for rejection. For
$e_{\pi o} < e \leq e_W$, the authority approves the merger. Both the outsider and
the insiders gain from this decision. In this case there is no contrast
between the authority and the national governments. Finally, for
$e_W < e \leq e_{\pi I}$, the authority rejects the merger. However, the insiders and
the outsider would gain if the merger were to be approved and lobby
the government of A and of B respectively to endorse the inefficient
merger.

The case of politically motivated governments is discussed in
figure 5.11.

An interesting example may be the *Aérospatiale-Alenia/De Havilland*
merger, the first merger ever prohibited by the European Commission.
This was not a purely EU merger as it involved two EU firms
(Aérospatiale and Alenia) and a Canadian firm, and as such our
example is not fitting perfectly the formal framework analyzed here
(but could easily be adapted to reproduce such an environment without
major complications). In that case the competent authority was the
European Commission (the merger had an EU dimension and the
relevant market was the world market), but while the Commissioner
for Competition (our welfare-maximizing authority) was clearly
opposed to the merger, some EU governments were favorable to it
(in particular, the French government strongly endorsed the merger).

$$0 \qquad e_B^G = e_{CS} = e_{\pi O} \qquad\qquad e_U^A = e_W \qquad\qquad e_A^G = e_{\pi I} \qquad 1 \quad e$$

Efficient merger endorsed by union authority	Efficient merger endorsed by union authority	Inefficient merger opposed by union authority	No merger takes place
O lobbies	No lobbying	*I* and *O* lobby together	
Government *A* (*B*) endorses (opposes) merger	Governments *A* and *B* endorse merger	Governments *A* and *B* endorse merger	

Figure 5.11
Political economy of *within-country EU mergers:* Politically motivated governments, insiders in *A* and outsider in *B*

In the end the Commission as a collegial body decided against the merger, which in our framework could be seen as a low realization of the parameters ξ_j.

Cross-Border Mergers   Differently from the previous sections, assume that merging firms are now located in different countries (i.e., one in *A* and one in *B*). Moreover assume that the outsider and the market are located in country *A* (again, this corresponds to the more interesting recent merger cases). We study first the effect of the merger on national social welfare (i.e., for benevolent national governments) and postpone the discussion of politically motivated governments to the last subsection.

BENEVOLENT NATIONAL GOVERNMENTS
When national governments are social welfare maximizers, the location of the market matters. Under this scenario, welfare in country *B* corresponds to the profits of one of the insiders. For this reason government *B* will endorse any merger (i.e., if and only if $e \le e_B^G = e_{\pi I}$) as whatever merger is proposed must be profitable for the insiders. This clearly implies that based on national welfare considerations, government *B* will endorse at least some inefficient mergers (i.e., $e_B^G \ge e_W$).

The situation in country *A* is more complex as several interests are present: consumers, the outsider and one of the insiders. It can be showed, however, that the effect of the merger on consumer surplus and on the profits of the outsider are always of opposite sign and that the first dominates the second for any level of realized efficiency gain

0	$e_{CS} = e_{\pi O}$	e_A^G	$e_U^A = e_W$	$e_B^G = e_{\pi I}$	1	e

Efficient merger endorsed by union authority	Efficient merger endorsed by union authority	Inefficient merger opposed by union authority	No merger takes place
No lobbying	No lobbying	No lobbying	
Governments A and B endorse merger	Government A (B) opposes (endorses) merger	Government A (B) opposes (endorses) merger	

Figure 5.12
Political economy of *cross-border EU mergers:* Benevolent governments, insider in B, insider, market and outsider in A

e. This implies that for any merger such that $e \leq e_{\pi o} = e_{CS}$, the benevolent government in A would endorse the merger as the increase in consumer surplus dominates the fall in the profits of the outsider. However, government A opposes at least some efficient mergers (i.e., $e_A^G \leq e_W$) as the welfare objective of this government neglects the effects of the merger on the other insider.

Figure 5.12 summarizes this case.

Notice that we might well have a conflict between domestic governments and union authorities that is simply based on the fact that their welfare objectives differ (i.e., for "economic" and not for "political" reasons).[12] This simple framework also helps us explain why it is important that within the EU, whenever there is a merger that affects several countries, it is the supranational authority that should decide on the merger: member states may have different positions on the merger due to the possible asymmetric distribution on firms' assets and market demands. It makes sense that overall welfare is taken into account to avoid that a national government (or an authority) may block a merger that would be beneficial to the Union as a whole.

POLITICALLY MOTIVATED NATIONAL GOVERNMENTS
In the opposite scenario where governments only care about political contributions from organized interest groups, the effects of the merger on consumer surplus, and therefore the location of the market does not matter.

Government B will always be induced by the insider to endorse any proposed merger, namely any merger such that $e \leq e_B^G = e_{\pi I}$. The situation in country A is more complex as there are realizations of e for

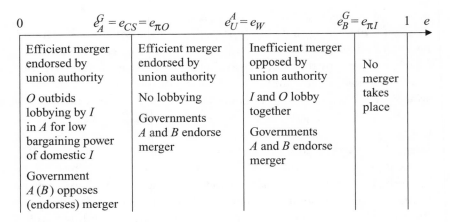

Figure 5.13
Political economy of *cross-border EU mergers:* Politically motivated governments, insider in B, insider and outsider in A

which the outsider and the insider have opposing interests. In particular, for low values of e (such that $e < e_{CS} = e_{\pi o}$) the union authority approves the merger and the outsider (domestic insider) has an incentive to lobby government A to oppose (favor) the merger. Whether the outsider can outbid the lobbying contribution of the domestic insider depends on the share of profits of the latter, which in turn reflect the bargaining power of the domestic relative to the foreign insider. For a low bargaining power, the outsider outbids the domestic insider and the politically motivated government of A opposes the (efficient) cross-border merger. This case is discussed in figure 5.13.

Our framework may shed some light on several recent merger cases. One highly debated case was *E-On/Endesa* where the German company E-On intended to take over the most important Spanish energy company Endesa. The Spanish government (as well as the Spanish energy regulator, partly responsible for the merger) strongly opposed the merger resulting in political tensions with the European Commission, which took action against measures introduced by the Spanish government to hinder the takeover. A similar case was *ABN-Amro/Antonveneta* where an Italian bank was the object of an attempted takeover by foreign EU banks. Under Italian law at the time, it was the central bank, as regulator of the banking sector, who had responsibility for the takeover. The then governor, Mr. Antonio Fazio, strongly opposed such takeovers and tried to organize counter-bids by other Italian banks.

5.3.4 An Extension: "Bureaucratic" Bias

While an interesting first step, this political economy analysis should be extended in a number of ways in the future. For instance, we assumed until now that antitrust authorities are always benevolent, not influenced by lobbies, and do not have concerns other than social welfare maximization. This neglects the fact that bureaucrats, not differently from politicians, face incentives and that their objectives are not necessarily aligned (or perfectly aligned) with those of society at large.[13] How would this affect our results so far?

Assume that the authority is run by a director who has career concerns and values the visibility that he can gain through interventionism, that is, by being tough on mergers. In other words, whenever the authority rejects a merger, the director obtains a visibility gain (or a prize for being tough). Clearly, the bureaucrat also cares about the stated goals of its organization that, under a welfare standard, coincide with social welfare. In this case career concerns of high-level bureaucrats might lead them to oppose socially efficient mergers, while inefficient mergers would always be rejected. That is, the political economy distortion of the authority might run exactly in the opposite direction of the bias of the politically motivated government, as shown in figure 5.14, where the intervention thresholds are to the left of the benevolent planner for the bureaucrat and to the right for the politician: $e_U^A \leq e_W \leq e_U^G$.[14]

As it is apparent from figure 5.14, contrasts between antitrust authorities and governments are the combination of bureaucratic and political biases. More generally, a better understanding of the incentives of antitrust authorities and the interaction of governments and

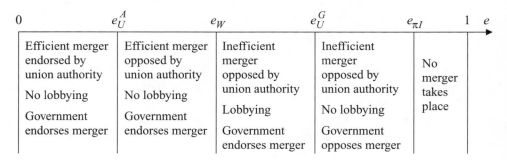

Figure 5.14
Political versus bureaucratic bias

(national and supranational) authorities are important avenues for future research in this area.

5.4 Conclusions

This chapter discussed strategic trade policy and political economy arguments to explain merger policy in open economy. These arguments are (obviously) not exhaustive of the determinants of merger decisions. Other factors might include the need for stability of the system (as in banking), or the security of supply (as in energy markets)—perhaps invoked opportunistically by national policy makers—or mere economic nationalism (i.e., a preference for national firms and/or a distrust of foreign firms). We do not address these factors in the present work.

Independently of the origin of distortions in merger control, it is clear that welfare losses are bound to take place whenever such distortions do occur: bad mergers may happen, or good ones may not (implying allocative, productive, and dynamic inefficiencies). An interesting question that we leave for future research is to what extent the current regulatory environment is fit to avoid distortions in merger decisions. For instance, do the existing tools of the European Commission suffice to discipline governments of member states? What is certain is that with a better "culture of competition" citizens would understand the costs of distorted merger policy aimed at preferring inefficient national champions.

Acknowledgments

We are grateful to Christian Gollier and Ludger Woessmann, the conference organizers, and Regis Renault, our discussant. We would like to thank Chiara Fumagalli, Isabel Grilo, Rainer Lanz, Joelle Latina, Stefano Vannini, and participants to the Working Group in Competition Policy at the EUI and to the "Alexis Jacquemin" seminar at the European Commission for comments.
Disclaimer: The opinions expressed in this paper should be attributed to the authors. They are not meant to represent the positions or opinions of the WTO and its Members and are without prejudice to Members' rights and obligations under the WTO.

Notes

1. For a recent survey, see Brander and Spencer (2010).

2. A similar rent-shifting mechanism occurs when subsidies are given for the R&D activities of domestic firms. Further, to the extent that the subsidies increase sales in the home market, they could also decrease allocative inefficiencies.

3. Note that if consumers existed in country H, the subsidy will have an even more positive effect because it would decrease the allocative inefficiency created by the oligopolistic distortion.

4. We focus throughout on horizontal mergers, that is, mergers between competitors. This is because most of the mergers at the center of disputes were indeed horizontal. Furthermore we do not consider the possibility that after the merger the industry might switch to a collusive equilibrium. None of these hypotheses is crucial for the arguments we are going to make, although the mechanisms to be discussed would be very different.

5. See Motta (2004: ch. 5) for details. An exception to this general result is when actions are strategic substitutes and the merging firms have a very small share of the market and face large outsiders. In that case the increase in output by the (large) outsiders may outweigh the decrease in output by the (small) insiders. But mergers between small firms are unlikely to raise the attention of policy makers and are therefore not considered here.

6. See Salant et al. (1983).

7. In other words, the domestic government could favor the merger among domestic firms only if the actions are strategic complements and the market for the product is mostly located elsewhere. As we will see later in the chapter, there may therefore be a conflict with the government where the market is mostly located.

8. For a formal model, refer to our related paper (Motta and Ruta 2010).

9. In the real world, authorities also have the possibility to approve mergers subject to certain conditions (called "remedies"). In our simple model there are no meaningful remedies authorities may resort to.

10. Consumers have weak incentives to lobby the government to influence merger policy because a specific good generally takes a small part of their budget. Moreover consumers often fail to organize politically because free-riding problems are more difficult to overcome compared to business owners (as in Olson 1965).

11. The case of a consumer standard is a straightforward extension of this model.

12. However, if such governments/authorities had consumer surplus as objective function, then such tensions would be eliminated in the simple economic model of this section, although they could reappear in the political economy framework.

13. See Alesina and Tabellini (2007).

14. For simplicity, the figure only refers to domestic mergers. A similar argument should apply to the other cases.

References

Alesina, A., and G. Tabellini. 2007. Bureaucrats or politicians? Part I: A single policy task. *American Economic Review* 97 (1): 169–79.

Bernheim, D. B., and M. D. Whinston. 1986. Menu auctions, resource allocation, and economic influence. *Quarterly Journal of Economics* 101 (1): 1–31.

Brander, J. A., and B. J. Spencer. 1983. International R&D rivalry and industrial strategy. *Review of Economic Studies* 50 (4): 702–22.

Brander, J. A., and B. J. Spencer. 1985. Export subsidies and international market share rivalry. *Journal of International Economics* 18 (1–2): 83–100.

Eaton, J., and G. Grossman. 1986. Optimal trade and industrial policy under oligopoly. *Quarterly Journal of Economics* 101 (2): 383–406.

Grossman, G., and H. Helpman. 1994. Protection for sale. *American Economic Review* 84 (4): 833–50.

Motta, M. 2004. *Competition Policy: Theory and Practice*. Cambridge: Cambridge University Press.

Motta, M., and M. Ruta. 2010. A political economy model of merger policy in international markets. Forthcoming. Economica.

Olson, M. 1965. *The Logic of Collective Action*. Cambridge: Harvard University Press.

Salant, S., S. Switzer, and R. Reynolds. 1983. Losses from horizontal mergers: The effects of an exogenous change in industry structure on Cournot-Nash equilibrium. *Quarterly Journal of Economics* 98 (2): 185–99.

6 The Hidden Costs of Political Sponsorship of Industrial Firms

Paul Seabright

6.1 Introduction

When in the spring of 2005 the Airbus A380 made its maiden flight, there was an upsurge of enthusiasm in Europe about the Airbus project as a testimony to the virtues of publicly supported, internationally collaborative industrial policy. This enthusiasm was not confined to France, but it found particularly heady expression there: President Chirac described the flight as "a magnificent result for European industrial cooperation and an encouragement to pursue this path of building a Europe of innovation and progress."[1] At the A380's unveiling three months earlier, in an even more lyrical flight of prose, he had hailed "the success of a European industrial policy, which has helped make Airbus the world's leading aircraft manufacturer." He continued: "Let us pursue the success of Airbus in other fields. Let us achieve the same outcome for the energy of the future, for tomorrow's transport and telecommunications, for the medicines of the future. Let us do it together, with a truly European ambition. . . . It is to rise to this challenge that France recently decided to establish an agency for innovation in industry. To my mind, this is the first step in what should be a major European undertaking, underpinned by the strength of our companies and our laboratories, to put European industry at the cutting edge of innovation and at the heart of tomorrow's markets."[2]

The sequel is now too well known to need spelling out in painful detail. Little more than a year later, a combination of the falling dollar, in which Airbus sales are denominated, and delays in delivery of the first aircraft, triggering large financial penalty clauses, caused significant losses to Airbus and its parent company EADS, leading to a 26 percent fall in the share price and eventually to the resignation in July 2006 of Airbus CEO Gustav Humbert (as well as to that of his boss,

EADS joint CEO Noel Forgeard, in the wake of revelations about his making large profits from the sale of EADS shares). Since then, the bicephalous management structure of Airbus has been reviewed and extensively reformed (though the importance of French or German nationality, and a rough balance between them in determining eligibility for top jobs in the company, does not seem notably to have diminished). A restructuring program called Power 8 is involving a reduction of some 10,000 jobs, though there is still strong resistance, both within the company and among its various political sponsors, to rationalizing the production map in a way that makes no reference to political geography. And the continuing gyrations in the value of the dollar raise important questions about the viability of the Airbus model of geographically concentrated production with and internationally diversified sales.

There are two questions that might strike even a moderately curious observer about these events. First, why should Airbus have faced a crisis of such magnitude at a time when demand for its products had never been higher (the problems significantly predated the onset of the recent economic crisis)? Restructuring programs, resignations of CEOs, and so forth, are typically symptoms of industries in either structural or temporary decline. Second, even if the fall of the US dollar against the euro were hard for the Airbus management to foresee and offset, the inability of Airbus to meet some highly foreseeable delivery deadlines for aircraft, as well as the banality of the reasons given for this failure (cabling problems at the Hamburg assembly plant), seem superficially to suggest an alarming degree of incompetence in a firm that, after all, makes extraordinarily safety-critical products. How confident can a detached observer feel that a firm that is unable to solve a problem of timing in its cabling can make aircraft that will not one day fall out of the sky through some malfunctioning in their highly sophisticated software, electronics, or composite materials?

This short chapter will suggest a broadly reassuring answer to the second question, which also in passing answers the first. The gist of the answer is that the problems at Airbus have little or nothing to do with incompetence and everything to do with conscious, strategic decision-making under uncertainty. Managers of assembly plants facing deadlines subject to stochastic shocks will choose their rhythm of work to balance the costs of working faster or better against the benefits of avoiding overruns. Factors that affect the risk or the cost of overruns will affect managers' choices in equilibrium, and therefore also the likelihood that overruns will occur. Two factors in particular matter here. The first is the nature of the division of the rents between different divisions of a firm. Firms with international political sponsorship, I will suggest, divide the rents differently, with more ex post bargaining, than do normal private firms (there is, of course, some bargaining between divisions even in private firms, but there is less, so I will simplify by assuming it away). This ex post bargaining will—obviously—have efficiency costs. But the extent and nature of these costs is sensitive to a second factor, which is the extent to which effort choices translate reliably into overruns. It will turn out that the more safety-critical the product, the more rather than less likely it is that overruns will occur—but this in no way implies that the firm that incurs the overruns is in any way in danger of creating unsafe products. The key point will be that firms with international political sponsorship choose consciously to incur the risk of overruns to a greater extent than private firms, and they are relatively more, not less likely to do so in safety-critical industries.

The logic of this result is simple. Overruns impose a cost, whether through contractual financial penalties or through other losses such as reputation. Managers of a firm, or a division within a firm, will be willing to exert some effort in order to avoid this cost. Typically an industrial process takes its course and a product emerges that has to pass certain tests before it can be delivered. If it fails the tests, it will be delivered late (or not at all, in which case the order will be fulfilled by a replacement product that may take further time to manufacture). The more stringent are the tests, for example, as in safety-critical industries where the standard of tests is enforced by external regulation or by the fear of truly catastrophic reputational loss, the more a prudent manager will wish to build in a safety margin, at a cost in effort, expecting to deliver the product early in order to give it time to be fixed before the deadline if it happens to fail the initial test. If the benefits of this prudence accrue to the manager concerned, she will have an incentive to make this trade-off optimally. To the extent that instead she fears her prudence will result in a clawing-back of the rents by other divisions (on such grounds as "if you can manage to produce so far before the deadline, you can't really need more human resources in your division"), she will exert less than optimal effort so that, on average, the products will fail the tests an inefficiently large proportion of the time. So firms with international political sponsorship, characterized by ex post bargaining that threatens the ability of a division manager to appropriate the rents from her prudence, will have more overruns than private firms, and they will do so relatively more often if they face stringent product tests. If the missed delivery deadlines at Airbus were really the product of simple incompetence, one might really have something to fear about the safety of the aircraft. Instead, it is precisely because safety is assured by draconian tests that are enforceable by outside authorities that the dysfunctional internal governance of Airbus shows up in missed deadlines.

So far, of course, I have simply asserted that a firm with international political sponsorship will be more prone to ex post internal bargaining over the share of the rents accruing to different divisions than a normal private firm, but I have said nothing about why this should be. In the second part of the chapter, therefore, I examine this question more directly, drawing on joint work with Mathias Dewatripont.

6.2   The Model

6.2.1   The Technology
A firm consists of two teams, $i = 1, 2$. Each team undertakes a task that contributes to the overall success of the project: both tasks must succeed for the project to succeed as a whole. To succeed, the task must pass an inspection; its probability of passing depends on both the rigor of the inspection and the effort the team has exerted. One natural way to interpret effort is as the speed of production: if the task is complete well before the deadline, there is more time for flaws to be corrected before the "final" inspection.

Each team exerts effort $e_i \in [0, 1]$ subject to an increasing convex cost function $\theta_i c(e_i)$, where $\theta_i \in [\theta_{min}, \theta_{max}]$. The probability that once effort has been exerted, the team's task fails the inspection is given by $p_i = (1 - e_i)\phi$, where $0 < \phi < 1$ and ϕ is the rigor of the inspection. The probability that the project succeeds overall is therefore given by $(1 - \phi + \phi e_1)(1 - \phi + \phi e_2)$. A successful project yields a gross benefit π; an unsuccessful project a gross cost R (the costs of effort are not included in either of these).

If all parameters, including the teams' values of θ_i, are known, then the expected value of a project is given by

$$V = \pi(1 - \phi + \phi e_1)(1 - \phi + \phi e_2) - R(1 - e_1)(1 - e_2) - \theta_1 c(e_1) - \theta_2(e_2). \tag{6.1}$$

We can now solve for the effort choices of teams in two types of context. The first is a profit-maximizing firm that can implement an efficient outcome through an incentive mechanism giving each team a full share of its marginal contribution to the project's value (this will be feasible in the absence of asymmetric information on the values of θ_i).

6.2.2 Profit Maximization

A profit-maximizing firm will choose the effort levels of the teams to satisfy

$$\frac{\partial V}{\partial e_i} = \pi\phi\left(1-\phi+\phi e_j\right)+R\left(1-e_j\right)\phi^2 - \theta_i c'\left(e_i\right)=0, \tag{6.2}$$

which yields

$$c'\left(e_i\right)=\frac{\pi\phi+\phi^2\left(R-\pi\right)\left(1-e_j\right)}{\theta_i}. \tag{6.3}$$

From this a simple result follows immediately:

Lemma 1 The effort levels of the two teams are (strict) strategic substitutes if and only if $R>\pi$.

Proof The derivative of $c'\left(e_i\right)$ (and therefore of e_i, by the convexity of $c(.)$) with respect to e_j is $-\left[\phi^2\left(R-\pi\right)\right]/\theta_i$. This is negative if the term inside the square brackets is positive, which implies that the two are strategic substitutes if and only if $R>\pi$. ∎

To obtain an explicit analytic solution for e_i, we assume a simple quadratic form for $c(.)$, and specifically that $c(e_i)=be_i^2$. To ensure an interior solution, it is assumed that $R, \pi < b\theta_{\min}$. This yields immediately that

$$e_i = \frac{\pi\phi+\phi^2\left(R-\pi\right)\left(1-e_j\right)}{b\theta_i}. \tag{6.4}$$

Solving for the equilibrium yields

$$e_i = \frac{A_i - B_i A_j}{1 - B_i B_j}, \tag{6.5}$$

where $A_i = \left[\pi\phi+\phi^2\left(R-\pi\right)\right]/b\theta_i$ and $B_i = \left[\phi^2\left(R-\pi\right)\right]/b\theta_i$. The assumption that $R, \pi < b\theta_{\min}$ implies that $|B_i| < 1$, which ensures that the equilibrium is stable in the space of the reaction functions. It also implies that $B_i < A_i < 1+B_i$.

We now compare this outcome with the outcome that would emerge from a more explicitly political governance structure.

6.2.3   A "Political" Firm

What do we mean by a "political" governance structure? The key assumption here will be that the managers of the firm (as distinct from the managers of its teams) cannot commit ex ante to a division of rents. It is only after effort choices have been made and outcomes realized that bargaining will be completed (even if some initial bargaining takes place beforehand).

The details of such bargaining are not important for the argument here. For the purpose of this argument all that matters is that individual teams incur all the costs of effort but receive only some proportion of the benefits. A natural interpretation is that costs are incurred prior to the receipt of benefits, and there is bargaining over the distribution of benefits only after sunk costs have been incurred. In the Airbus context a natural example might be that if a plant in one country demonstrated a capacity to complete manufacture comfortably in advance of deadlines, instead of being given more resources (as might occur in a profit-maximizing firm), it would receive fewer resources on the ground that it apparently did not need the resources as much as the plant that had difficulty meeting the deadline.

Formally, let the negotiations over the rents be such that each team receives a share γ ($0 \leq \gamma \leq 1$) of its marginal contribution to the value of the project. Given that there are two teams, γ could be one-half, but we can examine the result for more general values. Unsurprisingly, we can show the following:

Lemma 2 e_i is strictly decreasing in γ.

Proof   If each team receives a proportion γ of its marginal contribution, each will set

$$c'(e_i) = \frac{\gamma\left[\pi\phi + \phi^2(R-\pi)(1-e_j)\right]}{\theta_i} = \gamma(A_i - B_i e_j), \tag{6.6}$$

which means that

$$e_i = \frac{\gamma A_i - \gamma^2 B_i A_j}{1 - \gamma^2 B_i B_j}.$$

Differentiating e_i with respect to γ and re-arranging yields

$$\frac{\partial e_i}{\partial \gamma} = A_i - \gamma B_i A_j - (A_j - \gamma B_j A_i)\gamma B_i. \tag{6.7}$$

Then multiplying through by $\gamma/(1-\gamma^2 B_i B_j)$ yields

$$\frac{\partial e_i}{\partial \gamma} > 0 \quad \text{iff} \quad e_i > \gamma B_i e_j \, ,$$

which follows immediately from equation (6.6).   ∎

The result is straightforward and intuitive, though not entirely trivial since it holds even for asymmetric values of θ_i and therefore of e_i. More important, though, are the cross-derivatives, and signing these is not straightforward in the asymmetric case. Intuitively the reason is that a parameter change has two effects on a team's choice of effort: a direct effect via the returns to its effort ignoring the behavior of the other team, and an indirect effect via changes in the behavior of the other team. When effort decisions are strategic substitutes (when $B_i < 0$), the direct and indirect impacts of a parameter change work in opposite directions. Normally (and always when costs are symmetric), the indirect effect will be smaller in absolute magnitude than the direct effect, so that knowing the sign of the direct effect is sufficient for knowing the sign of the overall effect. However, when one team's effort level is much higher than the other's, the direct effect of a parameter change on the low-effort team's choice may be offset by a larger indirect effect. Finding general necessary and sufficient conditions on the parameters to sign the general effect turns out to be very difficult in this example.

For this reason we now look at the special case of symmetric costs. The main result of this section shows that the extent to which political firms invest lower effort than profit-maximizing firms is increasing in the rigor of the inspection, as well as in the size of the rents at stake, R and π.

Proposition 1 If $\theta_1 = \theta_2$,

$$\frac{\partial^2 e_i}{\partial \gamma \partial \phi} > 0, \quad \frac{\partial^2 e_i}{\partial \gamma \partial \pi} > 0, \quad \frac{\partial^2 e_i}{\partial \gamma \partial R} > 0.$$

Proof Differentiating equation 6.6 with respect to γ yields

$$e_i = \gamma(A_i - B_i e_j)$$

$$\frac{\partial e_i}{\partial \gamma} = A_i - B_i \frac{\partial e_j}{\partial \gamma}$$

If $\theta_1 = \theta_2$, $e_1 = e_2$ and we can substitute $\dfrac{\partial e_j}{\partial \gamma} = \dfrac{\partial e_i}{\partial \gamma}$ to yield

$$\frac{\partial e_i}{\partial \gamma} = \frac{A_i}{1 + B_i}$$

Differentiating with respect to ϕ yields

$$\frac{\partial^2 e_i}{\partial \gamma \partial \phi} = \frac{(1 + B_i)\frac{\partial A_i}{\partial \phi} - A_i \frac{\partial B_i}{\partial \phi}}{(1 + B_i)^2},$$

$$(1 + B_i)\frac{\partial A_i}{\partial \phi} - A_i \frac{\partial B_i}{\partial \phi} > 0, \qquad \text{since } (1 + B_i) > A_i \text{ and } \frac{\partial A_i}{\partial \phi} > \frac{\partial B_i}{\partial \phi}.$$

We can similarly derive

$$\frac{\partial^2 e_i}{\partial \gamma \partial \phi} = \frac{(1 + B_i)\frac{\partial A_i}{\partial R} - A_i \frac{\partial B_i}{\partial R}}{(1 + B_i)^2},$$

$$(1 + B_i)\frac{\partial A_i}{\partial R} - A_i \frac{\partial B_i}{\partial R} > 0, \qquad \text{since } (1 + B_i) > A_i \text{ and } \frac{\partial A_i}{\partial R} = \frac{\partial B_i}{\partial R},$$

and

$$\frac{\partial^2 e_i}{\partial \gamma \partial \pi} = \frac{(1 + B_i)\frac{\partial A_i}{\partial \pi} - A_i \frac{\partial B_i}{\partial \pi}}{(1 + B_i)^2},$$

$$(1 + B_i)\frac{\partial A_i}{\partial \pi} - A_i \frac{\partial B_i}{\partial \pi} > 0, \qquad \text{since } \frac{\partial B_i}{\partial \pi} < 0. \qquad \blacksquare$$

This result has a straightforward interpretation. Teams in political firms choose lower effort levels—this much is well known. More interestingly the extent to which political governance structures affect effort levels is increasing in the rigor of inspections and in the magnitude of the rents available (both the profits from the success and the penalties for failure). So it is entirely unsurprising that Airbus should be facing overruns at a time when its order book is full, and that this should be happening in a safety-critical industry. This may be a source of frustration for taxpayers and buyers of aircraft. But it should not be a matter of alarm to the safety-conscious traveling public.

6.3   Political Sponsorship and Commitment

6.3.1   Why Do Political Firms Face Commitment Problems?

It may be true that firms with significant political sponsorship face commitment problems, but why is it true? What is it about political sponsorship that makes it hard for firms to commit to efficient distributions of the rents?

There are (at least) two reasons that may be of relevance here. The first is simply that political authorities are sovereign powers, and (unless under constitutional restraints, which apply only to a limited range of contexts and rarely if ever to decisions about the management of industrial enterprises) therefore unable to bind themselves not to revisit previous promises and previous agreements. This much is well known, and there is little more to be added here. In this context the explanation for the fact that political bargaining gives teams only a fraction of their marginal contribution to output is that, once the sunk costs have been committed by the team, only bargaining between the parties matters.

However, there is a second argument that may be of relevance here. This addresses the fact, which may seem puzzling, that ex post bargaining over rents often has consequences for future production decisions. When resources are transferred between divisions of a firm, this is rarely done in simple cash terms: more typically physical capital equipment or human resources are transferred, and these remain in place, affecting production outcomes in the future. For instance, in the example cited above of a division of Airbus being unwilling to complete production a long way before the deadline because that would be cited as showing that it did not "need" human resources as much as some other division, the resulting allocations of human resources would have adverse consequences for future production efficiency: a less efficient division would be given more resources and a more efficient division would be given less than efficient allocations would require. Can we understand why political decision-making might be prone to lead to this kind of result? Why should politicians make allocation decisions they know to be inefficient?

Much of the literature on political decision-making would answer such a question in terms of failures of accountability of politicians to taxpayers and voters. The ability of taxpayer/voters to monitor what politicians do with their money is limited, so the argument goes, and for this reason politicians often spend money in ways that favors privileged lobbies. Though often true, this explanation has difficulty accounting for the striking fact that, rather than cover up such spending so as to limit accountability, politicians frequently trumpet their decisions to spend taxpayers' money on projects of dubious economic value, and actively seek out maximum publicity for such actions. In joint work with Dewatripont (Dewatripont and Seabright 2006, 2009)

I have been trying to explore reasons why it might be in politicians' interests to do this, and how the explanation can be compatible with rational behavior on the part of voters. The idea is that politicians sometimes engage in wasteful spending not out of negligence but rather out of a desire to improve their chances of reelection by signaling their commitment to supplying public goods. Funding projects, even wasteful ones, is a conspicuous way to signal this. We develop a model that shows (1) how this may be rational on the part of politicians, and (2) how the increased probability of reelection that follows from the wasteful spending decisions nevertheless reflects rational behavior on the part of voters too. Voters reward conspicuous spending because it is evidence of effort on the part of politicians—even though it is associated, on average, with some degree of waste.

We now set out the model that explains this argument, drawing on Dewatripont and Seabright (2006).

6.3.2   A Model of Wasteful Political Spending

There is a project that has a cost c and generates a value $v \in \{\underline{v}, \overline{v}\}$ that is observed by the politician and may or may not be observed by the voters. Voters are risk neutral and care about $v - c$. Therefore in the first-best outcome the project should go ahead iff $v \geq c$, and to make the problem interesting, we assume that $\overline{v} > c > \underline{v}$.

The decision as to the future of the project is made by a politician whose interests are not the same as those of the voters. We represent the politician's choice by $a \in \{0, 1\}$, with $a = 1$ meaning that the project is funded. Politicians care less about the benefits generated by the projects than voters do. Specifically, the politician cares about αv, with $\alpha \in \{\underline{\alpha}, \overline{\alpha}\}$ with probability p that $\alpha = \overline{\alpha}$ and probability $(1-p)$ that $\alpha = \underline{\alpha}$, and $0 < \underline{\alpha} < \overline{\alpha} < 1$. Only the politician knows α. In principle the $\overline{\alpha}$-type is the "better" politician from the voters' point of view, though as we show below this involves a subtle trade-off between moral hazard and adverse selection considerations. We call α the politician's degree of "concern" for the interests of voters, and politicians with higher α are the more concerned types.

The moral hazard arises because the politician has to invest (at a cost) to find a good project. Let the probability that the politician finds a project with $v = \overline{v}$ be $i \in (0, 1)$, where i is her investment level and costs her $\psi(i)$, which is increasing and convex in i.

We also assume that all politicians care about reelection, which yields them a rent B.

The timing of the model is as follows:

Stage 0: Nature chooses α.

Stage 1: The politician chooses i, then learns v.

Stage 2: The politician decides whether to fund the project or not, choosing a.

Stage 3: The voters decide whether to reelect the politician or not.

Since the project generates returns too late to be verified in advance of the election, the reelection decision is taken simply according to whether or not the project is funded. We assume for now that if the project is funded, the politician is reelected with a probability r, while if it is not funded, she is not reelected; we show below that this is rational for voters.

The politician's problem is as follows:

$$\max_{i}\{i(\alpha\bar{v}+Br-c)+(1-i)\max[\alpha\underline{v}+Br-c,0]-\psi(i)\}. \tag{6.8}$$

We make the following explicit assumption in order to investigate the possibility that politicians may "overbid" for projects:

$$\bar{\alpha}\bar{v}+Br > \min\left[\underline{\alpha}\bar{v}+Br, \bar{\alpha}\underline{v}+Br\right] \geq c > \underline{\alpha}\underline{v}+Br. \tag{6.9}$$

This implies that a relatively "unconcerned" politician—one of type $\underline{\alpha}$ —takes actions that are ex post efficient, while a "concerned" politician—one of type $\bar{\alpha}$—overfunds due to reelection concerns, in the sense that she funds the low-value project and not just the high-value project. Nevertheless, voters may still rationally prefer to reelect the type $\bar{\alpha}$ politician even in the knowledge that she will overfund. The reason is that she will exert more effort than the unconcerned politician, and the value of this effort may outweigh the efficiency cost of overfunding.

Given assumption (6.9), we can rewrite (6.8) for the concerned politician as

$$\max_{i}\{i(\bar{\alpha}\bar{v}+Br-c)+(1-i)(\bar{\alpha}\underline{v}+Br-c)-\psi(i)\}, \tag{6.10}$$

which yields the first-order condition for effort $\bar{\alpha}(\bar{v}-\underline{v})=\psi'(i)$.

For the unconcerned politician we can rewrite (6.8) as

$$\max_{i}\{i(\underline{\alpha}\bar{v}+Br-c)-\psi(i)\}, \tag{6.11}$$

which yields the first-order condition for effort $\underline{\alpha}\bar{v}+Br-c=\psi'(i)$.

Writing $\bar{i}$ and $\underline{i}$ for the utility-maximizing choices of effort for the concerned and unconcerned politician respectively, it is straightforward to show that $\bar{i} > \underline{i}$. To see this, note that $\bar{\alpha}(\bar{v} - \underline{v}) > \underline{\alpha}(\bar{v} - \underline{v}) = (\underline{\alpha}\bar{v} + Br - c) - (\underline{\alpha}\underline{v} + Br - c) > (\underline{\alpha}\bar{v} + Br - c)$, where the last inequality follows from assumption (6.9).

Since voters do not internalize the effort cost of the politician, they strictly prefer more effort to less. This will outweigh the less efficient funding choices of the concerned politician, and therefore lead them to reward a politician who reveals herself with greater probability to be the concerned type, iff

$$\left(\bar{i}\bar{v} + \left(1 - \bar{i}\right)\underline{v} - c\right) > \left(\underline{i}\left(\bar{v} - c\right)\right), \tag{6.12}$$

where the left-hand side represents the voter's gain with the high-α type, and the right-hand side represents her gain with the low-α type. This condition will hold iff the expected gain from the higher probability of a good project outweighs the expected loss from overfunding by an overzealous politician, namely iff:

$$\left(\bar{i} - \underline{i}\right)(\bar{v} - c) - \left(1 - \bar{i}\right)(c - \underline{v}) > 0. \tag{6.13}$$

The expression on the left-hand side is increasing in $\bar{i}$ and $(\bar{v} - c)$ and decreasing in $\underline{i}$ and $(c - \underline{v})$. Given the first order conditions for $\bar{i}$ and $\underline{i}$, this allows us to state the following result (from Dewatripont and Seabright 2006):

Proposition 2 Assume condition (6.9). Then, faced with a choice between reelecting a politician with probability r and refusing with probability 1 to reelect, voters will reelect politicians who fund projects and refuse to reelect politicians who do not (even though they know that concerned politicians will fund bad projects as well as good ones), provided that (1) the degree of concern of concerned politicians is sufficiently high relative to that of unconcerned politicians and (2) that the net value of good projects is sufficiently high relative to the net cost of bad projects.

In Dewatripont and Seabright (2009) we examine the characteristics of various forms of ex post auditing mechanism, explore the impact of ex post monitoring on the incentives for politicians to exert ex ante effort, and extend the model to take into account multiple interest groups, in which context we show that politicians may have an interest not only in implementing some inefficient projects in order to show that they have been "busy," but in failing to implement some efficient but "divisive" projects that create large aggregate benefits but at the cost of some interest group, in order to signal that they care about the costs inflicted on the group concerned.

The relevance of these arguments to the model of this chapter is that they could explain why political firms not only distribute ex post profits in ways that may damage ex ante incentives, but more precisely may do so in ways that increase the likelihood of inefficient decisions being made in the future, by directing resources toward inefficient divisions and inefficient activities. The reason why they do so is that the politicians who sponsor them are reluctant to prevent the allocation of resources to inefficient divisions because, in so doing, they will "reveal" themselves to voters to be the type of politician who cares relatively little about the benefits that such allocations create for their recipients.

There is much anecdotal evidence that politicians really do think in this way (we summarize much of this in the two papers referred to above). Jean-Claude Juncker, then Prime Minister of Luxembourg, once said to reporters after a European Council had failed to agree on measures for reducing public sector deficits that the reason for the impasse was that "we all know what has to be done. But none of us knows how to get reelected after doing it."

It may well be that this phenomenon—the unwillingness of politicians to halt projects that they privately know to be of poor quality—is quantitatively more important in accounting for poor uses of public money than any alleged inability of politicians to find good projects to spend taxpayers' money on. In Seabright (2005) I suggest that "it would be hard to show convincingly that executives of private firms are any better than public officials in their selections of projects to support (they may be, but there is no rigorous evidence that I know of, and anecdotal evidence can be used to show anything in this domain)." The problem, in other words, may be less the temptation to pick winners than the unwillingness to pull out the rug from under losers. The fact that Airbus overall has been something of a winner should not disguise the fact that, in its internal allocations of resources, it may have favored losers more often than would have been efficient. It could afford to do so both because of its weighty political sponsors and because, after all, it has been operating in a comfortably duopolistic market.

6.4   Conclusions

This chapter developed a model in which firms knowingly incur risks of delivery delays on important projects, and political firms (defined as firms that do not maximize profit but determine the division of rents between their divisions by ex post bargaining after important productive investments have been undertaken) do so to a greater extent than profit-maximizing firms. More interestingly the extent to which political firms "underperform" relative to profit-maximizing firms is increasing in the rigor of the inspections faced by their products and is therefore higher in safety-critical industries. The reason is that in safety-critical industries, profit-maximizing firms rationally exert effort to produce well in advance of deadlines, to ensure that problems can be fixed in time with high probability. However, political firms have less incentive to do this since they keep a smaller proportion of the rents from this prudent behavior.

The chapter also asked why political firms should behave like this, particularly given the fact that such behavior not only rewards past inefficiency but typically directs resources toward less efficient divisions and thereby affects future production efficiency. It has suggested that this may be rational behavior on the part of politicians who thereby signal to voters their degree of zeal at finding spending projects, and voters may rationally reward them for this even if, in equilibrium, politicians who act in this way are known to waste taxpayers' money to some degree.

The models are extremely simple and stylized, but if the phenomena to which they draw attention have any basis in reality, these will be important topics for future research.

Notes

1. See http://news.bbc.co.uk/2/hi/business/4488361.stm, http://www.nytimes.com/2005/04/27/business/27cnd-airbus.html?_r=1&oref=slogin.

2. See http://www.ambafrance-uk.org/Speech-by-M-Jacques-Chirac,4069.html.

References

Dewatripont, M., and P. Seabright. 2006. 'Wasteful' Public Spending and State Aid Control. *Journal of the European Economic Association* 4 (2–3):513–522.

Dewatripont, M., and P. Seabright. 2009. *"Rational Crowd-Pleasing and Electoral Accountability." mimeo.* Toulouse School of Economics.

Seabright, P. 2005. National and European Champions: Burden or Blessing? *CESifo Forum* 2/2005:52–55.

IV Analyses in Static Settings

7 National Champions under Credit Rationing

Christian Gollier and Bruno Jullien

7.1 Introduction

Oligopoly pricing yields a deadweight loss for society. The policy implication is to maintain competitive market conditions, providing the rationale for strong European laws which have been implemented to prohibit national governments from protecting national firms. However, over the last few years, there has been a strong tendency for governments to adapt their industrial policy to encourage the emergence of national champions. These firms have strong monopoly power in their home market, despite the absence of any obvious natural monopoly argument.

Air France provides a clear example of a national champion. The firm's market share recently reached 96 percent in the French domestic market after a number of its rivals were eliminated. This is in contrast to the stiff competition that Air France faces abroad. Another French illustration is the case of Suez, Enel, and Gaz de France. The proposed takeover of Suez by Enel was promptly opposed by the French government whose counterproposal was a merger of Suez and Gaz de France to create a national champion in the energy sector. The result was to reduce competition in the French energy market. More generally, it has been observed that many European governments delay the opening of their home markets to foreign competition until the last possible moment.

When a domestic firm charges monopoly prices at home, there are two effects. There is a monopoly profit for the firm. However, this is a transfer from consumers to shareholders that has no effect on welfare. There is also a deadweight loss owing to a wedge between the marginal production cost and the willingness to pay of the marginal consumer. This loss makes it socially desirable to promote more competition in the market. The problem is radically transformed when the situation is a domestic firm extracting a monopoly rent on foreign markets. This is because the welfare of foreign citizens is not taken into account by the domestic government. In such a situation it is in the best interest of domestic residents to promote competition at home, and monopoly for their national champion abroad.

Brander and Spencer (1985) have examined the strategic trade argument in favor of national champions. Promoting national champions could turn out to yield a negative-sum game and national welfare might rise at the expense of a greater loss for someone else. Domestic competition policy therefore tends to be too permissive toward mergers because it does not take into account the negative impact of less competition outside the country. The cases of Microsoft and Boeing are often invoked to illustrate this "transfer effect." The emergence of Airbus as a competitor for Boeing has been beneficial for European residents through the transfer of some duopoly rents to European soil. Yet this calculation does not take into account any economic loss for Boeing or lost economies of scale within the new industry structure. Neither does it count the benefit for consumers around the world who paid lower prices, as explained by Neven and Seabright (1995).

The puzzle we solve in this chapter is quite different. It concerns the observed willingness of some national governments to limit competition in their home markets. There are various possible explanations for this phenomenon. A standard, but flawed, explanation is based on domestic employment benefits. The flaw is that the monopoly power of national firms reduces output, and therefore demand for the factors of production, in particular labor. Another standard explanation is that the monopoly rent can, in part, be redistributed to public decision makers in charge of shaping the industrial policy. The explanation we present in this chapter is a different one. It is based on the observation that Air France has been able to expand abroad—and to extract extra profits from this expansion—through a mostly internal financing of these foreign investments and the merger with KLM. This self-financing of the airline's expansion has been possible, at least in part, because of the existence of a large profit margin on domestic flights. However, there is a missing element to this explanation. If this foreign expansion is profitable, it must be explained why external financing is not possible.

Our model is based on the well-established fact that firms face important constraints on their access to credit, which limits the ability to implement all of their profitable projects. Following Tirole (2006), we assume that this credit rationing is the consequence of an asymmetric information problem on the credit market. Namely we assume that lenders cannot observe whether managers allocate their loan to efficient activities. In particular, lenders do not observe whether managers invest effort to increase the probability of the project being successful. The capacity of the market for external financing is limited because it is optimal for managers not to exert effort if the size of the loan exceeds some threshold. This may explain why national governments choose to limit competition on their home market; they intend to increase the financial firepower of their national firms.

7.2 The Base Model

We consider a small country in a large export market. The country has a protected local market for some good that is produced by n firms, $i = 1,...,n$. The national demand for the good is $D(p)$ and the inverse demand is $P(Q)$. The firms have the same constant marginal cost c. We suppose that they compete à la Cournot. We denote by Π_n the Cournot profit of each firm, the price is p_n and the consumer surplus is $S(p_n)$. We are interested in determining the consequences of a change in the number of firms. In particular, we are interested in the special case with $n = 1$, which corresponds to the situation where the n firms merge to form a national monopoly, or a "national champion."

7.2.1 Entering the Foreign Market

Let us suppose that the firms have the possibility to use their resources to export to the foreign market. In order to export, firms first need to build an export capacity before investing in a commercial relationship with foreign distributors and in promotion activity as described below. Building export capacity Q_i for firm i costs γQ_i. Each firm has a maximum capacity $\overline{Q}$ large enough that the firm will not be at capacity.

If the firm that has an export capacity Q_i succeeds in distributing its product on the foreign market, it earns a profit μQ_i on this market that depends on an exogenous margin $\mu = \hat{p} - \hat{c}$, where $\hat{p}$ is the foreign price and $\hat{c}$ is the export cost.

Capacity must be built before the export market revenues are obtained. Thus capacity must be met either through self-financing or through external financing. External financing is by way of a competitive financial market. The interest rate is normalized to zero. To simplify matters, we assume that the foreign activity develops after cash flow is generated on the local market.[1]

Once the export capacity has been built, the firm has to find a foreign distributor to penetrate the foreign market. This requires that the firm devote proper resources to this activity. We ignore the verifiable financial costs of this activity by assuming that they are embedded in the cost of capacity γ. But the way the firm uses these resources also matters. If the resources are used adequately, the firm succeeds in penetrating the foreign market with probability x. We say that such a firm behaves. The firm may also misbehave by using resources in a less efficient way: that firm has then a smaller probability $x_0 < x$ to distribute its product successfully, but it enjoys some private benefits BQ. Private benefits are nonmonetary. We denote private benefits by $b = xB/(x - x_0)$.

We assume that $x\mu - \gamma > 0 > x_0\mu + B - \gamma$ so that building capacity and behaving is the efficient decision for each firm from the point of view of the national planner.

7.2.2 The Game

To address the question of the number of firms, we assume that there are N potential firms that could be active on the market and that the government chooses the number of firms. The timing is as follows:

- A number $n \leq N$ of firms is chosen.
- Firms compete on the local market and receive the associated cash flow.
- Firms decide how much cash flow to invest in export capacity and how much to borrow. Financial contracts are signed.
- Firms build export capacity and attempt to enter the foreign market.
- Firms succeed or do not succeed in exporting.

Assessing whether $n < N$ then amounts to comparing the optimal number of firms n^* to N given the financial constraints. We will consider the determination of n^*.

7.3 The Financial Contract and Export

We first investigate the financial contract. Consider a firm with cash flow Π from its local market. It is willing to invest $S \leq \Pi$ and to borrow

D in order to finance an export capacity Q. We thus have $S = \gamma Q - D$. There are three verifiable variables for the financial contract: the capacity Q, whether the firm is successful in exporting, and the export revenue μQ in case of success. We assume that all cash flows from the local market not invested by the firm are consumed during the process so that at the time when the firm has to repay the debt, it can only use the revenue from its foreign activities.[2]

The financial contract can be written as a triple $C = (Q, D, R)$, where D is the face value of the debt and R is the reimbursement in case of success. They are derived in Holmström and Tirole (1997) and Tirole (2006). It can easily be shown that there cannot exist an equilibrium in which a firm misbehaves. Indeed the total expected reward $(x_0 \mu + B - \gamma)Q$ to be shared between the lender and the firm would be negative in that case. Thus at least one party would face a negative profit and would thus refuse to participate. Therefore we will consider financial contracts that induce firms to behave.

A contract is feasible only if two conditions are verified. First, there must be enough cash flow to cover self-financing:

$$\Pi \geq \gamma Q - D. \tag{7.1}$$

Second, enough cash must be extracted from the export market to repay the debt:

$$\mu Q \geq R. \tag{7.2}$$

If contract C can be signed, the firm invests Q and decides to behave or not. It will behave if the expected revenue from doing so, which is $x(\mu Q - R)$, is larger than the expected revenue from misbehaving $x_0(\mu Q - R) + BQ$. Thus the firm behaves if $\mu Q - R \geq [B/(x - x_0)]Q$. In other words, a feasible contract is incentive-compatible if

$$x(\mu Q - R) \geq bQ, \tag{7.3}$$

where $b = [Bx/(x - x_0)]$. Observe that a larger b makes the incentive-compatibility constraint more likely to be binding. Thus b measures the intensity of the moral hazard problem. Notice that this condition automatically implies condition (7.2). Finally, the participation constraints require that both parties receive a positive expected profit:

$$xR \geq D \tag{7.4}$$

and

$$x(\mu Q - R) + \Pi - S \geq \Pi. \tag{7.5}$$

Thus a contract can be signed if we can find Q, D, and R such that we can verify conditions (7.3), (7.1), (7.4), and (7.5). Since financial markets are competitive, if a contract is signed, the lender obtains zero expected profit so that $xR = D$. Combining this condition with the condition that $S + D = \gamma Q$ implies that the expected revenue of the firm is $(x\mu - \gamma)Q + \Pi$, which is larger than the cash flow Π. This means that the participation constraints (7.4) and (7.5) are automatically satisfied with $D = xR$.

Thus, the firm will sign a contract $(Q, D, R = D/x)$ if this contract is incentive compatible (condition 7.3) and if enough capital can be raised on the credit market to finance the project (condition 7.1). This is summarized by the following condition:

$$\gamma Q - \Pi \leq D \leq (x\mu - b)Q. \tag{7.6}$$

As in Holmström and Tirole (1997), the cash that a firm can raise on the credit market is limited by the expectation of the lenders that if the firm borrows too much, it will prefer not to exert enough effort for the success of the project. We assume that $\gamma > x\mu - b$, which means that a firm with a larger export capacity is confronted with a stricter constraint (7.6) on its pledgeable income.

A contract satisfying condition (7.6) exists if

$$(b - (x\mu - \gamma))Q \leq \Pi. \tag{7.7}$$

This condition shows that the moral hazard problem existing on the credit market puts an upper limit on the export capacity that a firm may build. Because we assume that there is a positive markup $x\mu - \gamma$ on the foreign market, it is optimal for the firm to borrow as much as possible to invest in the export capacity, so that the firm's investment is constrained by the financial capacity, given by

$$Q = \alpha\Pi, \quad \text{where } \alpha = \frac{1}{b - x\mu + \gamma}.$$

To reach this optimal level of investment, the firm invests all the cash flow $S = \Pi$ and borrows the complement $D = \gamma Q - \Pi = [(x\mu - b)/(b - x\mu + \gamma)]\Pi$. The investment is thus proportional to the firm's profit Π on its national market. As long as $b > x\mu - \gamma$, the ability to find external resources to fund the export project is inversely related to the intensity b of the moral hazard problem.

Remember that we assume that the firm is always constrained.[3] In being constrained, the total profit of the firm is equal to

$\Pi + (x\mu - \gamma)Q = \alpha b\Pi$.

Observe that αb is larger than unity. This illustrates the importance of raising local profit to relax the credit rationing constraint to expand the firm on its profitable foreign markets. The limit case is when the foreign profit margin $x\mu - \gamma$ tends toward zero, in which case $\alpha b = 1$, and there is no reason to export.

7.4 The Optimal Concentration

Let us examine the welfare consequences of a change in the number n of national firms. For this analysis we ignore entry cost and fixed cost. We assume that there are $N \geq 2$ firms in the market and consider whether a merger from N to n could be favored by the national authority. We assume that there are strong barriers to entry so that merging two firms does not invite entry of a new firm. We further assume that merging firms have the same technology post merger. Notice that in the case of a Cournot game, firms may not benefit from a merger if n is large. Thus reducing the number of firms may require an active policy. The total surplus as a function of n is denoted W_n, which is equal to

$$W_n = S(p_n) + n\alpha b\Pi_n, \tag{7.8}$$

where p_n is the equilibrium price on the local market, and Π_n is the equilibrium local profit of each local firm. Because αb is larger than unity, we see from this equation that financial markets' imperfection raises the weight that the planner allocates to the firms' local profit in the social welfare function. This implies that the efficient solution is not necessarily with the smallest local profit for the firms, as in the first-best case with no credit rationing. Reducing the number of firms raises the deadweight loss on the local market, but it offers extra revenues for local firms to self-finance their foreign investment. Given the inefficiency on the credit market, the smaller number of firms may be good for social welfare.[4]

A first remark for what follows is that export opportunities and financial markets imperfection will not affect the behavior of the firm on the domestic market. What they will affect is the value of domestic profits for the firm, whose optimal strategy, in any case, is to maximize profits. This is a particular feature of our model in that we assume technologies to be fixed on the domestic market. So our equilibrium price with n firms will correspond to the Cournot equilibrium price.

EXAMPLE

To illustrate, we want to consider the special case with a linear demand function $P(Q) = a - Q$, with $a > c$. As is well known, the Cournot equilibrium in this case is characterized by

$$Q_n = \frac{n}{n+1}(a-c),$$

$$p_n = \frac{a + nc}{n+1},$$

$$n\Pi_n = \frac{n(a-c)^2}{(n+1)^2},$$

$$S(p_n) = \frac{n^2(a-c)^2}{2(n+1)^2}.$$

This set of equations implies that the social welfare equals

$$W_n = \frac{(a-c)^2}{2} \frac{n(n+2\alpha b)}{(n+1)^2}. \tag{7.9}$$

The export margin is null when $x\mu - \gamma = 0$ or $\alpha b = 1$, so foreign markets are not attractive, and we are back to the standard welfare analysis of the Cournot equilibrium: W_n is increasing in n and the competitive equilibrium ($n \to \infty$) is efficient. But when αb is larger than 1, W_n is not increasing in n.[5]

Let us compare the duopoly solution and the monopoly (national champion) solution in particular. The national champion is socially more desirable locally if

$$W_1 \geq W_2,$$

or if

$$\alpha b = \frac{b}{b - (x\mu - \gamma)} \geq \frac{7}{2},$$

or if

$$b \leq \frac{7}{5}(x\mu - \gamma).$$

Obviously monopoly would be the efficient solution if the foreign profit margin $x\mu - \gamma$ is large. Monopoly raises the benefits from foreign investment and thus the attractiveness of a policy that favors cash flows at the expense of domestic efficiency. But the surprising fact is that the monopoly solution is also more likely to be efficient if the intensity b of the moral hazard problem is small. We discuss this point below.

Let us consider the general case of Cournot competition with identical firms. Since all firms have the same cost, the total surplus is given by

$$W_n = S(p_n) + \alpha b(p_n - c)D(p_n).$$

Thus the effect of the number of firms on welfare resumes to the effect of the equilibrium domestic price on consumer surplus and export investment. For what follows, we simplify the analysis by assuming that the welfare is quasi-concave in price: $S(p) + \alpha b(p - c)D(p)$ is strictly quasi-concave.

We next obtain that the derivative of the welfare with respect to the price p_n is

$$\frac{\partial W_n}{\partial p_n} = (\alpha b - 1)D(p_n) + \alpha b(p_n - c)D'(p_n).$$

Denoting the price-elasticity of demand by $\varepsilon(p)$, we see that this derivative is positive if the price satisfies

$$\frac{p_n - c}{p_n} < \frac{\alpha b - 1}{\alpha b} \frac{1}{\varepsilon(p_n)} = \frac{x\mu - \gamma}{b} \frac{1}{\varepsilon(p_n)}.$$

Given that the price decreases with n, the optimal number of firms is unique and finite and such that the price–cost margin is set at the socially optimal level. We then have:

Proposition 1 The national welfare is maximal for a number of firms n^* such that

$$\frac{b}{x\mu - \gamma} - 1 < n^* < \frac{b}{x\mu - \gamma} + 1.$$

Proof The Cournot equilibrium satisfies $[(p_n - c)/p_n] = (1/n)[1/\varepsilon(p_n)]$. Given the quasi-concavity assumption, welfare is thus optimal for $1/n = (x\mu - \gamma)/b$ up to an integer. Hence the result. ∎

According to the result it is optimal to merge two more firms as long as $n \geq [b/(x\mu - \gamma)] + 1$. In particular, a monopoly can be optimal only if $b < 2(x\mu - \gamma)$. More precisely, under our concavity assumption, a monopoly is optimal if and only if it is better than a duopoly. This yields:

Corollary 2 A monopoly national champion is optimal if and only if

$$\frac{S(p_2)-S(p_1)}{S(p_2)+2\Pi_2-S(p_1)-\Pi_1} > \frac{b}{x\mu-\gamma}.$$

Proof The monopoly is optimal iff

$$\alpha b = \frac{b}{b-(x\mu-\gamma)} > \frac{S(p_2)-S(p_1)}{\Pi_1-2\Pi_2}.$$ ∎

Thus we confirm the result that a national champion can only be optimal if the financial constraints are not too tight. More generally, the optimal number of firms is an increasing function of b:

Corollary 3 The optimal number of firms increases when the tightness of financial constraints increases, that is, when b increases; it decreases when the profitability of the export market increases, that is, when $x\mu-\gamma$ increases.

This corollary reflects a fundamental tension in the interaction between the financial constraints and the social return of export investment. As b increases, the level of export that the sector can generate decreases due to a lower credit multiplier of the cash flow. In other words, the ratio between debt and self-financing decreases, which reduces total investment. This result would suggest a more lenient competitive policy, fewer firms, and higher domestic profits, but such a conclusion would ignore the fact that the return from relaxing competition policy is reduced for the same reason as the one that reduces the level of investment. Indeed, when b increases, the social return of the cash flow generated on protected internal markets reduces; hence the social return of relaxing competition policy is reduced.

Of course, these conclusions are only valid in the range where financial constraints are binding, namely where $Q_n < \bar{Q}$, which occurs if $b > x\mu-\gamma+(\Pi_n/\bar{Q})$. For low values of b, there are no constraints on investment and welfare increases with the number of firms. Thus there is a fundamental nonmonotonicity in the effect of financial constraints on the optimal policy. The next section analyses this in more detail by allowing for decreasing returns in exports.

7.5 Decreasing Returns to Scale in Exports

In this section we maintain the assumptions of the model, but we assume that when the firm succeeds, it obtains $M(Q)$ instead of μQ. We assume that $M(0) = 0$, $M(Q)$ is twice differentiable, and we denote the marginal revenues by $\mu(Q) = M'(Q)$. There are decreasing or constant returns to scale up to some maximal capacity, $\mu'(Q) \leq 0$, and we now define $\bar{Q}$ as the optimal capacity in the absence of any financial constraints.[6] We assume that the export profit is strictly increasing, $x\mu(Q) > \gamma$, on the range $Q < \bar{Q}$, and that $0 > x_0 M(Q) + (B - \gamma)Q$ on the relevant range. Thus the only viable contracts are contracts such that the firm makes proper effort with high probability to succeed.

Allowing decreasing returns does not change the analysis of the financial contract for a given investment level Q provided that one replaces μQ by $M(Q)$. Thus the firm can finance an export capacity Q whenever the following condition holds:

$$(b + \gamma)Q - xM(Q) \leq \Pi.$$

Since the left-hand side is convex, Q can be financed if it is below some threshold. We assume that the financial constraint is binding on the relevant range and that $\bar{Q}$ cannot be financed:

Assumption

$$(b + \gamma)\bar{Q} - xM(\bar{Q}) > \max_p (p - c)D(p).$$

Under this assumption, the firm then invests an amount $Q(\Pi) < \bar{Q}$, solution of

$$(b + \gamma)Q - xM(Q) = \Pi. \tag{7.10}$$

Notice that it must be the case that $b + \gamma > x\mu(Q(\Pi))$, meaning that the financing of the marginal unit of capacity is cross-subsidized by the return on infra-marginal units. With this level of investment, the firm obtains a profit $\Pi + xM(Q) - \gamma Q = bQ(\Pi)$. The profit is equal to the nonpledgeable income. Increasing the cash flow allows increasing the export capacity by

$$Q'(\Pi) = \alpha(Q) = \frac{1}{b + \gamma - x\mu(Q)}. \tag{7.11}$$

Notice that $\alpha(Q)$ decreases with Q, implying that the investment is a concave function of the cash flow. Replicating the analysis above, we see that the welfare is

$$W_n = S(p_n) + bnQ_n, \quad \text{with} \quad Q_n = Q\left(\frac{(p_n - c)D(p_n)}{n}\right).$$

Treating n as a continuous variable, we obtain

$$\frac{dW_n}{dn} = [(b\alpha(Q_n) - 1)D(p_n) + b\alpha(Q_n)(p_n - c)D'(p_n)]\frac{dp_n}{dn}$$
$$+ b(Q_n - \alpha(Q_n)\Pi_n).$$

The first term is similar to the one obtained for the linear case and vanishes at a value n^* solution of

$$n^* = \frac{b}{x\mu(Q_{n^*}) - \gamma}. \tag{7.12}$$

Since the marginal return to export capacity $\mu(Q_n^*)$ is nondecreasing with n, this defines n^* uniquely. The second term is a correction due to the nonlinearity of the investment function. The fact that $Q(\Pi)$ is a concave function under decreasing returns to scale implies that $Q_n - \alpha(Q_n)\Pi_n > 0$. Due to decreasing returns, there is an extra benefit of duplicating the firms, which is that export productivity increases as the size decreases. This effect is due to the financial market imperfection that creates a linkage between domestic market profitability and export investment.

Let us take a closer look at the first effect, namely the impact of technology on the trade-off between consumer surplus and export revenues. When the tightness of financial constraint increases, the effect on the optimal number of firms n^* is given by the impact of b on the right-hand side of equation (7.12). Thus $\partial n^*/\partial b$ has the same sign as $\{\partial(b/[x\mu(Q_{n^*}) - \gamma])/\partial b\}$.

Using $\partial Q/\partial b = -\alpha(Q)Q$, we obtain that

$$\text{sign}\frac{\partial}{\partial b}\left(\frac{b}{x\mu(Q_{n^*}) - \gamma}\right) = \text{sign}\left(1 + \frac{bx\mu'(Q_n)\alpha(Q_n)Q_n}{x\mu(Q_{n^*}) - \gamma}\right).$$

We confirm the fact that when there are little decreasing returns, the optimal number of firms increases with b. However, with strong returns to scale, when $\mu'(Q_n)$ is large and negative, the sign may be reversed.

7.6   Increasing Returns on the Domestic Market

Let us extend the model of the preceding section to include a fixed cost K to set up a firm. If the profit of a firm is $[(p_n - c)D(p_n)/n] - K$, then total welfare is written as

$$W_n = S(p_n) + \alpha b((p_n - c)D(p_n) - nK). \tag{7.13}$$

The optimal number of firms then is the solution of

$$\frac{\partial W_n}{\partial n} = ((\alpha b - 1)D(p_{n^*}) + \alpha b(p_{n^*} - c)D'(p_{n^*}))\frac{dp_n}{dn} - \alpha bK \simeq 0. \tag{7.14}$$

Recall that in the case where there is no financial constraint, the level of export is independent of the cash flow generated on the domestic markets. To compare the situations with and without the financial constraint, we need to specify what happens when there is no financial constraint. In the fixed-cost case, the cash flow generated on the domestic market does not affect the export investment. In order to see the effect of a financial constraint, we assume that the number of firms does not affect the export capacity absent any financial constraint.

Suppose that there are N firms, each investing the maximal export capacity $\overline{Q}$. The reduction of the number of firms from N to n is done through merger and the potential production capacities are pooled. The total production capacity is assumed to be $N\overline{Q}$. By this assumption, where there is no financial constraint, the welfare is

$$S(p_n) + (p_n - c)D(p_n) - nK + N(x\mu - \gamma)\overline{Q},$$

and welfare is optimal at

$$(p_n - c)D'(p_n)\frac{dp_n}{dn} - K \simeq 0.$$

Comparing the two conditions, we see that the former calls for fewer firms since $(\alpha b - 1)D(p_{n^*})(dp_n/dn) < 0$, which reflects the value of raising export investment through a larger total profit. This can be established quite generally:

Proposition 4   If there is a fixed cost per firm, the optimal number of firms is smaller when there is credit rationing than without credit rationing.

Proof $W_n = S(p_n) + (p_n - c)D(p_n) - nK + (\alpha b - 1)((p_n - c)D(p_n) - nK)$.
Since $(\alpha b - 1)((p_n - c)D(p_n) - nK)$ decreases with n, a simple revealed
preference argument shows that n^* is smaller than the optimal number
of firms with no financial constraints.   ∎

7.7   The Case of States in a Common Market

So far we have considered a domestic market of a single small economy.
In the European Union, markets are integrated, but states continue to
follow national objectives. The question with regard to states with a
common market is then whether national states have excessive or
insufficient incentives to follow policies raising market concentration.
To address this question, consider J states that are part of the same
common market. The states have identical demands apart from
size. We let $D(p)$ be the market demand; the demand from state j is
$\theta_j D(p)$, where θ_j is the population in state j, and $\sum_{j=1}^{J} \theta_j = 1$. For the
common market case let us assume that there is a fixed cost K to set
up a firm.

Suppose that in each state the government controls the number of
firms. Let n_j be the number of firm in state j and $n = \sum_{j=1}^{J} n_j$ be the total
number of firms. Then the welfare in state j is

$$W_j = \theta_j S(p_n) + \frac{n_j}{n} \alpha b (p_n - c)D(p_n).$$

Suppose that states fix the number of firms in a noncooperative way.
Then the optimal number of firms for state j is solved as

$$n_j \in \arg\max_{n_j} \left(\theta_j S(p_n) + \frac{n_j}{n} \alpha b (p_n - c)D(p_n) - n_j \alpha b K \right),$$

$$st \, n = n_j + \sum_{l \neq j} n_l.$$

This yields an approximate first-order condition

$$\left[\left(\frac{n_j}{n} - \frac{\theta_j}{\alpha b} \right) D(p_n) + \frac{n_j}{n}(p_n - c)D'(p_n) \right] \frac{dp_n}{dn} + \left(\frac{n - n_j}{n^2} \right)(p_n - c)D(p_n) = K. \tag{7.15}$$

Summing over all countries, we find that

$$\left[\left(\frac{\alpha b - 1}{\alpha b} \right) D(p_n) + (p_n - c)D'(p_n) \right] \frac{dp_n}{dn} + \left(\frac{n-1}{n} \right)(p_n - c)D(p_n) = nK, \tag{7.16}$$

which gives the total equilibrium number of active firms. We then conclude:

Corollary 5 Assuming concavity of W_n, in a common market, states choose to allow too many firms from a collective point of view iff

$$\frac{(p_{n^*} - c)D(p_{n^*})}{n^*} > K.$$

Proof Using (7.14) there are too many firms if

$$K > n^*K - \left(\frac{n^* - 1}{n^*}\right)(p_{n^*} - c)D(p_{n^*}),$$

which reduces to $(p_{n^*} - c)D(p_{n^*}) > n^*K.$ ∎

Thus there is insufficient concentration if the profit of the firms is positive in equilibrium. This result is due to a typical rent shifting effect: raising the number of firms allows a state to capture a larger share of profit at the expense of other states.

Another consequence of equation (7.16) is that the total number of firms is independent from the relative size of member states, since consumers are homogeneous across countries. Taking the difference between conditions (7.15) for two states j and l, we obtain

$$\alpha b\left(\frac{n_j - n_l}{n}\right)[(D(p_n) + (p_n - c)D'(p_n))]\left(\frac{dp_n}{dn} - \frac{(p_n - c)D(p_n)}{n}\right)$$

$$= (\theta_j - \theta_l)D(p_n)\frac{dp_n}{dn}.$$

As a consequence we have:

Corollary 6 Larger states tend to favor a larger number of domestic firms.

Proof Since

$$(D(p_n) + (p_n - c)D'(p_n))\frac{dp_n}{dn} - \frac{(p_n - c)D(p_n)}{n} < 0$$

and

$$D(p_n)\frac{dp_n}{dn} < 0,$$

we have that $n_j > n_l$ if $\theta_j < \theta_l$. ∎

The reason for larger states favoring larger numbers of domestic firms is that states internalize the negative impact of concentration on the domestic consumers, and this effect is larger for larger states. As a consequence the smaller states have a more lenient competition policy.

7.8 Alternative Policies

While we have shown that there may be some rationale for relaxing domestic competition policy when financial markets are imperfect, this does not mean that such is "good" policy. Indeed there are alternative policy instruments to consider, which we discuss next.

7.8.1 Direct Subsidy to Investment

One alternative for the government is to subsidize the investment. Consider a fixed subsidy s per firm. The impact on the firm is the same as increasing cash flow. Thus the firm invests $\alpha(\Pi_n + s)$ instead of $\alpha\Pi_n$, and obtains a profit $\alpha b(\Pi_n + s)$. Of course, this policy has the advantage of reducing the allocative inefficiency on the domestic market that a reduction in the number of firms would generate. But subsidies have their own costs and drawbacks. Therefore the social cost of market power on the domestic market should be balanced with the social cost of public funds in determining the optimal policy mix.

To illustrate this, suppose that there is a social cost $\lambda > 1$ of giving a subsidy to the industry. The policy instruments are now the number of firms n and the subsidy per firm s. Suppose that there are decreasing returns; then the investment of a firm is $Q(\Pi_n + s)$ defined as above.

Given n firms and a subsidy s, the total investment is $nQ(\Pi_n + s)$, total profit is $bnQ(\Pi_n + s)$, and total welfare is $W(n,s) = S(p_n) + bnQ(\Pi_n + s) - \lambda ns$.

Thus the optimal subsidy is given by

$$bQ'(\Pi_n + s) = \lambda, \tag{7.17}$$

where $Q'(.)$ is defined in equation (7.11). This defines a decreasing relation between the cash flow generated on the domestic market and the amount of subsidy.

Corollary 7 If both concentration and investment subsidies can be used, then the optimal subsidy decreases with concentration.

Proof The proof follows from the fact that $Q''(.) < 0$.   ∎

Similarly the number of firms solves $\partial W/\partial n = 0$, where

$$\frac{\partial W}{\partial n} = [(b\alpha(Q)-1)(p_n-c)D'(p_n)+b\alpha(Q)D(p_n)]\frac{dp_n}{dn}+b(Q-\alpha(Q)\Pi_n)-\lambda s.$$

We then obtain:

Corollary 8 If both concentration and investment subsidies can be used, an increase in the social cost of public fund raises the optimal level of concentration.

Proof Using the first-order condition for subsidy, we obtain that at the optimal n,

$$[(b\alpha(Q)-1)(p_n-c)D'(p_n)+b\alpha(Q)D(p_n)]\frac{dp_n}{dn}$$
$$+b[Q-\alpha(Q)(\Pi_n+s(n,\lambda))]=0,$$

where $s(n,\lambda)$ is the solution of equation (7.17). Denote by $Z(n,\lambda)$ the left-hand term. Given that Z depends only on s and n, and that $s(n,\lambda)$ decreases with λ, the sign of $\partial Z/\partial\lambda$ is the opposite of the sign of $\partial Z/\partial s$, which writes as

$$\frac{\partial Z}{\partial s} = b\left[\alpha'(Q)[(p_n-c)D'(p_n)+D(p_n)]\frac{dp_n}{dn}\frac{\partial Q}{\partial s}\right.$$
$$\left.+(1-\alpha'(Q)(\Pi_n+s))\frac{\partial Q}{\partial s}-\alpha(Q)\right].$$

Using $\partial Q/\partial s = \alpha(Q)$

$$\frac{\partial Z}{\partial s} = b\alpha(Q)\left[\alpha'(Q)[(p_n-c)D'(p_n)+D(p_n)]\frac{dp_n}{dn}-\alpha'(Q)(\Pi_n+s)\right],$$

which is positive since $\alpha'(Q)<0$.

Thus $\partial Z/\partial\lambda < 0$, implying that the optimal level of n decreases when λ increases. ∎

The same analysis applies to a proportional subsidy $\hat{s}Q$. In this case, the effect on the financial constraint is the same as the effect of a reduction in the investment cost γ. The investment is now $Q=\Pi/(b+\gamma-s-x\mu)$. In our context this is equivalent to a fixed subsidy $s=[\hat{s}/(b+\gamma-\hat{s}-x\mu)]\Pi$. Notice, however, that this policy may be more attractive with heterogeneous firms as it is better targeted at firms with more ability to leverage the subsidy into export.

The main point that we can make here is that subsidies and lenient competition policy are two substitutable instruments with similar effects on trade with foreign markets. Thus any motive that puts a ban on subsidy to exporting firms should also call for careful scrutiny of competition policy.

7.8.2 Privileged Loan

An alternative to direct subsidy is to grant firms investing in export privileged access to financial markets. Suppose that the government recognizes that there is credit rationing, so it entitles exporting firms to borrow some fixed amount d to solve this issue while letting the private market provide the extra financing. It can immediately be seen that in our model, if the privileged access to credit is granted at the market rate of return, this has no effect on export.

Indeed let the public contract be d with reimbursement r. Suppose that the loan is such that the rate of return is $xr = 1 - \theta$, where $\theta = 0$ corresponds to competitive market conditions. As long as $d < (\gamma\alpha - 1)\Pi$, the new constraints are $xr = (1-\theta)d$, $xR = D$, $d + D = \gamma Q - \Pi$, and the incentive compatibility condition is $x(\mu Q - R - r) \geq bQ$. We find that investment solves

$$\Pi + \theta d = (b + \gamma - x\mu)Q.$$

Thus, at competitive market conditions $\theta = 0$, the policy is ineffective in affecting foreign investment. This means that an effective policy must provide access to the financial market at a subsidized rate. The effect is similar to the effect of a subsidy analyzed above.

One alternative would be to fully substitute the credit market by providing credit d larger than what the private sector would do. Clearly, the massive intervention would interfere in a nondesirable way with market efficiency. Moreover, even if the state is as efficient as the private sector at managing financial contracts, there is no incentive compatible contract that can be written at the market rate of return for an amount larger than what the private sector would grant. Such a policy would only be feasible if the rate of return is smaller than the market rate, in our model if $\theta > 0$. Thus, in any case, there must be some interest rate subsidy.

7.9 Conclusion

It is shown in this chapter that the presence of inefficiencies on the credit market may lead some governments to promote national champions by granting protection against competition on the domestic market. The optimal competition policy at the local level is the result of a compromise between the wish to limit the deadweight loss of monopoly pricing and the wish to raise corporate profits to allow national champions to self-finance their rent-extracting investments abroad. However, several counterarguments can be made against this theory.

A first argument is that an industrial policy promoting national champions is based on pure national self-interest. It is assumed that there is an absence of cooperation among nations. There is an international prisoner's dilemma. In equilibrium, each nation will dissipate resources to create firms that will fail, in most cases, to emerge as global champions. Like arms races, the race to support national champions usually leads to an escalation in deadweight losses with little substantial benefit. In practice, cooperation to avoid this negative outcome may be possible via a repeated game.

A second argument is that the development of national champions relies on the fuzzy notion of corporate nationality. A national firm extracting a monopoly rent abroad will be beneficial to its stakeholders, who are assumed to be domestic citizens. These benefits are assumed to take the form of larger dividends for shareholders, larger wages for employees and greater employment. However, this picture is far from accurate. Véron (2006) examines the national shares of revenues and employment among Europe's 100 largest listed companies. The share of their customer base in their home market is on a rapidly declining trend, from 50.2 percent in 1997 to 36.9 percent in 2005. The move is particularly striking in sectors like energy, telecommunications, pharmaceuticals, and chemicals. The proportion of the workforce that is domestic was also less than 40 percent in 2005.

Finally, by providing protection against local competition to domestic champions, a country can preserve domestic firms and their jobs, but only in the short run. The strategy only delays necessary adjustments and constrains the beneficial process of creative destruction. When public policies reduce competitive pressure, more efficient companies cannot replace less efficient ones. As argued by Porter (1990), creating domestic champions "rarely results in international competitive advantage. Firms that do not have to compete at home rarely succeed abroad."

Notes

1. We can presume that this assumption is void when cash flow on the local market is verifiable (can be used as a collateral) and the financial contract not observable by the competitor (no strategic effect).

2. Allowing for verifiable residual cash flow would not alter the analysis.

3. A sufficient condition is that the monopoly is constrained, that is, $\alpha \max_p (p-c)D(p) < \bar{Q}$.

4. Notice that we take a total welfare perspective. This may not coincide with the view of an antitrust agency whose objective may be more aligned with consumer welfare (see Motta and Vasconcelos 2005).

5. By taking n as a continuous variable, it is easy to check that W_n is decreasing in n iff b is smaller than $n(x\mu - \gamma)$.

6. The analysis also applies for increasing returns as long as a stability condition is satisfied, but we wish to ignore any technological motive for raising concentration on the domestic market.

References

Brander, J. and B. Spencer. 1985. Export subsidies and international market share rivalry. *Journal of International Economics* 18 (1–2): 83–100.

Holmström, B., and J. Tirole. 1997. Financial intermediation, loanable funds, and the real sector. *Quarterly Journal of Economics* 112 (3): 663–92.

Motta, M., and H. Vasconcelos. 2005. Efficiency gains and myopic antitrust authority in a dynamic merger game. *International Journal of Industrial Organization* 23 (9–10): 777–801.

Neven, D., and P. Seabright. 1995. European industrial policy: The Airbus case. *Economic Policy* 10 (21): 313–58.

Porter, M. E. 1990. *The Competitive Advantage of Nations*. New York: Free Press.

Tirole, J. 2006. *The Theory of Corporate Finance*. Princeton: Princeton University Press.

Véron, N. 2006. Farewell national champions. Bruegel Policy Brief 4.

8 Market Integration with Regulated National Champions: Winners, Losers, and Cooperation

Sara Biancini

8.1 Introduction

Historically monopoly regulation has been a response to market failures, such as increasing returns to scale and externalities. In most countries government intervention took the form of the creation of public monopolies. More recently the poor performance of public enterprises has motivated widespread reforms introducing partial privatization and liberalization. However, regulation remains important when market failures impede the development of pervasive competition, as in the case of increasing returns to scale industries (e.g., telecommunications, energy, transports, and the water industry). In these markets the national leader typically stays dominant even after the reforms. This dominance can be challenged by the entry of foreign producers, operating in the neighbor countries. For example, the European Union is fostering competition in regulated markets through market integration. Firms are allowed to provide services in all member states, and raising barriers to entry is no longer permitted. As a result the main players of the liberalized markets are the former national monopolies.

Other processes of integration have created regional markets for electricity in Africa and Latin America. In all these cases supranational competition poses new challenges to the national regulatory policies.

This chapter analyzes this kind of situations where supranational competition complicates the optimal regulatory policy, studying the optimal regulation of national firms in a common market. In this context the regulation of the former monopoly becomes regulation of the "national champion." Often the former monopoly is subject to ex ante regulation, while competitors are less regulated or unregulated (we refer to this situation as to *incomplete* or *asymmetric* regulation). Asymmetric regulation is aimed to correct the consequences of market power, placing additional requirements on incumbent or dominant suppliers. In addition incomplete regulation can arise when regulated and unregulated firms compete producing subsitute goods and services.[1]

When barriers to trade are removed, competition takes place at the supranational level, while regulation typically acts at the national one. Market integration increases the opportunity for efficient firms to expand their business, and it can promote efficiency through a more competitive environment. However, competition also implies a loss of control for national regulators. In particular, when public funds are costly, the optimal regulated price is in general a Ramsey tariff: in this context, as Armstrong and Sappington (2007) observe, unregulated entry can have the adverse effect of undermining the tax base of the tariffs. The revenues of regulated tariffs have traditionally been used to cross subsidize non competitive segments of the network, such as network expansion and universal service obligations. Even after liberalization, in many markets we observe integration between the incumbent and firms operating in competitive segments. Profits earned the in competitive segments can help to satisfy the firm's participation decision in the non competitive ones. The erosion of these profits can be costly to society.

The chapter offers a welfare analysis of the impact of integration in regulated markets. I first show that under complete information, competition is welfare enhancing if and only if the variable costs of the two firms are sufficiently different. The high-cost country benefits from a price reduction and the low-cost country from export revenues. When the costs are similar, the (negative) business stealing effect prevails. Competition is not very beneficial to consumers (small price effect), and it harms the national firm, and hence tax payers, through business stealing.

Indeed market integration creates winners and losers in both countries: I thus identify and discuss the impact of market integration on consumers, taxpayers and firms. In particular, in the presence of asymmetric information, supranational competition produces nontrivial effects on the rent-seeking behavior of regulated firms. Competition is in general thought to put constraints on regulated firms and to limit their capability of capturing information rents. My analysis shows that this is not always the case and that the direction of the effects depends crucially on the stochastic distribution of the shocks on production costs.

In the last part of the chapter, I consider the possibility of cooperation between regulators. In a process of regional integration, regulators can try to achieve collective gains: however, at the globally optimal allocation of production, the country with the less efficient technology is, in general, a loser of the integration process. For this reason the efficient solution cannot be sustained without side transfers. Each decentralized cooperative solution has to repay the negative impact of business stealing and the costs related to restructuring. These results suggest that cooperation in the form of transfers should be used in order to provide funding for infrastructure and restructuring policies.

8.1.1 Market Integration and Regulated Markets

There are several examples of regulated markets which have progressively been exposed to foreign competition. A natural example is the process of market integration in the European Union, which has progressively involved all regulated markets. In telecommunications, the process of liberalization and market integration is probably the most advanced. The larger providers operate at the European level and have reciprocally challenged their monopoly position in their home countries. Some of the main players are public or mixed-public firms, others are completely privatized. For instance, in the United Kingdom, British Telecom has fully been privatized since 1987. In continental Europe the situation is different. The French government kept the majority of the capital of France Telecom until 2004. At the time, 80 percent of the workers were civil servants (Berne and Pogorel 2004). In 2007 the share passed to 27 percent, while almost half of the workers (and the vast majority of the ones working inside France) are still civil servants. Similarly in Germany Deutsche Telekom is only partially privatized. Even if the privatization process goes on, the role of governments in this industry will remain important because of universal service obligations and price regulation. Moreover direct government intervention seems to be the rule in case of crisis, sometimes conflicting with the general antitrust and non discrimination policies. An example is the intervention of the French government in favor of France Telecom, which has been under scrutiny of the EU Commission under the legislation on state aid.

Other regulated industries are by far less competitive than telecommunications, but market integration and the removal of barriers to trade still put some competitive pressure on the incumbents. An example is postal service. Here the extent of effective competition is lower, but efforts are made at the EU level to increase market integration. As a reaction, in the last years many former postal monopolies have bought private parcel operators to consolidate their presence in other member states.

In the same way energy markets are progressively being integrated. Market integration is further developed in northern countries, independently of the more general process of integration at the EU level. Norway and Sweden have liberalized their markets, allowing neighbor operators to enter the national market. The incumbent public monopolies have been privatized to a very small extent, but foreign competitors are allowed to serve the market. Likewise European directives promote the formation of an European market for energy through liberalization and interconnection.

The situation is similar for transports. Every national leader has transport market power in its country. For railways, public ownership and government funding are widespread due to the social value of the industry and the persistent economies of scale. For this reason the industry is still quasi-monopolistic in most of the countries. Nonetheless, competition is allowed and the European institutions are trying to develop a common transport policy for the integrated market. For airlines, the process of privatization is more pervasive. However, some direct government participation remains. For instance, the French government controls 44 percent of Airfrance, which represents 81 percent of the merged entity Airfrance–KLM. Moreover the crisis of the industry in the early 2000s has shown that direct government intervention takes place whenever the national carrier encounters a major threat. Even in the United States, government officers are usually in favor of rescuing airlines, creating barriers to exit and soft budget constraints (the government does not allow firms to fail). Moreover, even when the degree of deregulation increases, the attribution of slots in the airports tends to maintain market power of the national leader. Despite the attempts to make the market more competitive in the last years, concentration has increased at the EU level due to important mergers such as British Airways–Iberia or Airfrance–KLM. Beside the European experience, other processes of regional integration have interested regulated markets. One important example is the creation of regional markets for electricity like the African Power Pools (West, East, and South Africa Power Pools), the Greater Mekong subregion, and the regional markets of Central and South America. In all these cases market integration is expected to generate high-efficiency gains, allowing energy industries to exploit economies of scales related to large infrastructures (e.g., dams) and creating a more competitive environment. However, the possible conflicts arising from lack of coordination of government interventions are a source of concern and a potential brake on development of the regional markets.

8.1.2   Related Literature

The literature concerning the interactions between regulation and market integration is not very developed. On a clearly related topic, the strategic trade policy literature, starting from the seminal paper of Brander and Spencer (1983),[2] concentrates on the strategic effects of trade subsidization policies under adverse selection. Brainard and Martimort (1996, 1997) introduce asymmetric information in a Brander and Spencer framework, showing how the interaction of regulatory policies can reduce the agency cost associated with subsidization policies. In their case the consumers on the home market are unaffected by the policies, except for the fact that firms' rent-seeking behavior is costly to society. On the contrary, market power per se is not detrimental to welfare, since it is exerted only on *foreign consumers*. Combes, Caillaud, and Jullien (1997) develop Brainard and Martimort's framework, adding domestic production and national consumers to the problem. They use a common market model in which states may subsidize domestic producers. The regulatory instrument is a quantity subsidy (associated with a lump sum tax on profits). They do not consider the fiscal effect of competition which arises whenever the public funds are costly. With no budget constraint for the government, market integration is always welfare improving (for both countries). However, the public finance aspect of monopoly regulation is an important one. Traditionally monopoly Ramsey pricing has constituted a way to raise funds in order to cover fixed costs or cross-subsidize consumption of less favored groups of consumers. Adding positive costs of public funds, Biancini (2008) finds strikingly different results in the welfare analysis. In this chapter I build on these results and analyzes the distributive impact of market integration on consumers, firms and taxpayers. Moreover I characterize the global optimum for the integrated market and discuss how cooperation can help achieve the fully efficient solution.

This chapter is also related to the work of Calzolari and Scarpa (2009). They consider the optimal regulation of a firm which is a monopoly at home, but competes abroad with a foreign firm. They study the effects of foreign activities on home welfare, but without allowing for the entry in the home market. Yet economic integration is a process of reciprocal market opening. Adding this aspect to the picture, I provide different insights on the impact of market integration on the rent seeking behavior of regulated firms in a common market.

8.2   The Model

The model is based on Biancini (2008). I consider two symmetrical countries, identified by $I = 1, 2$. The (inverse) demand in country i is given by

$$p_i = d - Q_i, \tag{8.1}$$

where p_i is the price and Q_i the national demand. In a closed economy, Q_i corresponds to, the quantity produced by the national monopoly of country i. When markets are integrated, total demand is given by:

$$P = d - \frac{Q}{2}, \tag{8.2}$$

where $Q = Q_1 + Q_2$ is the total demand in the integrated market which can be satisfied by firm 1 or 2 ($Q = q_1 + q_2$). The specification in (8.2) assumes perfect integration (no segmentation), but this is not crucial for the result which holds under segmented markets (it simplifies the exposition avoiding the emergence of many corner solutions). I also neglect the possible existence of transportation costs: for a discussion of their impact, see Auriol and Biancini (2009).

Before market integration there is a monopoly in each country. Each monopoly is regulated following an incentive contract determining the quantity[3] and a regulatory instrument (transfer or tax). In the integrated market, each of the two regulators maximizes the home welfare, given by the sum of national consumer surplus and the profit of the national firm. The regulator of country i is not allowed to contract with firm j. This aims to describe a situation where regulation is incomplete in each jurisdiction. For simplicity, I consider the case where the national firm is public. Even in the case of privatized firms, asymmetric regulation is used in practice, and it has already received some attention in the literature.[4]

The welfare in country i is

$$W_i = S(Q_i) - P(Q)Q_i + \Pi_i - (1 + \lambda)t_i, \tag{8.3}$$

where $S(Q_i)$ represents national gross consumer surplus, the profit of the national producer and t_i the regulatory instrument. The presence of a positive λ can capture the idea that public funds are raised through distortive taxation.

When t_i is positive (transfer), paying a subsidy to a regulated firm creates distortions in other sectors. Conversely, when t_i is negative (tax), it helps reduce distortive taxation and to finance investment in infrastructure or other public projects. More generally, this modeling strategy captures in a reduced form the idea that the operating profits of the national champion are valuable to society because they can be "extracted" through the regulatory contract. It can thus be applied to several contexts in which the operating profits of the national firm are valuable to society.

The profit of the national firm can be written as

$$\Pi_i = (P(Q) - \theta_i)q_i + t_i - K,$$

where θ_i is the constant marginal cost of firm i and K a fixed cost that measures the economies of scale in the industry. Regulator i maximizes national welfare W_i under the participation constraint of the national firm $\Pi_i \geq 0$. When the regulator cannot observe production costs, which are private information of producers, an incentive compatibility constraint has to be added to the problem. For the moment we neglect this issue, which is separately addressed in section 8.5.

8.3   The Impact of Market Integration

Each regulator maximizes national welfare with respect to q_i. By convention, we denote Δ the cost difference between producer 2 and producer 1, that is, $\Delta = \theta_2 - \theta_1$. When $\Delta > 0$, country 1 has the more efficient technology. Solving for the Nash–Cournot equilibrium of the model, we find the quantity produced by firm i in the integrated market. When $|\Delta| \leq 2(d - \min(\theta_1, \theta_2))/(3 + 2\lambda)$, both firms produce and

$$q_i^O = \frac{2(1+\lambda)\{d - [(\theta_1 + \theta_2)/2]\}}{2+3\lambda} + \theta_j - \theta_i. \tag{8.4}$$

When $|\Delta| > 2[d - \min(\theta_1, \theta_2)]/(3 + 2\lambda)$, only the most efficient firms produces, and the total quantity is given by $Q^O = [4(1+\lambda)(d - \min(\theta_1, \theta_2))]/(3 + 4\lambda)$.

Then, at the noncooperative equilibrium, for any level of λ the lowest cost firm has the highest market share. Market integration increases efficiency, expanding the market share of the most efficient producer. This quantity can be compared with the regulated monopoly benchmark:

$$q_i{}^C = \frac{(d - \theta_i)(1 + \lambda)}{1 + 2\lambda}. \tag{8.5}$$

When $\lambda = 0$, $q_i{}^O$ is smaller than $q_i{}^C$ whenever the foreign firm is more efficient than the national producer. In this case the former monopoly leaves some space to the more efficient competitor and consumers enjoy lower prices. When $\lambda > 0$, regulator i may be willing to expand the regulated quantity even if the competitor is slightly more efficient. The reason is that in this case competition decreases the net profits of firm i without generating a drastic price decrease. Regulator i is thus willing to reduce the business stealing effect caused by competition and the quantity is reduced *less* often.

Replacing the expressions for the quantities in the welfare functions, we can now compare welfare levels under closed economy and market integration. When the national firm's relative efficiency is high, the country gains from market opening due to export profits. Conversely, the consumers in the relatively inefficient region benefit from a decrease in the price which increases welfare. However, if λ is positive, business stealing is costly to society. As a consequence, when the difference in marginal costs is small and no country has a drastic cost advantage, this negative effect outweighs the efficiency gains and welfare losses occur in one or both countries.

The following holds:

Result 1 For $\lambda = 0$, market integration increases welfare in both countries. For any λ strictly positive, market integration increases welfare in both countries if and only if the difference in the marginal costs is large enough.

This main welfare result, which highlights the negative effect of business stealing on welfare, is not related to the assumption of a duopoly in the integrated market. On the contrary, increasing the number of unregulated competitors would worsen the business stealing effect (though possibly increasing efficiency gains).

Summarizing, for a given country, market integration is welfare enhancing in two cases:

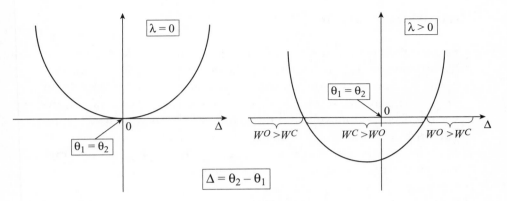

Figure 8.1
Welfare gains, $W_1^O - W_1^C$

• If the foreign firm is significatively *less* efficient than the national firm because the increase in the profit of the national firm drives an increase in total welfare.

• If the foreign firm is significatively *more* efficient than the national firm because the price reduction caused by competition increases consumer surplus enhancing total welfare.

The welfare gains $W_1^O - W_1^C$ are represented in figure 8.1 for $\lambda = 0$ and $\lambda > 0$ respectively. The gains of country 2 are clearly symmetric.

When $\lambda = 0$, an increase in Δ increases the welfare gains identically in country 1 and 2: the result is driven by the efficiency gains related to the reallocation of production among the two countries. When public funds are not costly, the regulators can prevent inefficient business stealing by expanding the production of the national firm: this has no cost because the information rent is not an issue in this case (if public funds are not costly, a subsidy to the regulated firm is a pure transfer and has no impact on welfare).

When $\lambda > 0$, the minimum of the welfare gains shifts downward and to the left. As a result the intercept (corresponding to $\Delta = 0$) is negative, which means that if $\theta_1 = \theta_2$, both countries lose from integration. For $\Delta \neq 0$, the welfare gains of the two countries are asymmetric. For the most efficient one, the gains are strictly increasing. For the less efficient one, they are U-shaped. Welfare gains first decrease and then increase. Eventually, for $|\Delta|$ large enough, the welfare gains are positive in both countries.

8.4 Winners and Losers

Beside this general result concerning total welfare, market integration has distributive effects and may generate winners and loser in both countries. For this reason, consumers may oppose market integration in countries in which total welfare is increased by integration. Conversely, a welfare maximizing regulator would promote market integration in cases in which national consumer welfare is reduced. We now decompose the total welfare effect in the impact on consumer welfare, transfers, and firms' profits (rents) respectively.

8.4.1 Price and Consumer Surplus

Substituting the relevant quantities (8.5) and (8.4) in the inverse demand functions (8.1) and (8.2), we obtain the value of the price in the cases of closed economy and market integration respectively.

Result 2   For $\lambda = 0$, the price in the integrated market is equal to the average marginal cost. Then $P(Q^O) > p(q_i^C)$ if and only if $\theta_j > \theta_i$. The price increases for the more efficient country and decreases for the less efficient one. For $\lambda > 0$, a threshold $\hat{\Delta} > 0$ exists such that

- if $\theta_j - \theta_i \leq \hat{\Delta}$, $P(Q_i^O) \leq P(q_i^C)$;
- if $\theta_j - \theta_i > \hat{\Delta}$, $P(Q_i^O) > P(q_i^C)$.

Then for $0 \leq |\Delta| \leq \hat{\Delta}$, the price decreases in both countries.

Proof   The result is obtained solving the inequality $P(Q_i^O) \geq P(q_i^C)$ with respect to $\theta_j - \theta_i$.   ∎

The impact of integration on the price is illustrated in figure 8.2, for $\lambda = 0$ and $\lambda > 0$, respectively. When λ is positive and the cost difference not very large, the price decreases in both countries.

Notice that, under our simplifying assumptions, the prices in the common market converge to a common value $P(Q^O)$ and no demand segmentation persists. Price convergence is usually considered positive by the European Commission because it is a sign of effective market integration. However, the possible adverse impact of price convergence on groups of consumers can be a source of opposition and discontent toward the integration process. The interests of the national firm and taxpayers are opposed to the ones of national consumers, as the following subsection shows.

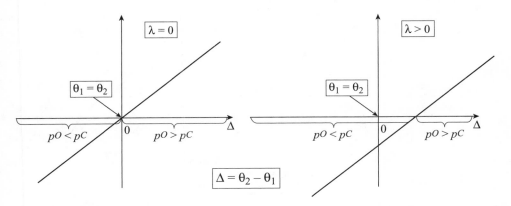

Figure 8.2
Impact on the price, $P^O - p_1^C$

8.4.2   Operating Profits and Transfers

We now consider the effect of market integration on the operating profit of the national champion. As shown above, competition generally decreases the price paid by consumers in the less efficient region as well as the market share of the relatively inefficient provider. Then the operating profits of relatively inefficient firms are reduced by competition in the common market. In our model this translates into an increase of the tranfer t (or a decrease in the tax). This has two aims: contrasting the business stealing effect and decreasing the market power of the foreign producer (because the foreign regulator does not take into account national consumer welfare and tends to produce an inefficiently small quantity).

Then, the following result holds:

Result 3   For $\lambda = 0$, $t_i^O < t_i^C$ if and only if $\theta_j > \theta_i$. The transfer decreases for the more efficient country and increases for the less efficient one.

For $\lambda = 0$, a threshold $\tilde{\Delta} > 0$ exists such that

- if $\theta_j - \theta_i < \tilde{\Delta}$, $t_i^O > t_i^C$;
- if $\theta_j - \theta_i \geq \tilde{\Delta}$, $t_i^O \leq t_i^C$.

Then for $0 < |\Delta| < \tilde{\Delta}$, the transfer increases in both countries (or the tax decreases).

Proof   The participation constraint of the firm is saturated at the equilibrium. Then under the closed economy the transfer is $t^C = -(p(q_i^C) - \theta_i)q_i^C + K$.   ∎

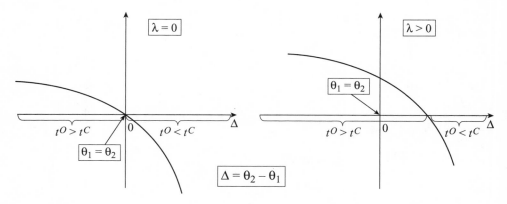

Figure 8.3
Impact on the transfer, $t_1{}^O - t_1{}^C$

Under the open economy

$$t^O = -(P(Q^O) - \theta_i)q_i{}^O + K.$$

The result is obtained by replacing the equilibrium quantities (8.4) and (8.5) and solving the inequality $t_i{}^O \geq t_i{}^C$ with respect to $\theta_j - \theta_i$.

Figure 8.3 shows the impact of integration on the transfer to the regulated firm when $\lambda = 0$ and $\lambda = 0$, respectively.

This results illustrate the claim of Laffont and Tirole (2000) who argue that pro-competitive reforms, limiting the scope for taxation by regulation, may have the effect of increasing the total transfers paid to the industry. When the operating profits of the national firm are valuable, this can induce relevant welfare losses. My analysis confirms this and shows that the efficiency benefits of competition need to be traded off against the loss of control of market activities. When public funds are costly, tariffs play an important role. Under competition, this has to be replaced by explicit taxation (and targeted subsidies): the cost of these policies has to be taken into account when considering the welfare impact of reforms.

8.5 Asymmetric Information

Until this point the regulator has been assumed to have complete information about the costs of the regulated firm. One may think that this induces to underestimate the welfare benefits of market integration, neglecting the impact of supranational competition on the rent-seeking behavior of regulated firms. As we argue in the following, this is not necessarily the case.

The impact of market integration on firm rents can be very important in practice because firms could oppose market integration if their rents were reduced. Then, the effects of integration on firm rents are very relevant to understand their possible lobbying decisions, aimed to delay or decrease the level of integration. Thus we now remove the hypothesis of complete information to study this issue. Under asymmetric information the cost parameter is private information of the firms and the regulator has to extract this information through the contract proposed to the different types. We restrict the attention to direct revelation mechanisms in which the regulator asks the national firm to reveal its costs and then assigns a contract (the revelation principle assures this is without loss of generality). The information rent of the regulated firm i, denoted by U_i, is computed applying the by now standard technique (e.g., see Laffont and Martimort 2002). Solving the optimization problem of the firm obtains

$$\frac{\partial U}{\partial \theta_i} = -\left[1 - \frac{\partial p}{\partial \theta_i}\right]q_i = -\left[1 - \frac{1}{2}\frac{\partial q_j}{\partial \theta_i}\right]q_i.$$

To illustrate the results, we make the following simplifying assumption:

Assumption 1 The marginal costs θ_i are uniformly distributed over the same support $[0, \bar{\theta}]$.

Then the information rent takes the form

$$U_i = \int_{\theta}^{\bar{\theta}}\left[1 + \frac{1}{2}\frac{\partial q_j}{\partial \theta_i}\right]q_i d\theta_i. \tag{8.6}$$

The regulator maximizes the expected welfare:

$$W_i^{AI} = E_{\theta_1, \theta_2}[S(Q_i) - P(Q)Q_i + \Pi_i - (1 + \lambda)t_i],$$

taking into account (8.6) and subject to the constraint

$$\Pi_i^{AI} = (P(Q_i) - \theta_i)q_i + t_i - K + U_i \geq 0.$$

In order to get explicit results, we consider the two limit cases of uncorrelated costs and perfect correlation. These are limit cases that approximate the more general cases of high or low correlation between the variable production costs.

8.5.1   Uncorrelated Costs

We start by considering the case of uncorrelated marginal costs. More precisely we assume that costs are distributed over the same support but are subject to idiosyncratic shocks. In this case $\partial q_j / \partial \theta i = 0$. Solving the problem obtains

$$q_i^{O,AI} = \frac{2(1+\lambda)\{d - [(\theta_1^v + E\theta_2^v)/2]\}}{2+3\lambda} + \frac{1}{3+4\lambda}(\theta_1^v - E\theta_2^v), \qquad (8.7)$$

where θ_i^v are the virtual costs under asymmetric information (which include the distortion related to the information rent, i.e., $\theta_i^v = \theta_i + [\lambda/(1+\lambda)]\theta_i$) and $E\theta_2^v$ are the expected virtual costs of firm 2. Moreover we have

$$q_i^{C,AI} = \frac{(d - \theta_i^v)(1+\lambda)}{1+2\lambda}. \qquad (8.8)$$

The following result holds:

Result 4   Under asymmetric information and uncorrelated marginal costs distributed as by assumption 1, if $\lambda = 0$, the rent increases for all types. If $\lambda > 0$, there are two cases:

• If

$$\frac{\bar{\theta} - \underline{\theta}}{d - \bar{\theta}} \le \frac{\lambda(1+\lambda)(3+4\lambda)}{1+3\lambda(2+\lambda(5+\lambda))},$$

the rent increases for all types.

• If

$$\frac{\bar{\theta} - \underline{\theta}}{d - \bar{\theta}} > \frac{\lambda(1+\lambda)(3+4\lambda)}{1+3\lambda(2+\lambda(5+\lambda))},$$

a threshold $\hat{\theta} \in (0, \bar{\theta})$ exists such that the rent increases if and only if $\theta_i \le \hat{\theta}$.

Proof   The proof is obtained by replacing the quantities (8.8) and (8.7), respectively, in the rent equation (8.6) and solving the inequality $U^O \ge U^C$.   ∎

When $\lambda = 0$, the rent decreases for all types θ_i. When λ is strictly positive, the results depend on the size of λ and of the term $(\bar{\theta} - \underline{\theta})/(d - \bar{\theta})$. The latter can be interpreted as a measure of ex ante technological risk because it captures the size of the uncertainty about

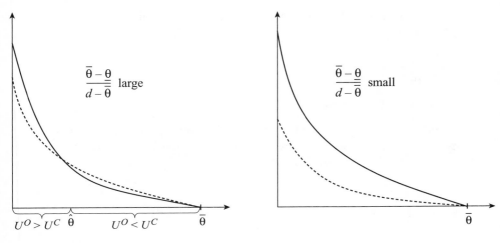

Figure 8.4
Information rent: Uncorrelated costs

θ_i, as compared to the size of the economy, as described by the parameter d. When the ex ante technological risk is low, the increase of the size of the market pushes regulators to increase the produced quantity (to control high market shares in the common market) and the information rent is always increased. When the ex ante technological risk is high, the regulator *increases* the quantity for the efficient types and *decreases* it for the inefficient ones. When the national firm is very efficient, the regulator expects the competitor to be less efficient. Then she expands the regulated quantity and the rent is also increased. As a consequence relatively efficient firms generally enjoy higher rents in the integrated market. These firms will thus be in favor of market integration. The opposite holds for very inefficient producers.

These results are represented in figure 8.4. The dotted line is the rent of firm i in the integrated market and the solid one is the rent in the closed economy case.

8.5.2 Perfectly Correlated Costs
We now consider the opposite limit case of perfect correlation $\theta_1 = \theta_2 = \theta$. Also in this case we solve for the case of θ distributed as by assumption 1. We obtain

$$q_1 = q_2 = q = \frac{2d(1+\lambda) - \theta(2+3\lambda) + \lambda\underline{\underline{\theta}}}{2+3\lambda}. \tag{8.9}$$

This is the case where the rent reducing impact of competition is maximized. We have

$$\frac{\partial q_j}{\partial \theta_i} = \frac{\partial q}{\partial \theta} = -1.$$

The following result holds:

Result 5 Under asymmetric information and perfectly correlated marginal costs distributed as by assumption 1, if $\lambda = 0$, the rent decreases for all types. If $\lambda > 0$, there are two cases:

- If

$$\frac{\bar{\theta} - \underline{\theta}}{d - \bar{\theta}} \leq \frac{2(1+\lambda)^2}{\lambda(3+4\lambda)},$$

the rent decreases for all types.

- If

$$\frac{\bar{\theta} - \underline{\theta}}{d - \bar{\theta}} > \frac{2(1+\lambda)^2}{\lambda(3+4\lambda)},$$

a threshold $\tilde{\theta} \in (0, \bar{\theta})$ exists such that the rent decreases if and only if $\theta_i \leq \tilde{\theta}$.

Proof The proof is obtained by replacing the quantities (8.9) and (8.8) respectively in the rent equation (8.6) and solving the inequality $U^O \geq U^C$. ∎

When $\lambda = 0$, the rent decreases for all types θ_i. When λ is strictly positive and the ex ante technological risk is high, the rent can increase for very inefficient types. For these types, under monopoly, the downward distortion of the second best quantity is large. Under market integration, the regulator induces lower downward distortion (i.e., higher quantity) and the rent can be increased.

Figure 8.5 shows the difference in the information rent under the closed and open economies. The dotted line represents the rent under the closed economy and the solid line the information rent in the case of an integrated market.

8.5.3 Concluding Remarks on the Impact of Asymmetric Information

Competition is, in general, thought to put constraints on regulated firms and to limit its capability of capturing information rents. The

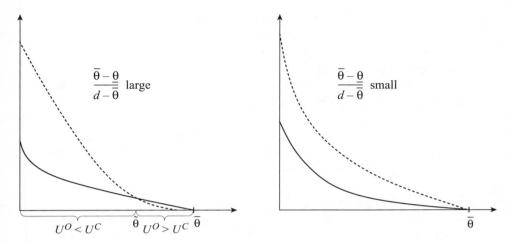

Figure 8.5
Information rent: Correlated costs

analysis of this chapter shows that this is not always the case and that the direction of the effect depends crucially on the stochastic structure considered. When shocks are uncorrelated, the information rent tends to increase, at least for the more efficient types. On the contrary, with high correlation, the rent generally decreases (though it may increase for very inefficient firms). Both scenarios could empirically be relevant, depending on the industry considered. Variations of the information rent would transmit to the transfer paid to the regulated firm (or the tax extracted). When the rent is reduced, the transfer decreases, and this has an additional impact on total welfare gains. Conversely, an increase in the rent has an adverse impact on the welfare gains as compared to the case with complete information. It can be shown that when the costs are not correlated, all the qualitative results of section 8.4 apply. When correlation is high, market integration is more valuable. Still there may exist values of the parameters for which a closed market is preferred to market integration.

8.6 Cooperation between Regulators

We are now interested in the possibility of solving the problem arising from the lack of coordination between the two regulators. The welfare-reducing effect of market opening is related to the fact that regulators do not take into account the impact of their policies on foreign consumers and taxpayers. When considering a process of market integration, we can imagine that some cooperation will emerge among regulators. For instance, in the European Union member countries seem concerned with the possibility of introducing policy harmonization. In such a situation, considering only the noncooperative Nash–Cournot solution is restrictive because it neglects the possible role for cooperation between institutions.

We now consider the case of cooperation between countries. As a first step, we focus on the solution chosen by a global welfare maximizing social planner (global optimum). Afterward, we discuss the possibilities of decentralized cooperation.

8.6.1   The Global Optimum

In the global maximization problem, a central benevolent government imposes a policy on the unified market. This problem somewhat captures the kind of integration that occurred in the German reunification process. In the reunification under one government one of the merged regions had a major productivity gap.. At the beginning of the reunification process, the physical productivity of East Germany was estimated to be about a third of that in West Germany (Czarnitzki 2005). As Röller and Hirchhausen (1996) point out, the particularity of the East German case was that restructuring and privatization were managed by the same institution. State aid has accompanied the restructuring process. The provision of public goods and governmental services were redistributed within the state sector: eastern Germany railways and telecommunications became part of the western German counterparts. As Siegmund (1997) observes, the budget constraint of the privatization agency *could be made politically soft because mainly western German taxpayers were paying and will pay for the losses.*

In this section we restrict our attention to the complete information benchmark. As we showed in section 8.5, the main welfare results are qualitatively similar to the case of asymmetric information, especially if costs are subject to idiosyncratic shocks. In our linear cost model, the global optimum prescribes a shutdown of the less efficient firm.[5] The optimal solution has the following characteristics:

- Only the most efficient firm produces.

- The quantity produced in the common market is twice the quantity of the regulated monopoly in the more efficient country.

Without less of generality, let firm 1 be the more efficient one (i.e., $\theta_1 \leq \theta_2$). Then firm 2 shuts down and firm 1 covers all the market producing a quantity $Q^* = 2q_1{}^C$.

By definition, at this globally optimal solution, total welfare in the common market is larger than the sum of the two welfares in the decentralized solution. A global welfare-maximizing social planner would also share the surplus equally among taxpayers. So all potential benefits related to market integration can be exploited. However, this framework does not seem particularly suitable to describe real-world situations whereby each country has an independent government and regulator—and profits and tariffs are not equally shared among the participants (the national taxpayers enjoy the increased profit of the national firm but not the foreign ones). If one firm shuts down, at least one of the countries would be worse off with respect to the noncooperative equilibrium. In particular, for λ large enough, the less efficient country will always oppose the solution dominated by both the noncooperative equilibrium and the closed economy outcome. Country 2 will then try to oppose integration. If barriers to trade are already removed, country 2 will prefer to stick to the non-cooperative solution rather than try enforcing the optimal allocation of production.[6]

8.6.2 Decentralized Cooperation and International Transfers

When λ is large, shutting down the national firm decreases the welfare of the less efficient country due to the costs related to restructuring. Eliminating (regulated) monopoly revenues is costly to society. In order to enforce cooperation, this country should be paid at least its outside option (the noncooperative payoff). Any cooperative solution will thus have to pay back the negative impact of business stealing. For instance, at a cooperative Nash bargaining solution, independently of the bargaining power attributed to country 2, a transfer from 1 to 2 would be needed to enforce the globally optimal solution (e.g., if the bargaining power of country 2 is zero, the transfer has to ensure the welfare level of the noncooperative benchmark).

The idea that it could be necessary to sustain the losers of the liberalization process is consistent, for instance, with the practical experience of the introduction of the National Competition Policy (NCP) in Australia. NCP was introduced in 1995: at the time the government commissioned a public enquiry as to the impact of the new policy on the different communities and social groups. This was explicitly aimed to evaluate the need for structural adjustment policies toward the losers of the liberalization process.

In the context of the European Union, the Structural Funds are the instrument used to reduce disparity in development and in particular "developing infrastructure, . . . targeting the development of trans-European networks in the area of transport, telecommunications and energy" (EC 1260/99).

In less developed regions, institutions such as the World Bank and international donors could coordinate a system of transfers, targeting the losers of the integration process.

In fact the result of our analysis above suggests that cooperation in the form of transfers should be used in order to provide funding for infrastructure and restructuring policies. In the absence of these resources, it is reasonable to expect countries to overprotect national firms. Cooperation with transfers may avoid other less desirable form of subsidies (state aid to inefficient national producers).

8.7 Conclusion

This chapter's analysis of the interactions between market integration and national regulatory policies has shown a way to study issues arising in many international contexts.where national regulators have to deal with firms operating in a supranational market. Adopting a two firms and two regulators model, we found that at the decentralized equilibrium market, integration may decrease welfare in one or both countries. Market integration can be welfare reducing because of its impact on the budget constraints of regulated firms. In general, what occurs then is that the interests of consumers, firms, and taxpayers come into conflict, generating winners and losers in both countries.

The chapter also advanced a globally optimal solution and identified the conditions under which such an efficient outcome could be sustained in a decentralized framework. Side transfers must be paid, and when the cost of public funds is an issue, the losses related to restructuring the national firm must be compensated. It may thus be necessary to facilitate market integration with subsidies to the restructuring countries in order for the globally optimal allocation of production to work. Cooperation is required to avoid globally suboptimal policies such as those resulting in countries opposing market integration and/ or in inefficiently subsidizing national producers.

Acknowledgments

I would like to thank Emmanuelle Auriol and Jacques Crémer for many helpful discussions and Bernard Caillaud and Gianni de Fraja for thoughtful comments. I also thank the participants of the CESifo Conference "Do We Need National or European Champions?" for their comments, which allowed me to significantly improve the paper.

Notes

1. For instance, trains and trucks compete in freight transportation, and in general, the truck industry is not regulated whereas railways are heavily regulated. Similarly high-speed railways compete with airlines, and in telecommunications, fixed lines operators are increasingly exposed to competition from mobiles and Internet providers.

2. For more details about the strategic trade policy literature, see also Brander (1995).

3. It could be argued that it is much more common to regulate prices than quantities. Indeed, under price regulation, the results are qualitatively similar when considering closely substitute goods, especially for what concerns the welfare analysis and the impact of market integration on information rents. More details are available on request to the author.

4. See, for instance, Caillaud (1990) and Biglaiser and Ma (1995).

5. This result arises because of the assumption of linear marginal costs and zero trans-portation costs. In a more general model, the quantity reduction would be smaller, but still larger than the one obtained at the equilibrium solution (see Auriol and Biancini 2009).

6. Without operating profit redistribution across countries, $W_2(q_1 = 2q_1^C, q_2 = 0)$ is smaller than W_2^C if and only if

$$\lambda > \frac{\Delta[d - (\theta_1 + \theta_2)/2]}{d - \theta_2}.$$

Moreover $W_2(q_1 = 2q_1^C, q_2 = 0)$ is smaller than W_2^O if and only if $\lambda > \Delta/(d - \theta_2 - \Delta)$. Both inequalities are satisfied if and only if λ is large enough.

References

Armstrong, M., and D. Sappington. 2007. Recent developments in the theory of regula-tion. In M. Armstrong and R. H. Porter, eds., *Handbook of Industrial Organization*. vol. 3. Amsterdam: North Holland, 1557–1700.

Auriol, E., and S. Biancini. 2009. Market integration and investment in regulated markets. Discussion paper 7296. CEPR.

Berne, M., and G. Pogorel. 2004. Privatization experiences in France. Working paper 1195. CESifo.

Biancini, S. (2008). Regulating national firms in a common market. Working paper 2209. CESifo.

Biglaiser, G., and C. Ma. 1995. Regulating a dominant firm, unknown demand and industry structure. *Rand Journal of Economics* 26 (1): 1–19.

Brainard, S., and D. Martimort. 1996. Strategic trade policy design with asymmetric information and public contracts. *Review of Economic Studies* 63 (1): 81–105.

Brainard, S., and D. Martimort. 1997. Strategic trade policy with incompletely informed policymakers. *Journal of International Economics* 42 (1): 33–65.

Brander, J. 1995. Strategic trade theory. In G. M. Grossman and K. Rogoff, eds., *Handbook of International Economics*. vol. 3. Amsterdam: North Holland, 1395–1455.

Brander, J., and B. Spencer. 1983. International R&D rivalry and industrial strategy. *Review of Economic Studies* 50 (4): 707–22.

Caillaud, B. 1990. Regulation, competition and asymmetric information. *Journal of Economic Theory* 52 (1): 87–100.

Calzolari, G., and C. Scarpa. 2009. Footloose monopolies: Regulating a national champion. *Journal of Economics & Management Strategy* 18 (4): 1179–1214.

Combes, P., B. Caillaud, and B. Jullien. 1997. Common market with regulated firms. *Annales d'Economie et de Statistique* 47: 65–99.

Czarnitzki, D. 2005. The extent and evolution of productive deficiency in eastern Germany. *Journal of Productivity Analysis* 24 (2): 211–31.

Laffont, J., and D. Martimort. 2002. *The Theory of Incentives: The Principal-Agent Model*. Princeton: Princeton University Press.

Laffont, J., and J. Tirole. 2000. *Competition in Telecommunications*. Cambridge: MIT Press.

Röller, L., and C. Hirchhausen. 1996. State aids, restructuring and privatization in the new German Länder. Discussion paper. WZB.

Siegmund, U. 1997. Was privatization in eastern Germany a special case? Some lessons from the Treuhand. Working paper 85. William Davidson Institute.

9 Economic Patriotism, Foreign Takeovers, and National Champions

Jens Suedekum

9.1 Introduction

In a recent paper Suedekum (2010) argued that globalization may buttress government aversion toward attempts of foreign corporations to acquire large domestic firms. In his model the government recognizes the positive aspects of cross-border mergers, particularly for domestic consumers who benefit from cost reductions due to merger synergy effects. However, governments also often entertain a bias against foreign takeovers of domestic target firms, and falling transport costs can initially reinforce this bias. Suedekum (2010) shows that even a biased government may accept a foreign takeover if transport costs are sufficiently high, essentially because the consumer gains are then substantial, but not if trade integration has proceeded too far. At such a later stage of trade integration, the government will rather attempt at creating a "national champion." In other words, the government will promote large-scale mergers between domestic firms in order to keep domestic profits from drifting to markets of foreign competitors.

These theoretical results may provide a rationale for some recent examples from the international business world. Maybe the clearest case is that of the SUEZ/ENEL/GAZ-de-FRANCE proposed merger. The Italian gas and electricity provider ENEL attempted to acquire its French counterpart SUEZ, in an endeavor to become a "European champion" in the relevant markets and to capture, in particular, market shares in France. The French government, which is well known to pursue a patriotic and biased industrial policy, heavily opposed the takeover and advanced the argument that foreign acquisition would lead to a buyout of national assets. The government instead promoted a merger of SUEZ with the national firm GAZ de FRANCE (GdF), which would create a "national champion," and one of the largest gas providers worldwide, with headquarters based in France. Several other merger cases have followed a similar pattern. Some of these proposed mergers, including the EON/Endesa/GasNatural, the ABN-Ambro/ Antonveneta, the Arcelor/Mittal, and the Danone/Pepsi cases, are discussed in other chapters of this book.

From the time line of merger events, it appears that cases of "national champions" have popped up quite frequently in recent years. In fact the general trend of economic integration in Europe is more often than not countered by instances of economic patriotism. This is despite the generally observed trend that cross-border mergers are becoming the dominant form of foreign direct investment (UNCTAD 2005). This dichotomy is precisely predicted by the model of Suedekum (2010). For an unbiased government that is not a priori opposed to foreign take-overs, he finds that falling transport costs make cross-border mergers more likely compared to purely national mergers, thereby confirming earlier results by Horn and Persson (2001). However, upon including a government's initial bias, he finds that trade integration makes national champions more likely.

In this chapter I study these issues using an alternative model of the underlying market structure. Suedekum (2010) assumes that firms compete in quantities of a homogeneous good; that is, he uses the standard model of Cournot competition. I assume instead that firms have differentiated products and compete in prices à la Bertrand. This alternative allows an important check of robustness because it is well known that Cournot and Bertrand models sometimes lead to drastically different results in merger analysis. For example, Salant et al. (1983) show that horizontal mergers without synergy effects are typically not profitable for the participating firms under Cournot conditions unless all firms that merge create a monopoly. This "merger paradox" does not hold in a model of Bertrand competitition with differentiated products where mergers tend to be profitable to insiders and outsiders (see Deneckere and Davidson 1985).[1]

In my model two domestic firms and one foreign firm compete in the domestic market. A foreign firm may produce more efficiently, namely at lower unit costs than the national firms, but it faces transport costs for servicing the market. Starting from this initial situation, I consider a three-stage game. In the first stage firms negotiate about changes in the ownership structure through mergers & acquisitions (M&A). In particular, the foreign firm wants to acquire one of the domestic firms in order to improve its market access; alternatively, the two domestic firms may merge to become a national champion that captures market shares from the foreign competitor. In the second stage, a domestic competition agency has to approve any change in the ownership structure (i.e., any merger type) but has no other tools of industrial policy available. The model is constructed such that some type of merger, be it national or international, will surely arise in equilibrium. The final equilibrium configuration depends on various factors, but mostly on the initial attitude of the government toward foreign takeovers—that is, whether the government's decision is influenced by an inherent patriotic bias.

Deriving the comparative statics of the equilibrium ownership structure, I found that higher levels of trade openness make national mergers less likely and foreign takeovers more likely if the government is unbiased. However, when considering a biased ("patriotic") government, I obtained the opposite result. The formation of a national champion is preferable at high levels of trade openness but not necessarily at low levels. These results confirm the insights of Suedekum (2010) who used the Cournot model to suggest that they are robust—with small deviations, as explained below—in a model where firms' actions are strategic complements rather than strategic substitutes.

9.2   The Model

My model closely follows Suedekum (2010), but I assume Bertrand price competition with differentiated products instead of Cournot quantity competition with homogeneous goods. I consider a domestic country where consumers have symmetrical preferences over three differentiated varieties (x_1, x_2, x_3), and for a homogeneous numeráire good x_0:

$$U(\cdot) = v \cdot (x_1 + x_2 + x_3) - \frac{3}{2(1+\gamma)}\left[(x_1^2 + x_2^2 + x_3^2) + \frac{\gamma}{3}(x_1 + x_2 + x_3)^2\right] + x_0,$$

$$(9.1)$$

where $v > 1, \gamma > 0$. The purpose of good x_0 is to eliminate income effects from the demand for the differentiated varieties. Each variety $i = 1, 2,$ 3 is produced by a single firm. The firms 1 and 2 and their shareholders are located in the domestic country, whereas firm 3 is located in a foreign country.

Standard utility maximization yields the following demands for the varieties x_i as a function of the prices p_j ($j = 1, 2, 3$):

$$x_i = \tfrac{1}{3}\cdot\left[v - p_i(1+\gamma) + (\gamma/3)\cdot\left(\textstyle\sum_{j=1}^{3} p_j\right)\right] \qquad \text{for } i=1, 2, 3. \tag{9.2}$$

I assume production costs of the two domestic firms 1 and 2 to be identical, constant, and normalized to one. The foreign firm 3 has unit production costs $0 < c \le 1$. Hence that firm may potentially produce its variety more efficiently, but it faces "iceberg" transport costs for servicing the domestic market: from every unit shipped, only a fraction $0 < g < 1$ arrives. Effective marginal costs for the foreign firm are $c/g > 0$.

In the initial situation, the three firms act independently and compete in prices. The profit functions of the three firms are given by $\pi_i = (p_i - 1)x_i$ for $i = 1,2$ and $\pi_3 = (p_3 - c)\cdot g\cdot x_3$, where x_i ($i = 1, 2, 3$) is as given in equation (9.2). From the first-order conditions, it is straightforward to compute the Bertrand–Nash equilibrium prices in the pre-merger situation:

$$p_1^{pre}* = p_2^{pre}* = \frac{c\gamma(3+2\gamma) + g\left(2(3+2\gamma)^2 + 3v(6+5\gamma)\right)}{2g(3+\gamma)(6+5\gamma)}, \tag{9.3}$$

$$p_3^{pre}* = \frac{18\,g\,v + 3c(2+\gamma)(3+2\gamma) + g\gamma(6+15v+4\gamma)}{2g(3+\gamma)(6+5\gamma)}. \tag{9.4}$$

Substituting these prices into the demand function yields the initial equilibrium quantities, which in turn imply the following equilibrium profit levels for the three firms:

$$\pi_1^{pre}* = \pi_2^{pre}* = \frac{(3+2\gamma)\left(c\gamma(3+2\gamma) + g(3v(6+5\gamma) - 2(9+\gamma(9+\gamma)))\right)^2}{36g^2(6+5\gamma)^2(3+\gamma)^2}, \tag{9.5}$$

$$\pi_3^{pre}* = \frac{(3+2\gamma)\left(18gv + g\gamma(6+15v+4\gamma) - c(18+\gamma(21+4\gamma))\right)^2}{36g(6+5\gamma)^2(3+\gamma)^2}. \tag{9.6}$$

Firm 3 is assumed to be active on the domestic market in this initial situation ($x_3* > 0$). This imposes a parameter restriction on its effective marginal costs, which can be written as

$$g > g_{trade} \equiv \frac{c(18+\gamma(21+4\gamma))}{2\gamma(3+2\gamma) + 3v(6+5\gamma)}. \tag{9.7}$$

A closer inspection of this initial equilibrium reveals that trade integration (rising levels of g) yield lower equilibrium prices for all firms. The equilibrium quantity of a domestic firm is decreasing in g; hence profits decline as trade openness increases. The quantity x_3* that the foreign firm is selling on the domestic market, and its profit level π_3*, are both increasing in g. Trade integration thus strengthens the position of the foreign firm by effectively lowering its marginal costs.

9.2.1   Structure of the Game

Starting from this initial situation, I consider a three-stage game:

First stage: Shareholders of the firms negotiate about bilateral M&A

Second stage: The domestic government has to approve any change in the ownership structure

Third stage: Firms compete noncooperatively à la Bertrand on the product market.

By using appropriate assumptions on the synergy effects of mergers, it can be ascertained that *some* change in the ownership structure will surely come about; that is, the current status quo as described above will not prevail as long-run equilibrium. Which merger form is going to be the equilibrium? As is common in the literature, I ruled out, by assumption, that all three firms merge to a monopoly. I rather focused on bilateral mergers between two firms only, and I focused on two possible ownership structures that may emerge: (1) the formation of a national champion through an alliance of the two domestic firms, or (2) a takeover of *one* national firm by the foreign competitor. In case of a merger of any type, a multiproduct company emerges that henceforth produces two varieties, but maximizes joint company profits.

In both merger cases the single outsider firm is either (1) the foreign firm or (2) the domestic firm that is not taken over. In case of the foreign takeover, the new multiproduct firm will also become a multinational enterprise (MNE) with its headquarters located in the foreign country. We can assume that operating profits of that firm accrue at this foreign headquarter location. Yet the domestic shareholders of the target firm receive a takeover price for their asset. That price is determined in the first stage of the game, which is equivalent to an auction for the target between the foreign firm (which seeks to improve its market access) and the other domestic firm (which tries to avoid becoming the outsider of the international takeover scenario).

In a successful foreign bid, shareholders of the target firm sell their asset abroad and thereby generate so-called takeover wealth.

A central aspect of this model, which crucially affects the equilibrium ownership structure, is how the government interprets the welfare implications of the two different merger options. We could think of the government as a welfare-maximizing competition agency that decides on the firms' proposals regarding a change in the ownership structure. Below, I distinguish between two types of governments, unbiased and biased. These two types of governments differ in the welfare measure that they use, specifically in their interpretation of the welfare significance of the takeover wealth that the shareholders of the target firm may generate when selling their asset abroad.

An unbiased government fully takes this wealth into account when comparing the two different merger scenarios from the point of view of domestic welfare. This type of agency evaluates the consequences of both merger types for domestic consumer surplus, profits of active national firms, and the wealth of domestic shareholders. It approves the type of merger that yields higher welfare gain for the domestic country; that merger deal may then take place provided that the firms are interested in it. A biased government, on the contrary, focuses on consumer surplus and operating profits of national firms in its welfare evaluation. It does not—or at least not fully—count "unproductive" foreign takeover wealth as welfare-relevant producer surplus. This is the notion of "economic patriotism" that I use in this model.[2]

9.2.2 An Example

Consider the following illustrative simple example. Suppose that each of the domestic firms is worth 8m€ in the pre-merger situation, and there is 15m€ worth of consumer surplus. Because of merger synergies, the firm value of the national champion exceeds the value of the participating firms. Say it is 20m€. Since the two involved national firms are symmetrical, it is natural to assume that each of the two shareholders receives 10m€ if there is a national champion formation. Furthermore after the merger the national champion generates a higher consumer surplus than it was pre-merger, say 30m€. The total surplus would be 50m€. The national champion formation is thus Pareto superior to the pre-merger situation.

The alternative to the national champion is the takeover of one of the domestic firms by a foreign corporation. This option precludes transport costs because the foreign corporation can draw on the existing distribution channel by the acquired national firm. This cost will nevertheless be partly passed on to consumers, so consumer surplus will typically be even higher with a foreign takeover than with a national champion—by how much depends on the level of transport costs. For the sake of argument, assume that consumer surplus is 31m€ with the foreign takeover.

The crucial question for the domestic government is: Which merger option generates the higher total surplus? To answer this, I should say something first about the magnitude of domestic producer surplus in the foreign takeover scenario. From the two national firms only one will remain in domestic ownership. So I will construct the model such that this domestic outsider firm suffers a negative profit externality from the merger of its two rivals. Suppose that the outsider is worth only 7m€ if the other domestic firm is bought, since it loses market share to the newly founded MNE. Further the magnitude of the profit loss for the domestic outsider will, in general, depend on the level of transport costs.

A comparison of the two merger scenarios shows that the foreign takeover generates 1m€ more consumer surplus than the national champion but 13m€ less in terms of profits of active domestic firms. The only way how this domestic profit loss can be compensated is through the takeover price for the target firm, namely the takeover wealth of domestic shareholders.

An unbiased government would fully count the takeover price that is paid by the foreign firm as relevant for domestic welfare. Anticipating this, the foreign firm knows that it would have to pay a takeover price that is sufficient to (1) win the takeover battle for the target against the other national firm (which tries to avoid becoming the outsider), and (2) to convince the domestic government to approve the foreign acquisition.

That latter requirement implies that the takeover price must at least be 12m€ so that total domestic surplus in the foreign takeover scenario (31m€ + 7m€ + 12m€) matches at least the 50m€ worth of total surplus in the national champion scenario. Any takeover price above the 12m€ would make the foreign takeover even more welcome from the perspective of the unbiased domestic government. The required 12m€ will also be enough to win the auction for the domestic target firm because the value of each firm (which are symmetrical and equally attractive targets for the foreigner) in the outside option—the national merger—is only 10m€. Without collusion among the domestic firms (which I neglect in this chapter), there is no way that one domestic firm could achieve a takeover price higher than 12m€, since another domestic firm could offer itself as a cheaper acquisition substitute. In sum, if the foreign firm is willing to pay 12m€, it can in fact successfully buy a domestic firm and get approval from the domestic government. Whether or not the foreign firm is actually willing to pay these 12m€ will depend on the endogenous value of the market access.

It turns out below that market access is most valuable when transport costs are high; that is, the foreign firm is willing to pay a higher price at high levels of transport costs. However, the takeover price itself is also endogenous in the fully specified model. At high transport costs the required takeover price is higher because the outsider would suffer a more severe profit externality. It therefore has a bigger interest to avoid the foreign takeover and stays longer in the auction for the target firm. When analyzing the effect of trade integration on the net profitability of the foreign takeover (gross profit gain minus the required endogenous price), it turns out that the foreign takeover would occur at intermediate levels of transport costs but not at high or low levels.[3] This result seems paradoxical: the foreign acquisition does not occur when it is most valuable (when transport costs are high). However, the explanation is that the takeover is more expensive in that case; it does not occur in equilibrium because of the endogenous takeover price that the foreign firm has to pay, which is too high relative to the value of market access. When transport costs are low, the takeover does not occur, even though it would be relatively cheap, because the gross value of market access is relatively too low.

Now consider the same setup, but with a *biased* domestic competition agency. The most extreme constellation is a government that completely disregards the welfare significance of takeover wealth. Whatever the actual takeover price for the target firm is, such a government would interpret the foreign acquisition *as giving away* the domestic firm for free. That is, this government would still acknowledge that the foreign takeover is associated with additional 1m€ worth of consumer surplus compared to the national merger. Yet the domestic profit loss equal to 13m€ cannot be compensated by the takeover price because the domestic government is reluctant to accept the takeover wealth of the domestic shareholders as relevant producer surplus. The government makes the following calculation: the national merger generates $30 + 10 + 10 = 50$m€ worth of total surplus, but the foreign takeover only $31 + 7 = 38$m€. Whatever the foreign firm is willing to pay for the target firm, the government simply cannot count that amount as relevant to welfare. Hence there is no way to convince the domestic government to approve the foreign acquisition in this case. The very restrictive and patriotic interpretation of national producer surplus imposes an insurmountable hurdle for a foreign takeover.

The main interest in this chapter is yet to analyze what trade integration does to the attitude of biased governments toward foreign takeovers. Therefore let us consider now a somewhat more mild government that has some bias but is not completely against a foreign takeover. The government is willing to count some part of the takeover price offered by the foreign firm as relevant producer surplus, but not the full price as an unbiased agency would. In particular, in the model I assume that the agency imposes a maximum amount that it is willing to consider in favor of the foreign takeover scenario. This maximum is equivalent to the value of the target firm should it experience a national merger, namely the 10m€ in the example.

The idea here is the following: the agency acknowledges—in principle—that foreigners should be able to acquire domestic firms. The agency also acknowledges the associated consumer gain. But the patriotic bias of this agency capitalizes on its conviction that foreigners should not outbid domestic firms in an auction for a domestic merger target. Recall that the acquisition ultimately hurts the domestic outsider firm. Aggressive bidding by the foreign firm is therefore considered excessive. The agency must instead impose a "reasonable" firm value for the target that it implicitly uses in its welfare evaluations. A reasonable firm value is given by the value of the firm under a national merger scenario, namely by the value that the firm would have if it joined with another domestic firm to form a national champion. Economic patriotism is surely not the only possible way to formalize government bias to a takeover of a target domestic firm, and it differs from the formalization used by Suedekum (2010). The main trade-off, however, as presented in this chapter does not in fact hinge on a precise formalization.

Returning to the example, say the foreign firm submits a proposal to acquire the target firm for the "reasonable" price of 10m€. The agency deliberates over this request by evaluating the implications for domestic consumers and the domestic outsider firm. From the point of view of the foreign firm, it is pointless, however, to offer more than 10m€ because the government will not take any higher price offers into account when deciding on a foreign takeover request. The government's restriction of the foreign firm's scope of action, of course, illustrates the patriotism implicit in this model. So the foreign firm effectively loses one tool in its pursuit to acquire the domestic firm. Simply paying a higher takeover price is not sufficient for success because price cannot alone be used to satisfy the domestic government.

The equilibrium offer by the foreign firm in this version of the game will be the maximum price that is set by the government, namely the 10m€. In the overall welfare evaluation the government compares the total surplus in the national merger scenario (30 + 10 + 10 = 50m€) and in the foreign takeover scenario (31 + 7 + 10 = 48m€). In this numerical example the government would therefore reject the foreign takeover and approve the formation of a national champion. There is the possibility to consider that a foreign firm could be compelled to pay a higher price to compensate for the domestic profit loss before a government will approve a foreign acquisition. For this to happen, the consumer gain must be substantial and outweigh the negative profit externality on the domestic outsider firm. I show below that this is likely to occur if high transport costs are involved. When transport costs are high, consumers stand to gain a lot from the foreign takeover because then the cost reductions are effectively high. This prospect then dominates the negative profit externality on the domestic outsider, and the foreign takeover is approved even for a relatively low "reasonable" price. As transport costs decline in the course of trade integration, the consumer gain from allowing the foreign acquisition becomes less important.

Therefore such a government will allow foreign acquisition of a domestic firm at high transport costs but not at low costs. In other words, trade integration encourages national mergers.

I now turn to the formal game structure mentioned above, and I use backward induction to solve for the subgame perfect Nash equilibrium.

9.3   Third Stage: Market Interaction

In the third stage of the game, there are two alternative ownership structures that can emerge: the national champion (with foreign outsider firm), or the takeover scenario with a MNE and one domestic outsider firm.

9.3.1   National Champion
When the two domestic firms 1 and 2 merge, the profit maximization problems are

$$\max \pi_{\{1+2\}} = (p_1 - s)\cdot x_1 + (p_1 - s)\cdot x_1 ,$$

$$\max \pi_3 = (p_3 - c/g)\cdot g\cdot x_3 , \tag{9.8}$$

subject to the demand functions (9.2). The national champion's firm {1 + 2} is now a multiproduct firm that can internalize the externality from the price setting p_1 on demand for good x_2, and vice versa. Furthermore, by merging, the two firms realize synergy effects that imply lower postmerger unit costs $0 < s < 1$. It is straightforward to compute the Bertrand–Nash equilibrium of this game, which reads as

$$p_1^{nat}{}^{*} = p_2^{nat}{}^{*} = \frac{c\gamma(3+2\gamma)+g(2s(3+\gamma)(3+2\gamma)+3\upsilon(6+5\gamma))}{6g(6+\gamma(6+\gamma))}, \tag{9.9}$$

$$p_3^{nat}{}^{*} = \frac{c(3+2\gamma)(3+\gamma)+g(s\gamma(3+\gamma)+\upsilon(9+6\gamma))}{3g(6+\gamma(6+\gamma))}. \tag{9.10}$$

Equilibrium quantities and profit levels follow immediately by plugging (9.9) and (9.10) into (9.2) and (9.8). The profit level of the national champion, which is also the national producer surplus in this scenario, is given by

$$PS^{nat} = \pi_{\{1+2\}}^{nat}{}^{*} = \frac{(3+\gamma)(c\gamma(3+2\gamma)+g(3\upsilon(6+5\gamma)-2s(9+\gamma(9+\gamma))))^2}{162g^2(6+\gamma(6+\gamma))^2}. \tag{9.11}$$

Consumer surplus can be now be computed as $CS_{nat} = V^{*} - \left(\sum_{j=1}^{3} p_j{}^{*}\cdot x_j{}^{*}\right)$. We can assume that the synergy effect is sufficiently strong (s sufficiently low) so that the national merger Pareto-dominates the pre-merger constellation. Inter alia, it will then also be the case that the national merger imposes a negative externality on the profits of the outsider firm—the foreign corporation—since the national merger allows capturing market shares on the home market.

9.3.2 Foreign Takeover

In the alternative scenario, one domestic firm is taken over by the foreign corporation whereas the other domestic firm stays as the independent competitor. We can assume without loss of generality that firm 2 has been taken over, whereas firm 1 is the outsider firm. The newly created MNE can use the existing distribution channel of the target firm so that transport costs vanish in the foreign takeover scenario. Yet, because we have assumed that general merger synergies exist as well for the national merger, we can also posit some additional cost reductions in an international takeover that are not related to transport costs. Specifically, I follow Suedekum (2010) and assume that the international merger gives rise to synergy effects identical in absolute strength to the effects of a national merger. The MNE thus has post-merger unit costs $c-(1-s)$. It also Pareto-dominates the pre-merger situation, and it imposes a negative externality on the outsider, which would then be the domestic firm 1.

The profit maximization problems are now

$$\max \pi_1 = (p_1-1) \cdot x_1,$$

$$\max \pi_{MNE} = (p_2 - (c+s-1)) \cdot x_2 + (p_3 - (c+s-1)) \cdot x_3, \tag{9.12}$$

subject to the demand functions (9.2). The equilibrium prices in this scenario are

$$p_1^{int*} = \frac{v(9+6\gamma)+(3+\gamma)(3+\gamma(c+s+1))}{3(6+\gamma(6+\gamma))}, \tag{9.13}$$

$$p_2^{int*} = p_3^{int*} = \frac{18(v+c+s-1)+3\gamma(5v+6c+6s-5)+\gamma^2(2c+2s-1)}{6(6+\gamma(6+\gamma))}. \tag{9.14}$$

The definition of consumer surplus is analogous, and it turns out that CS_{int} is generally higher than CS_{nat}. This represents the consumer-friendly aspect of the international takeover. This merger form has identical general synergy effects, but with additional transport cost savings that benefit consumers. Hence, if consumer surplus maximization were the ultimate goal of the domestic government, it would always strive for the foreign takeover.

The crucial task in this foreign takeover scenario is to determine domestic producer surplus. The gross profit levels of the two firms in this scenario are given by

$$\pi_1^{int*} = \frac{(3+2\gamma)[v(9+6\gamma)+3\gamma(c+s-4)+\gamma^2(c+s-2)-9]^2}{81(6+\gamma(6+\gamma))^2}, \tag{9.15}$$

$$\pi_{MNE}^{int*} = \frac{(3+\gamma)[18(v+c+s-1)+3\gamma(6c+6s-5v-7)+2\gamma^2(c+s-2)]^2}{162(6+\gamma(6+\gamma))^2}. \tag{9.16}$$

From (9.16) we see that the net profit level of the MNE is $\pi_3^{int*} = \pi_{MNE}^{int*} - \lambda$, where λ denotes the takeover price that the foreign corporation has to pay to the shareholders of the target firm 2. The magnitude of this takeover price will be determined below.

If and how this takeover price λ is included in the national producer surplus depends on the attitude of the government. An unbiased government would fully include λ as an integral part of total national surplus. An extremely biased government would implicitly assume a value of zero, whatever the actual takeover price is. To capture this potential discrepancy between the actual takeover price λ and its welfare-relevant counterpart that is used by the domestic government in the welfare evaluation of the foreign takeover, I introduce the variable $\tilde{\lambda}$ (with $0 \leq \tilde{\lambda} \leq \lambda$), which is $\tilde{\lambda} = \lambda$ for an unbiased government, $\tilde{\lambda} = 0$ for an extremely biased one, and $0 < \tilde{\lambda} < \lambda$ for a government that has some reservations against the foreign takeover, but that is not completely biased. In sum, the domestic producer surplus can be written as

$$PS^{int} = \pi_1^{int} * + \tilde{\lambda}. \tag{9.17}$$

9.4   The Traditional Infant Industry Argument

9.4.1   Second Stage: The Government
In this section the takeover game is shifted to the case of an unbiased domestic government that fully accounts for takeover wealth in its welfare evaluation ($\tilde{\lambda} = \lambda$). If a sufficiently large foreign takeover offer for one of the domestic firms is made, shareholders of the target firm counter the offer by submitting to the foreign firm their price λ. The government will approve the merger if that price yields a higher domestic welfare gain than a national champion formation alternative. When the foreign acquisition yields lower welfare than the national champion at price λ, it is rejected, and a national champion is formed. A national champion could also be formed if no acceptable foreign takeover offer arrives, so the domestic firm seek a national merger instead (recall that some type of merger will surely come about). The total surplus difference can be written as

$$\Delta\Omega = \left(CS^{nat} - CS^{int}\right) + \left(\pi_{\{1+2\}}^{nat} - \left(\pi_1^{int} + \lambda\right)\right). \tag{9.18}$$

If (9.18) is positive, then the national merger would generate higher total surplus in the domestic country than the foreign takeover, and vice versa. Due to the transport cost savings on top of the general synergy effects, the *consumer surplus difference* is always negative, $\Delta CS = \left(CS^{nat} - CS^{int}\right) < 0$. The *producer surplus difference* ΔPS is the domestic profit level of the national champion $\pi_{\{1+2\}}^{nat}$ (as given above in equation 9.11) minus the profit level of the domestic outsider firm in the takeover scenario (equation 9.15) and the takeover price/wealth λ whose equilibrium level is still to be determined. Equation (9.18) can be used to compute the minimum takeover price that is required to gain acceptance by the unbiased domestic competition agency. This is given by

$$\Delta\Omega = 0 \quad \Leftrightarrow \quad \lambda = \lambda_{min} = \left(\pi_{\{1+2\}}^{nat} - \pi_1^{int}\right) - \Delta CS . \tag{9.19}$$

Firm 3 can anticipate that, in order to be successful in the takeover battle with the other domestic firm, it has to place an offer that is at least as high as λ_{min}, in order to convince the (unbiased) domestic government.

9.4.2 First Stage: Takeover Auction
In the first stage of a takeover game for a target firm, there may be presumed two substages. First, the two domestic firms negotiate about the national merger by specifying a division rule of the aggregate profits $\pi_{\{1+2\}}^{nat}$ in case of the national champion formation. Second, after observing the result of this domestic negotiation, the foreign firm 3 can place a higher offer for one of the domestic firms if it is interested in doing so. When placing this offer, the foreign firm anticipates the decision of the domestic government; that is, it acknowledges the constraint $\lambda \geq \lambda_{min}$.

The foreign firm wants to take over whichever domestic firm is cheaper to acquire, without having any particular preference for either of the two potential targets. This setup is thus equivalent to a competitive auction where firms 1 and 2 offer themselves as acquisition objects to firm 3. The outside option for the two domestic firms is the formation of the national champion, hence the total profit level $\pi_{\{1+2\}}^{nat}$. Because of symmetry, that profit level would be equally split among the two domestic shareholders. To win the takeover auction in the first stage, the foreign firm would have to place an offer that exceeds this outside option. That is, it would have to offer at least $\pi_{\{1+2\}}^{nat}/2$. Lower price offers are not sufficient because the target firm would then rather join the national merger. Higher price offers are not needed to win the auction for target i, because the other firm j would offer itself as a cheaper acquisition object.

However, since the government is also involved, the domestic firms can anticipate that the takeover price must also exceed λ_{min} as given in (9.19). Hence the takeover price that the foreign firm would have to pay in equilibrium is

$$\lambda^* = \max\left[\tfrac{1}{2} \cdot \pi_{\{1+2\}}^{nat}; \ \lambda_{min}\right]. \tag{9.20}$$

If the foreign firm is willing to pay this price λ^*, it will successfully (9.20) acquire one domestic firm; hence the foreign takeover would be the equilibrium ownership structure (EOS) of this game. So the participation constraint for the foreign firm must hold, namely that the gain from the takeover (which includes the prevention of the national champion as the relevant aim for the foreign firm) is large enough to outweigh the required equilibrium takeover price:

$$\pi_3^{int} - \lambda^* \geq \pi_3^{nat} \ \Leftrightarrow \ \lambda^* \leq \pi_3^{int} - \pi_3^{nat}. \tag{9.21}$$

If this condition is violated, the foreign firm will not make an offer, and a national champion will be formed instead, with profits $\pi_{\{1+2\}}^{nat}$ equally divided among firms 1 and 2.

9.4.3 Equilibrium Ownership Structure

The relevant question to determine the EOS is whether firm 3 is *willing* to pay the price λ^* for the target firm. If it is willing, the takeover actually takes place. Otherwise, the foreign firm places no offer, and the national champion is formed.

Since the analytical expressions of this Bertrand model are quite cumbersome, we suffice to present some representative numerical results. Figure 9.1 depicts the gross profit gain of the takeover for the

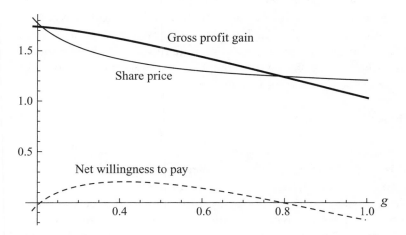

Figure 9.1
Foreign firm's willingness to takeover price λ^*: Unbiased government. Parameter values are $v = 3.5$, $\gamma = 1/2$, $c = 6/10$, $s = 7/10$.

foreign firm (thick solid line), the required takeover price λ^* (thin solid line, given by equation 9.20), and the net willingness to pay (broken line).

A priori we might have expected the foreign takeover to be more attractive the *lower* trade openness because the improvement of market access is then more valuable. Notice, however, that the takeover prices are endogenous and entail precisely a market access advantage. It is apparent from the figure that the *gross* profit gain for the foreign firm from entering the domestic market is higher the lower g is. Yet higher are also the endogenous prices that the MNE has to pay for this market access, which can be verified by noting that $\partial\lambda^*/\partial g < 0$. In sum, the foreign takeover is found to only arise for intermediate trade costs. At high trade costs, when market access is most valuable, it is also most expensive, and in fact it is too expensive for the foreign firm. The domestic firm will thus form a national merger in that case. If trade costs g are low, there will be no foreign takeover, either because the gross profit gain is relatively low and does not justify the required price. For intermediate levels of g, however, the foreign firm is willing to pay the required price, and the foreign takeover will effectively occur as the equilibrium ownership structure.

There is a slight difference between these results for the Bertrand model, and the results derived by Suedekum (2010) for an analogous Cournot model. He finds that the foreign takeover will not occur at low levels of g for the same reason, that it is then too expensive for the foreign firm. However, once trade costs have fallen short of a critical level, Suedekum finds that the foreign takeover will always arise, even if g is close to one. In the Bertrand case there will also be a national merger at low levels of g because the gross profit gain of the takeover tends to decline sharper with trade openness g.

9.5 Biased Government

9.5.1 Second Stage: The Government
There is ample evidence for nationalistic biases in industrial policy (e.g., see Brülhart and Trionfetti 2001), and more specifically for reservations against acquisitions of domestic firms by foreign corporations. Governments tend to favor domestic ownerships because nationally owned firms are more likely to commit to production in the home country, since politicians find it easier to interact with (and eventually

to tax) domestic owners, and so on. A foreign acquisition, in contrast, raises concerns that the MNE may no longer maintain relationships with local inputs suppliers or lay off domestic workers.

In the model I capture these concerns by assuming that the government can be biased against the foreign takeover when making its approval decision. This bias can clearly also be the result of political economics mechanisms. Seminal work in this area is due to Motta and Ruta who show in their chapter 5 of this book that a government bias against foreign takeovers of domestic firms can be caused by the lobbying effort of well-organized domestic interest groups (e.g., representatives of the outsider firm, worker councils, or input suppliers) who would be harmed by the takeover. Motta and Ruta present a political model of merger policy where they distinguish between approval decisions are carried out by an independent antitrust agency (maximizing standard social welfare) and by a government that maximizes some combination of social welfare and contribution payments. If politicians can influence merger decisions, prospective losers will engage in lobbying activities and certain merger types are ruled out if the respective outsiders are efficient lobbyists. In this chapter I have simply postulated that the government may be biased against the foreign takeover. However, as in the model of Motta and Ruta, I have also treated government authority as not an independent competition agency but subject to lobbying influences. The prospective losers of the foreign takeover scenario have access to domestic policy makers, which may explain the origin of the bias. Clearly, the foreign firm that has no power to influence domestic politicians could lose in a national merger attempt.

In this final section of the model, I analyze the takeover game when the government is biased. As explained above, I do not consider an extremely patriotic government that completely disregards the welfare significance of the takeover wealth ($\tilde{\lambda} = 0$), but it fixes a maximum amount $\tilde{\lambda} = \pi_{\{1+2\}}^{nat}/2$ up to which it is willing to accept takeover wealth as welfare relevant in its decision whether or not to approve the foreign acquisition. Notice that this amount would be the "normal" value of the target firm under the alternative M&A option, the national champion, where shareholders of the two domestic firms could expect to earn exactly this profit level. The government must decide whether the foreign takeover acquisition price is equal to this normal value. In other words, the patriotic agency assumes a value of the target firm that it thinks is reasonable. The foreign firm may be willing to pay a higher price, but higher offers are not taken into account.

One reason for such government behavior could be public pressure. It may be accepted that a foreign takeover is approved on the basis that it generates positive outcomes for consumers, competition, and so on, but an outbidding of a domestic firm by a foreign corporation is not considered acceptable but "excessive" or "unpatriotic." Hence the agency decides on the foreign takeover on the basis of the reasonable reference price that also the domestic bidder would have to pay, but it is unwilling to let its decision depend on the fact that the foreign corporation is able to outbid a domestic competitor and offer more for the acquisition target.[4]

This type of government behavior effectively creates a hurdle for the foreign bidder because the government disregards all payments beyond the maximum amount when making its policy decision. Hence firm 3 cannot simply safeguard the cross-border merger by paying a much higher price. Since this additional burden is only relevant for the *foreign* bidder, it is clear that this type of government behavior may be called *nationalistic* and not just a general anti-merger attitude on the part of government.

9.5.2   First Stage: Takeover Auction

Given this behavior of the competition agency, there is in fact no reason for firm 3 to pay more than $\pi_{\{1+2\}}^{nat}/2$, since (1) this price is sufficient to outbid the other domestic firm in the takeover battle for the acquisition target and (2) payments beyond $\pi_{\{1+2\}}^{nat}/2$ do not affect the government's approval decision in the subsequent welfare evaluation. The resulting actual equilibrium takeover price in this scenario is

$$\lambda^{**} = \tfrac{1}{2} \cdot \pi_{\{1+2\}}^{nat}, \tag{9.22}$$

and the respective participation condition for firm 3 is now $\pi_3^{int} - \lambda^{***} \geq \pi_3^{nat}$. This "mild" form of economic patriotism will effectively make foreign takeovers less likely, even though it capitalizes in a lower takeover price (notice that $\lambda^{**} \leq \lambda^{*}$), because higher price offers cannot be used by firm 3 to convince the government.

9.5.3   Equilibrium Ownership Structure

Using $\tilde{\lambda} = \lambda^{**}$ in (9.17), it is possible to show that $\Delta PS(\lambda^{**}) > 0$ and $\lambda^{**} < \pi_3^{int} - \pi_3^{nat}$. That is, the foreign firm is generally willing to take over one domestic competitor for a price as low as λ^{**}. Yet the national champion always yields higher domestic producer surplus than the foreign takeover if the price is λ^{**}. That price is too low to compensate the negative profit externality that the domestic outsider firm has to suffer if the MNE is formed.

Consequently higher domestic producer surplus would accrue if the two national firms merge. In other words, the foreign takeover implies a "buyout" of national producer surplus in this scenario, which seems to be one main worry of policy makers in real world cases (e.g., recall the SUEZ/ENEL/Gaz-de-France case described above where the concern of the French government was precisely such a buyout). To be sure, the foreign takeover still generates the consumer gain, $\Delta CS < 0$, regardless of the price λ.

The final decision of the government will thus require trading off the consumer gain against the lower domestic producer surplus. When evaluating this trade-off, a robust pattern emerges as illustrated in figure 9.2. It implies that the national champion is the welfare-maximizing ownership structure for high transport costs, whereas the foreign takeover is the preferred option—even for the biased domestic agency—at low levels of trade openness. Importantly the national champion becomes more attractive for the domestic competition agency in the course of trade integration: there is a critical level of trade openness below which the agency would prefer the international takeover, but above which it would rather approve the national champion.

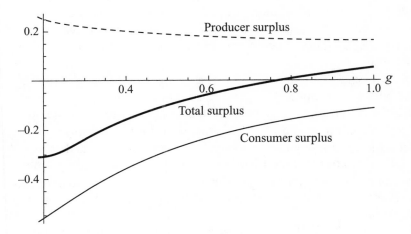

Figure 9.2
Welfare implications of a national champion: Biased government. Parameter values: $v = 3.5$, $\gamma = 1/2$, $c = 6/10$, $s = 7/10$.

The national champion always yields higher domestic producer surplus when the price is λ^{**}. It is nevertheless always associated with lower domestic consumer surplus. Total national surplus aggregates producer and consumer interests. At low levels of trade openness the foreign takeover yields higher welfare because the positive effect on consumers prevails. Yet, if g should rise to a critical level, the national champion becomes the preferred option for the domestic competition policy.

9.6   Conclusion

Studied in this chapter was a model where two domestic and one foreign firm produce differentiated commodities and compete in Bertrand fashion on the domestic market. The initial constellation of this model was the case where there would be either a national merger or a takeover of one domestic firm by the foreign rival. A competition agency is added to this game whose role was to approve any type of M&A. We saw that whether the national champion or the multinational enterprise arises in equilibrium depends crucially on the level of trade openness and on the attitude of the government. Globalization makes the foreign takeover more likely if the government is not biased against foreign acquisitions of national firms. Such a result suggests that trade integration makes cross-border mergers more likely, and this is consistent with the general surge of international mergers observed in the data (UNCTAD 2005). Yet this result is at odds with the more the casual recently observed fact that at least some countries (e.g., France) have increasingly attempted to deter foreign takeovers.

Introduced also into the model was a measure of "economic patriotism," and it was found that *globalization makes national mergers more likely* if the government has a patriotic bias to begin with. Even a patriotic government may allow a foreign takeover if trade openness is low because the consumer gain from vanishing transport costs is then substantial. As trade becomes freer, however, the domestic competition agency opts for the national champion beyond a certain point, in order to prevent a buyout of domestic producer surplus by a foreign corporation.

A qualitatively similar result was derived by Suedekum (2010) in a model of Cournot competition. The analysis of this chapter suggests that Suedekum's main result, that globalization reinforces the case for promoting national champions if the government is biased, remains robust under Bertrand competition where firms' actions are strategic complements rather than strategic substitutes.

Acknowledgment

The author is indebted to Michele Ruta and to the seminar participants for very helpful suggestions and comments on an earlier draft of this chapter.

Notes

1. The underlying cause for this discrepancy is the distinction between strategic substitutes and strategic complements, as introduced by Bulow et al. (1985). For an excellent textbook exposition of these issues, see Motta (2004, ch. 5).

2. This formalization of the government bias is not crucial for the results. Similar results would be obtained under different specifications. In the model of Suedekum (2010), for example, the government bias is endogenously rooted in a political economy framework where the domestic firm owners may engage in lobbying activities in order to promote their preferred merger type. Here I abstract from those explicit political economy considerations, which are discussed in greater detail in chapter 5 of this volume by Motta and Ruta.

3. A similar result has been shown by Horn and Persson (2001), who use a Cournot model to argue that trade integration makes cross-border mergers more likely. I find instead that the impact of trade integration on the "likelihood" of the foreign takeover is nonmonotonic.

4. One could argue that even a patriotic government should try to maximize the actual takeover price that the foreigners pay, and then tax away and redistribute the takeover wealth from the shareholders of firm i. However, the government in my model is a competition agency that has no power of taxation or subsidization.

References

Brülhart, M., and F. Trionfetti. 2001. Industrial specialisation and public procurement: Theory and empirical evidence. *Journal of Economic Integration* 16 (2): 106–27.

Bulow, J., J. Geanakoplos, and P. Klemperer. 1985. Multimarket oligopoly: Strategic substitutes and complements. *Journal of Political Economy* 93 (3): 488–511.

Deneckere, R., and C. Davidson. 1985. Incentives to form coalitions with Bertrand competition. *Rand Journal of Economics* 16 (4): 473–86.

Horn, H., and L. Persson. 2001. The equilibrium ownership of an international oligopoly. *Journal of International Economics* 53 (2): 307–33.

Motta, M. 2004. *Competition Policy: Theory and Practice*. Cambridge: Cambridge University Press.

Salant, S., S. Switzer, and R. Reynolds. 1983. Losses from horizontal mergers: The effects of an exogenous change in industry structure on Cournot–Nash equilibrium. *Quarterly Journal of Economics* 98 (2): 185–99.

Suedekum, J. 2010. National champions and globalization. *Canadian Journal of Economics. Revue Canadienne d'Economique* 43 (1): 204–31.

UNCTAD. 2005. *World Investment Report 2005*. Geneva: United Nations.

Index